DIVINE-HUMAN SYMPHONY

DIVINE-HUMAN SYMPHONY

A Comparative Reading of Ecclesiastes and Paṭṭiṉattār

Yesu Karunanidhi

Christian World Imprints

First Published in 2020 by

Christian World Imprints
Christian Publishing & Books from India
C-3, Wazirpur Industrial Area
Delhi-110052
cwidelhi2017@gmail.com
www.ChristianWorldImprints.com
Phone: +91 11 41526079

ISBN: 978-93-5148-461-5

Printed in India.

Picture Courtesy: M. Silvestri, La Sapienza del Cuore

"So teach us to count our days
that we may gain a wise heart."
(Psalm 90:12)

Fondly dedicated
to
my mother
who sacrificed her sleep
to pay my school fees

CONTENTS

A BOUQUET OF THANKS

To א (Aleph) beginning - the அkaram & ஆti pakavan̲ of Life, Light and Sweetness.

To ב (Beth) home, the roots of my being.

To ג (Gimel) important ideas, Rev. Dr. Selva Rathinam, SJ, the Guide, who introduced me to the world of Hebrew and Tamil Literature then and now, for his guidance, corrections, and suggestions.

To ד (Daleth) door, Most Rev. Dr. Antony Pappusamy, Archbishop of Madurai, my co-priests and friends for their unfailing support.

To ה (Hey) window, Most Rev. Dr. Peter Fernando, Archbishop-Emeritus of Madurai, who sent me to pursue my LSS.

To ו (Waw) hook, Most Rev. Dr. J. Susaimanickam, the Bishop of Sivagangai, who ignited the spark in me to explore Sacred Scripture.

To ז (Zayin) sword, Rev. Dr. Jose Thayil, SJ, Rev. Dr. Francis Gonsalves, SJ, the Chairman of Doctoral Committee then & now, who defined my area of research.

To ח (Cheth) fence, Rev. Dr. Mohan Doss, SVD, the Dean of the Faculty of Theology, Rev. Fr. Vincent Crasta, SJ, the Registrar, Rev. Fr. G. Alex, SJ, the Treasurer, who paved way for my research.

To ט (Teth) new life, Mrs. Philomena Arockiasamy, who is my Bethany.

To י (Yod) hand, Rev. Dr. Konrad Noronha, SJ, Rev. Dr. Paulraj Mariapushpam, who helped me in formulating the questionnaire for the research survey.

To כ (Kaf) holding, A. Selvi, SMSM, A. Gnana Soundari, CIC, F. Jenitha Mary for accompanying me in the survey.

To ל (Lamed) ox, Mrs. Rosa Pasquini of Rome, for her life-lessons.

To מ (Mem) waters, the libraries at Pontifical Biblical Institute, Rome, JDV, Pune, Tamil University, Tanjore, and Madurai Kamaraj University, Madurai.

To נ (Nun) individual, the Diocese of Rome, that welcomed me to work at Parrocchia di San Giuda Taddeo, and to study at PIB.

To ס (Samech) surrounding, the PG Block for the welcome and hospitality.

To ע (Ayin) eyes, Ms. Santhosa Mary, my Tamilamma, who helped me understand Tamil Grammar and Syntax.

To פ (Peh) mouth, Rev. Dr. Anthony Forte, SJ, Rev. Dr. Dominik Markl, SJ,

Rev. Dr. Henry Pattarumadathil, SJ, Rev. Dr. J. Chrzanowski, SJ, for inducing me to perform better always.

To צ (Tsade) fish-hook, Jegankumar, OMI, Naveen Rebello, SVD, my friends.

To ק (Kof) needle-eye, Maria Dhanaraj Thivyarajan, SAC, S. Dhinakaran, who spell-checked my paper.

To ר (Resh) head, doctoral colleagues, for helping me focus in my research.

To ש (S/Shin) tooth, all my dear ones.

To ת (Tav) eternity, all of you, thanks - now and always.

Thank You and God Bless!

ABBREVIATIONS AND NOTES

1. Biblical Abbreviations are from ***The New Revised Standard Version***

2. Other Abbreviations

ABD	Anchor Bible Dictionary
AG	Ad Gentes
ANE	Ancient Near East
ASV	American Standard Version
BDB	Brown-Driver-Briggs, *A Hebrew and English Lexicon of the OT*
BCE	Before Common Era
BETL	Bibliotheca ephemeridum theologicarum lovaniensium
BHQ	Biblia Hebraica Quinta
BHS	Biblia Hebraica Stuttgartensia
Bib	Biblica
BZAW	Beihefte zur Zeitschrift für die alttestamentliche Wissenschaft
CBQ	Catholic Biblical Quarterly
CE	Common Era
cent.	century
cf.	confer, compare
ch. / chs.	Chapter(s)
ed. / eds.	edited; edited by; edition; editors;
e.g.	exempli gratia, for example
Eccl	Ecclesiastes (Book)
et al	and others
etc.	et cetera, and so on
Eng	English Translation Variant
ff.	following
FOTL	Forms of Old Testament Literature
GS	Gaudium et Spes
HALOT	The Hebrew and Aramaic Lexicon of the Old Testament
HB	Hebrew Bible

hap. leg.	hapax legomenon
JBL	Journal of Biblical Literature
JBQ	Jewish Bible Quarterly
JNES	Journal of the Near Eastern Studies
JPS	Jewish Publication Society
JQR	Jewish Quarterly Review
JSOT	Journal for the Study of the Old Testament
JSOTS	Journal for the Study of the Old Testament Supplement
KAT	Kommentar zum Alten Testament
KJV	King James Version
lit.	literally
Lxx	Septuagint
MLB	Modern Language Bible
MM	Masorah Magna
MP	Masorah Parvah
Mss	Manuscripts
n.	footnote
no.	number
NA	Nostra Aetate
NAB	New American Bible
NASB	New American Standard Bible
NEB	New English Bible
NET	New English Translation Bible
NIV	New International Version
NJPS	New Jewish Publication Society
NRSV	New Revised Standard Version
p. / pp.	page / pages
RSV	Revised Standard Version
RivBib	Rivista Biblica
SA	See Also
TDNT	Theological Dictionary of the New Testament
TDOT	Theological Dictionary of the Old Testament
TLOT	Theological Lexicon of the Old Testament
Uṭal	Uṭalkūṟṟuvaṇṇam
v. / vv.	verse / verses (Biblical verses; and the stanzas in Uṭalkūṟṟuvaṇṇam)
x	occurrences
YLT	Young's Literal Translation
/	or; corresponds to
+	and

3. Notes

- 'Qohelet' stands for the author of Ecclesiastes, while 'Ecclesiastes' for the book.
- The language used is UK English. If citations are from American authors US English is retained.
- The use of masculine gender is for convenience. It includes the other genders too.
- The stanzas of *Uṭalkūṟṟuvaṇṇam* are called 'verses' and abbreviated as v./or vv.
- The footnotes, bibliographic details, citations, references, and notes are formatted according to the recent methodology followed in biblical research circles in Pontifical Universities in Rome as prescribed in S. BAZYLIŃSKI, *A Guide to Biblical Research* (Rome, 2009).
- When we cite an author's text we use "..." and refer to the source in the footnote.
- When we paraphrase an author, at the end of the line or argument or the paragraph we make a note and refer to the source as 'cf.'
- Many of the Tamil writers mention their surname with their initials. Hence, when their surnames are not deciphered from their texts we retain their first name as their surname. For example, A. Maria Selvam is referred to as A. MARIA SELVAM.
- When a work is referred second time in the notes, instead of repeating the entire citation we mention the author by the surname and the work by the key words.
- When an author's only work is referred the second citation carries only the name of the author.

A NOTE ON TRANSLITERATION

The Hebrew words are not transliterated except in the citations.

For the transliteration of Tamil words, we have followed this: (a) When citing the popular words (e.g., Tamil, Siddha, Veda) the commonly accepted spelling is retained; (b) In all other instances we have adopted the transliteration method used by the Tamil Lexicon (read from the top to the bottom), which has by now become more or less the standard one.[ℵ] In the transliteration of Tamil words, the names of books, places and persons begin with uppercase letter, while the rest are in lowercase.

Vowels		Consonants		
a	அ	Hard	k	க்
ā	ஆ		c	ச்
i	இ		ṭ	ட்
ī	ஈ		t	த்
u	உ		p	ப்
ū	ஊ		ṟ	ற்
e	எ	Soft	ṅ	ங்
ē	ஏ		ñ	ஞ்
ai	ஐ		ṇ	ண்
o	ஒ		n	ந்
ō	ஓ		m	ம்
au	ஔ		ṉ	ன்
		Medial	y	ய்
			r	ர்
			l	ல்
			v	வ்
			ḻ	ழ்
			ḷ	ள்
	Āytam			
	ḵ	ஃ		

ℵ A. Maria Selvam, *The Song of Songs and Ancient Tamil Love Poems*. Poetry and Symbolism (roma 1988) 13. Also V. S. Rajam, *A Reference Grammar of Classical Tamil Poetry* (Philadelphia, 1992), 1.

HEBREW TRANSLITERATION GUIDE (LAMBDIN METHOD)

NAME	LETTER		OUR TRANSCRIPTION
ʼǻlep̄	א		ʼ
bêṯ	בּ		b
	ב		ḇ
gîmel	גּ		g
	ג		ḡ
dǻleṯ	דּ		d
	ד		ḏ
hē	ה		h
wāw	ו		w
záyin	ז		z
ḥēṯ	ח		ḥ
ṭēṯ	ט		ṭ
yōḏ	י		y
kap̄	כּ	ךּ	k
	כ	ך	ḵ
lǻmeḏ	ל		l
mēm	מ	ם	m
nûn	נ	ן	n
sǻmeḵ	ס		s
ʻáyin	ע		ʻ
pēh	פּ	ףּ	p
	פ	ף	p̄
ṣāḏēh	צ	ץ	ṣ
qōp	ק		q
rēš	ר		r
śîn	שׂ		ś
šîn	שׁ		š
tāw	תּ		t
	ת		ṯ

Name of Sign	Plain		With *mater* י *y*		With *mater* ו *w*		With *mater* ה *h* (final only)	
páṯaḥ	בַ	*ba*	—		—		—	—
qǻmeṣ	בָ	*bā* or *bo*	בָי	*bâ* (rare)	—	—	בָה	*bāh*
ḥîreq	בִ	*bi* (or *bī*)	בִי	*bî*	—	—	—	—
ṣērê	בֵ	*bē*	בֵי	*bê*	—	—	בֵה	*bēh*
səḡōl	בֶ	*be*	בֶי	*bệ*	—	—	בֶה	*beh*
ḥṓlem	בֹ	*bō*	—	—	בוֹ	*bô*	בֹה	*bōh* (rare)
qibbûṣ	בֻ	*bu*	—	—	בוּ	*bû*	—	—

And the reduced vowels:

בְ	*bə*	חֲ	*ḥă*	חֱ	*ḥĕ*	חֳ	*ḥŏ*

PROLOGUE

1. The What

Let us begin with the end. The last verses of the texts of our study - Ecclesiastes 11:4-12:8 and Paṭṭiṉattār's Uṭalkūṟṟuvaṇṇam - are: "*hăḇēl hăḇālîm 'āmar haqqôheleṯ hakkōl hāḇel*" ["Vanity of vanities, says the Teacher, all is vanity"] (Eccl 12:8). "*Ōr piṭiṉīṟum ilāta uṭampai nampum aṭiyēṉai iṉi āḷumē*" ["not even a handful of ash remains of body – rule over me the servant who trusts this"] (Uṭal v. 24). These two verses instead of approving the title of our research - Divine-Human Symphony - seem to oppose it. That is the beauty of a poem. No one really ever comprehends a poem fully because the poem reveals as much as it hides. The poems written with a religious outlook are all the more appalling. For, by reading them we transcend human limitedness and embrace the transcendental infiniteness. That is why I have chosen to study poems.

The interest to choose a Śaivite poem is an inspiration from my *ayyāmai* ('grandmother') Late Lakshmiammal, a folk-singer and an ardent devotee of the Lord Śiva. As is the custom in Śaivite funeral rites to sing Paṭṭiṉattār's *Uṭal*, she used to rehearse the singing at home. She would often tell me that this song has nothing to do with the dead but is concerned entirely about the living, and this song sums up the entire human life – from birth to death. Later, when I started my Licentiate at Pontifical Biblical Institute with the study of Hebrew language, I began to admire the lexical and syntactical links between Hebrew and Tamil. To cite an example: Conceptually to refer to a human person in Greek and English we use an idiom 'flesh and blood' ["Blessed are you, Simon son of Jonah! For *flesh and blood* has not revealed this to you, but my Father in heaven" (Mt. 16:17)]. But in Hebrew and Tamil, the way it is expressed is 'bone and flesh' ["This at last is *bone* of my bones and *flesh* of my flesh; this one shall be called Woman, for out of Man this one was taken" (Gen 2:23)]. This aroused my interest to study Hebrew and Tamil texts comparatively. The first impressions of the reading of Ecclesiastes 11:4-12:8 and Paṭṭiṉattār's *Uṭal* are: (i) they are poems, (ii) they are narrative poems, and (iii) they metaphorize the reality of light, sweetness, and rhythm of human life.

Eccl 11:4-12:8 is a Jewish Wisdom poem written in Hebrew by Qohelet in the 3rd cent. BCE, in the context of post-Exilic trauma when the metanarratives such as God, Temple, Torah, and Land failed miserably. And *Uṭal* ('beauty of the composition of the body') is a Śaivite Bhakti poem written in Tamil by Second Paṭṭiṉattār in the 12th cent. CE, at the onset of Chola Bhakti movement which tied people to women, wine, and world.

The *status quaestionis* reveals that Eccl 11:4-12:8 has so far been looked through (i) parallel-literature, (ii) figurative-literal, (iii) historical, and (iv) ethical approaches, and *Uṭal* through (i) religious literature, and (ii) spiritual commentary approaches. But in the current study, (i) as a Christian I approach a Jewish and a Śaivite text; (ii) in English I attempt to devour Hebrew and Tamil worldviews; and (iii) I blend three streams of hermeneutics: narrative analysis, socio-scientific criticism, and comparative literature study.

My research statement is: a close and comparative reading of two narrative poems, Ecclesiastes 11:4-12:8 and Paṭṭiṉattār's *Uṭalkūṟṟuvaṇṇam*, emerging from two socio- cultural and religious traditions opens up a new hermeneutical arc to understand human life transition insofar as they (i) portray light as a metaphor to life, (ii) set human life in four stages; and (iii) establish divine-human symphony as an imperative to find meaning amidst meaninglessness.

Our hermeneutical locus, i.e., the place from which we look at the text, is the mid-life transition. A man about 36 years, who is just in mid-life transition, when he begins to lose sense of meaning in life, when the hard-earned friendships and relationships walk out for no reason, when impressing people becomes a nonsense, when priorities change, and, above all, when he realizes that he has but one life to life, seeks Ecclesiastes and Paṭṭiṉattār for an answer.

2. The Why

The scope of our research is (i) to affirm that the basic aspirations and expressions of humans are same across the cultures, the faiths, and the languages; and (ii) to enter into a dialogue with the poems and the poets, taking our understanding of the self and the other (the transcendental, the social, and the environmental) to them to be transformed by them, and to challenge their positions when needed; and (iii) to understand human life transition.

The strengths of the research are (i) the novelty; (ii) doing the research in my own soil; and (iii) contribution to Tamil, my mother tongue and Śaivism, the religion of my father. Its limitations are (i) the space-time gap between the poets, the poems, and us; (ii) the scarce resources on Paṭṭiṉattār corpus; and (iii) the loss of meaning and word-play in transliterated or translated texts. The new avenues that this research will open up are (i) possibilities of more studies on comparative literature; (ii) understanding Qohelet and Paṭṭiṉattār in a more optimistic perspective; and (iii) drawing life-lessons offered by the poems. The possible dangers that I have carefully tried to avoid in this research are: (i) eisegesis (i.e., reading oneself into texts or forcing meaning into them); (ii) setting degrees (i.e., creating a superiority ladder); and (iii) amalgamation (i.e., making a fruit salad and spoiling the taste of each fruit in it).

The uniqueness of this study and its contribution to the present scholarship rests in the following: (i) The present study is a contribution to the research on the Wisdom Literature of the Hebrew Bible in general and Book of Ecclesiastes in particular because of the method employed to study the text. The present study looks at the Eccl 11:4-12:8 through the tools of narrative analysis. There has been no narrative reading of the Book of Ecclesiastes in early or recent Biblical scholarship. (ii) The studies done on Paṭṭiṉattār's *Uṭal* are very minimum. Moreover, these studies are of the genre of pious interpretations or religious discourses. They merely paraphrase the poems with synonymous words. But, the present study analyses the poem by applying differing literary tools. This paves way for analysing other poems of the same genre with these tools. This study also will be source of reference for the later studies on Paṭṭiṉattār. (iii) The only extra-biblical literature so far compared with the Book of Ecclesiastes is that of Omar Khayyám.[1] There have been some studies to see the influence of the Ancient Near East texts to establish how they have influenced the Qohelet's thinking.[2] Our study is unique insofar as it tries to embrace Qohelet and Paṭṭiṉattār together. Though the poets and the poems are distant to one another in space, time, language, culture, and worldview, they do have common grounds. This shows that the human aspirations and longings are same across cultures, regions, and faiths. (iv) This study is a milestone in the history of interfaith dialogue and *enculturation*.[3] There is a blend of Jewish, Śaivite, and Christian faiths,

1 J. F. Genung, *Ecclesiastes and Omar Khayyám. A Note for the Spiritual Temper of Our Time* (New York 1901). Here the author takes some texts from Ecclesiastes and looks for their echoes in Omar Khayyám songs.

2 At this juncture let me mention the noteworthy work of Dr. A. Maria Selvam, who has undertaken a comparative study approach to symbolism and poetry in the Song of Songs and Tamil Akam Poems as his doctoral dissertation at Pontifical Biblical Institute in Rome. See, A. Maria Selvam, *The Song of Songs and Ancient Tamil Love Poems. Poetry and Symbolism* (Roma 1988).

3 Christianity in India also to a certain extent tries to incorporate Jesus of the West into Indian categories. Efforts have been made in the past to give expression to its faith in the lingua franca of the deeply religious people. To cite a few, Michael Amaladoss (b. 1936) warned how inculturaion, inter-religious dialogue and liberation would be alienating if they do not influence and involve each other. D. S. Amalorpavadoss' (1932-1990) keen sensitivity to God's ways in other religious traditions and cultures made him a theologian of dialogue and inculturation. A. J. Appasamy (1891-1975) merged Hinduism and Christianity through yoga. Vengal Chakkarai (1880-1958) attempted to liberate Christ of experience from the

where one tries to embrace the other without eclipsing it. and (v) To see the contextual, conceptual, and communicative similarities between Hebrew and Tamil worldviews.

3. The How

The research is done (i) By clearing the already existing exegetical space and creating a new methodological framework; (ii) By setting the poems and the poets in their respective space-time, translating the poems, clarifying the texts in the light of their textual traditions; (iii) By employing the tools of synchronic study - narrative analysis (structure, setting, style [e.g., parallelism, imagery, pause, order, word-play, and word-picture], characterisation, and themes and motifs), and comparative literature in the close-reading of the poems; (iv) By juxtaposing the poems side by side to understand their contextual, communicative, and conceptual similarities and dissimilarities through the help of comparative literature analysis tools; and (v) By entering into a hermeneutical dialogue with the poems and the poets, taking our understanding of the self, the transcendental other, the social other, and the environmental other to them to be transformed by them, and to challenge their positions when needed.

The methods employed in our study is narrative analysis and comparative literature. The present work is divided into six chapters.

Chapter One consists of three parts: (a) The presentation of our first impressions on the poems under discussion. The poems are questioned as to see whether they are inset hymns or narrative poems. The basic themes that run through the two poems, the metaphor of light, sweet, and rhythm of human body are reviewed; (b) The state of question of the two poems – in other words, how these two poems have been studied so far in critical scholarship, is carefully analysed; and (c) A brief survey of human life-stages and life transition.

In Chapters Two and Three we read the poems closely. This is the crucial part of our study. In Two, we study Eccl 11:4-12:8, and in Three, Paṭṭiṉattār's *Uṭal*. We have chosen so because chronologically the former precedes the latter. Each poem is studied under seven headings: (i) Poet, (ii)

---

western pre-occupation with Jesus of history and Christ of experience. Francis X. D'Sa (b. 1936) calls for interculturation. Sebastian Kappen (1924-1993) has echoed the cries of the subaltern in his writings. Raimundo Panikkar (b. 1918) contributed cosmotheandric worldview. George M. Soares-Prabhu (1929-1995) gave birth to Jesus of faith, dialogue, and Indian Biblical interpretation. Brahmabandhab Upadhyay (1861-1907) stood immortal as a trendsetter in incarnating the gospel in the cultural ethos of India. This list is not exhaustive. For a brief look at Indian Christian thinkers and their works see A. Amaladoss, ed., Indian Christian Thinkers (Chennai 2005).

Text and Translation, (iii) Delimitation and Structure, (iv) Setting, (v) Style, (vi) Characterisation, and (vii) Themes and Motifs.

Chapter Four is divided into two sections. In section one, we place the poets and the poems side by side and look for the contextual, communicative, conceptual similarities and differences between them and observe whether both are in duet or duel. Section two is our dialogue with the poems, the poets, and their worldviews.

In Chapter Five we see the poems in their literary contexts – Eccl 11:4-12:8 in the context of the Book, Wisdom Literature, and the Hebrew Bible; *Uṭal* in the context of the Paṭṭiṉattār corpus, and Śaivite Bhakti Literature – and establish the literary and hermeneutical arc between them.

The Final Chapter, on the one hand, stretches and embraces the title of our study – 'Divine-Human Symphony', and finds the significance of the poems for the readers in different human life-stages.

Our research work is limited insofar as we try to grasp the milieu of Hebrew and Tamil through the palms of English. The poems reveal themselves better in their own languages. The translated and the transliterated texts at times do not divulge the richness completely. However, we have tried our best to translate the poems into English.

This present book is the abridged and updated version of my doctoral dissertation submitted and defended on 14 March 2017 at Jnana-Deepa Vidyapeeth, Pune. I place on record my sincere thanks to Rev. Dr. Selva Rathinam, SJ, Moderator of the Dissertation, Rev. Dr. Maria Arul Raja, A., SJ, the First Reader, and Rev. Dr. Irudayaraj Manickam, SJ, the Second Reader. A bouquet of thanks to the Mr. and Mrs. Kanda of the Christian World Imprints, New Delhi, for publishing it.

I. FIRST THINGS FIRST

Chapter One is the foundation to the entire research for three reasons: (a) It presents the first impressions of our poems; (c) It critically reviews the early and recent scholary research on our poems and brings to light their contributions and the lacunae; and (c) It surveys the human life-stages and life transition.

A. Two Poems: First Impressions

1. Poem or Inset Hymn

The first question that arises in our study is whether Eccl 11:4 – 12:8 is a poem. There have been various studies undertaken on the literary genre of the book of Ecclesiastes. The proposals of these studies can be classified under three groups:[4] (i) The first group considers the entire book as a prose except for 3:2-8; (ii) The second group treats a number of passages and recurring proverbs as poems or verses and the rest as prose; and (iii) The third group, which is represented in the recent critical edition of BHQ (2004), divides almost all of Qohelet into bipartite lines. The TOB (*Traduction oecuménique de la Bible*, 1977) formats Eccl 1:1 and 2:25-26 alone as prose. Based on the second and third proposals we can state that 11:4-12:8 is a poem.

Eccl 11:4-12:8 is filled with variegated literary genres. As far as the content of the book is concerned the scholars agree that the book in general and 11:4-12:8 in particular must have been inspired from the ancient wisdom tradition, which stretched beyond the narrow borders of Israel – Mesopotamian, Babylonian, Assyrian and Egyptian.[5] The content of the book also reflects Hellenistic influence or the mindset of the Greek philosophy,

---

4 Cf. J. F. Hobbins, "The Poetry of Qohelet," 170-73.

5 W. S. Towner, "The Book of Ecclesiastes. Introduction, Commentary, and Reflections," in *New Interpreter's Bible*, Vol. 5, 273-76. The Song of the Harper comes very close to Eccl 11:7-10. Cf. J. B. Pritchard, *Ancient Near Eastern Texts Relating to the Old Testament* (New Jersey [3]1969), 438-40.

which tries to determine the good by the application of human reason alone, without appeal to tradition or revelation.[6]

Hence, from the point of view of form and genre criteria, we assert that Eccl 11:4-12:8 is a poem.

After having established Eccl 11:4-12:8 as a poem, let us consider yet another question whether this text is an inset hymn.[7] An inset hymn usually continues the plot of the prose text that precedes immediately. In an inset hymn, the characters that are present in the precedent text are mentioned directly or indirectly in poetic form. Our poem does not continue the plot or characterisation[8] found in the precedent prose text. Hence, Eccl 11:4-12:8 is not an inset hymn but an independent hymn.

Paṭṭiṉattār songs are titled after the places in which they have been composed.[9] All the songs of Paṭṭiṉattār corpus except two contain the names of the places where they were sung: one is that which he sang at the funeral pyre of his beloved mother and the other, *Uṭal*, the poem of our study. From the context of the poem the funeral pyre song can be set in the context of his birthplace Kāvēripūmpaṭṭinam. *Uṭal* is an independent poem written or sung by Paṭṭiṉattār. Until today this song is sung during the funeral rites in some of the villages near Chengalpattu and Chennai.[10] The Tamil word 'vaṇṇam' means "hue, colour, pigment" and also "nature, characteristic, or quality."[11] "Vaṇṇam" also means "skill either given or learned," "disposition of the heart or the mind" or "the manner of being and doing."[12] "Uṭal kūṟṟu" refers

6 H. L. Ginsberg – M. V. Fox, "Ecclesiastes," in *Encyclopaedia Judaica*, vol. 6 (Detroit [2]2007), 89.

7 J. W. Watts, *Psalm and Poetry. Inset Hymns in Hebrew Narrative*, JSOTS 139 (Sheffield 1992).

8 The character 'young man' is found only here.

9 How do we arrive at the text that we have today? The editors and compilers having made copies from various palm-leaf scripts and printed texts arrived at 36 books of verses as written by Siddhars. Of such editors Va. Saravaṇa Muttu Piḷḷai gathered 44 books and named the compilation as Periya Ñaṉakkōvai (publication date unknown). Following this Āṟu. Rāmanātaṉ published Ñaṉakkōvai in 1959 with a detailed introduction to the compilation and an enormous glossary of terms. But there is no consensus on the total number of Siddhās. While there are only 18 Siddhās in standard collections, G. Māṇikka Vācakaṉ (1995) has included 34 Siddhās. The text we have taken for our study is from T. V. Kalyānasundaranār, who had adopted from Ñaṉakkōvai. Cf. T. V. Kalyānasundaranār, Paṭṭiṉattār Pātalkaḷ (Chennai [4]2010). The controversy as to the total number of Siddhars still continues and can be debated.

10 Kalyānasundaranār, 7.

11 J. Carman – V. Narayanan, *The Tamil Veda. Piḷḷāṉ's Interpretation of the Tiruvāymoḻi* (Chicago 1989), 299, n. 46.

12 The Poet Kampar in Kamparāmāyaṇam (Pāla Kāṇṭam, Akalikai Paṭalam, 24) employing all these meanings plays with the word vaṇṇam by using it eight times within a single

to "the rhythm of the body," "the harmony of the parts in the whole," or "the human life cycle." The poem details life from its inception to extinction. M. D. Jeyabalan calls this poem an epigraph or an inscription on the statue of human being.[13] When we read the poem the striking metaphor that comes to the mind is the building. The human body, like a building, comes to existence from nothing. It grows tall, attracts people, and is admired by all. And after a while begins to fall to the ground and becomes nothing.

Uṭal is an independent poem though it reflects many intertextual links with the rest of the Paṭṭiṉattār corpus (discussed in Chapter Five).

2. Narrative Poem

Alter arugues that, "The Hebrew writers used verse for celebratory song, dirge, oracle, oratory, prophecy, reflective, and didactic argument, liturgy, and often as a heightening or summarizing inset in the prose narratives – but only marginally and minimally to tell tale."[14] Though the poetry is not used to *narrate* a life or story of individual or a people, the poetry at times functions as a mirror of narrative as in Eccl 11:4-12:8. This we call a narrative poem. A narrative poem is a poem that presents a series of events using poetic devices such as rhythm, rhyme, precise language, imagery and attention to sound. In other words, a narrative poem tells a story, but it does it with poetic flair. Many of the same elements such as characters, setting, conflict and plot, that are found in a short story are also found in a narrative poem. Narrative poems are born in the context of oral tradition. In order to help recall details of the events, people began to use rhyme and rhythm to give their stories a musical quality that would allow the story to be remembered and recalled much more easily. For it is much easier to remember the words of a song than to recall all of the words of a short story. That is exactly how narrative poems were originally created.[15]

The texts Ecclesiastes 11:4-12:8 and Paṭṭiṉattār's *Uṭal* can be treated as narrative poems for the following reasons: (i) These two texts are filled with imageries, which are organized in a rhythmic pattern of well-knit lines; (ii) Both these poems tell the story of the rhythm of human life – from conception to death. Though *Uṭal* is very explicit in this aspect, Eccl 11:4-12:8 is very

stanza:

"Ivvaṇṇam ('thus') nikaḻnta vaṇṇam ('in this manner') ini inta ulakukku ellām
Uyvaṇṇam ('manner of things') aṉṟi maṟṟu ōr tuyar vaṇṇam ('mental disposition') uṟuvatu uṇṭō
Mai vaṇṇatu ('colour') arakki pōril maḻai vaṇṇatu ('colour') aṇṇalē un
Kai vaṇṇam ('skill') aṅku kaṇṭēn kāl vaṇṇam ('magic' or 'skill') iṅku kaṇṭēn"

13 Cf. Vē. Kōpālaṉ, *Paṭṭiṉattāṭikaḷiṉ Pātalkaḷ* (Chennai 2001) 5.

14 R. Alter, *The Art of Biblical Poetry* (New York 1985) 27.

15 Cf. D. C. Rubin, *Memory in Oral Traditions. The Cognitive Psychology of Epic, Ballads, and Counting-out Rhymes* (Cleveland 1991), 35-36.

implicit, because being implicit is the hallmark of its author; and (iii) Both these poems have a narrative function in the oral tradition. Eccl 11:4-12:8 (and the entire book) is narrated on the feast of Booths[16] while *Uṭal* is narrated or sung in the Śaivite funeral passages. Both the texts have evolved from the oral tradition and then have been born as written texts. Even after taking the written form, the texts survive in oral tradition not as something which is transmitted, but as something which is sung.

3. Metaphors and Reality

The two poems share a common ground in three motifs: (i) Metaphor of light; (ii) Tasting 'sweet;' and (iii) Rhythm of human life.

3.1. Metaphor of Light

'Light' in Hebrew Bible

The word *'ôr* ('light') is derived from the root *'r*,[17] which means 'to be bright, to illumine.'[18] In Egyptian literature light is associated primarily with the sun-god, who is the creator, and the originator of life and well-being. But, in the HB, the light primarily refers to daylight. The creation account in Gen 1 sets the sun in an inferior position to the light for the simple reason that the sun was a pagan god and the worship of which was strictly forbidden to the Israelites. "For a correct understanding of the OT idea of light, the distinction between light and sun is important. Of course, the sun shines during the day, but the moon and the stars do the same thing at night, and in spite of this the night is not really bright. Thus, by itself a shining body in heaven does not cause brightness."[19] In "Eccl 12:2, *'or*, probably meaning daylight, stands alongside the sun, the moon, and the stars."[20]

Though the darkness is linked to chaos in Gen 1:2 it is not a power hostile to God. The HB "does not speak of a battle or a dualism between light and darkness … it is an 'organized power of chaos.' God is the creator of both light and darkness (Isa 45:7)."[21]

16 "The Book of Ecclesiastes forms one of the five Megilloth (rolls or scrolls), and it was read by the postbibilcal Jewish community on the Feast of Booths (Tabernacles)." J. S. Wright, "The Interpretation of Ecclesiastes," in R. B. Zuck, *Reflecting with Solomon. Selected Studies on the Book of Ecclesiastes* (Grand Rapids 1994), 173.

17 Let us note its similarity to Tamil language, where eri means 'to light.'

18 Cf. *TDOT*, I, 149. Cf. In Akkadian urru is 'day.' TDOT, I, 149.

19 *TDOT*, I, 151.

20 *TDOT*, I, 153.

21 *TDOT*, I, 157.

However,

> the inferiority of darkness is shown in different ways: in the association of light and life, of darkness and the Underworld, of darkness and evil men; in the figurative use of light in the sense of success and salvation and of darkness in the sense of failure and destruction; in the idea that darkness is a potential power of chaos; and finally, in the expectation that darkness will be eliminated in the eschatological state of salvation.[22]

At times the HB equates 'light' with 'life' and 'darkness' with 'death.'[23] In Ps 36:10 [Eng v. 9], "For with you is the fountain of life; in your light do we see light," 'light' probably means 'salvation, way, orientation.'"[24] "The light of the day is reflected in the light of the eyes (Prov 29:13). An increase of this light means increased vitality and joy (Ezr 9:8; Prov 15:30). The verb form *ha'ir* (hiphil) also used in this sense (Ezr 9:8; Ps 13:4; cf. Eccl 8:1). When the light of the eyes fails, a person is approaching death (Ps 38:11; 13:4)."[25]

Darkness stands for suffering and failure (Isa 8:22; Jer 23:12; Amos 5:18, 20; Ps 23:4; Job 17:12; 29:3; Lam 3:2) and light for well-being, success (Amos 5:18, 20; Job 17:12; 18:5f; 22:28; Prov 13:9; Lam 3:2; Est 8:16).[26] "In religiously oriented texts, light is a symbol for the salvation given by God (Isa 9:1; 58:8; Ps 18:29; 36:10; 43:3; 97:11; Job 29:3)."[27]

God also is referred to as light in the HB: "'my light' in Ps 27:1; 'my lamp' in 2 Sam 22:29; 'the light of Israel'in Isa 10:17; 'your light' in 60:1; 'a light to me' in Mic 7:8."[28]

"'To see the light' also means to experience salvation or deliverance (Isa 9:1; 53:11; Lxx and 1QIsa)."[29] The expression 'light of the countenance' of God probably means 'God's favor and grace' (Ps 4:7); 44:4 [Eng v. 3].[30] "The light which God gives represents his protecting and preserving guidance (Ps 43:3; Prov 4:18; Job 22:28; 29:2ff.; Isa 9:1; 42:16)."[31]

Light also suggests an ethical meaning. Walking in light or being in light means to be in life or to be wise. "Without this light, man gropes in darkness (Prov 6:23; Ps 119:105; Eccl 2:13ff.). Light is used in parallelism with wisdom

---

22 *TDOT*, I, 157.

23 See Job 3:16; 33:28; Ps 58:9, Eng v. 8; 49:20, Eng v. 19;

24 Cf. *TDOT*, I, 158.

25 *TDOT*, I, 158.

26 Cf. *TDOT*, I, 160.

27 *TDOT*, I, 160.

28 *TDOT*, I, 161.

29 *TDOT*, I, 161.

30 Cf. *TDOT*, I, 161.

31 *TDOT*, I, 161.

or understanding, and darkness with folly (Eccl 2:13ff.; Dan 5:11, 14; cf. Job 37:19, 21; 38:2; 22:11-14; Mic 3:6)."[32]

In Isa 42:1-3, the Servant Song, the idea of light is combined with justice. The servant will cause justice to appear to the best of the nations. Here it means "bringing (the nations) to light or making manifest (see e.g., Job 12:22; 28:11)."[33] "When the servant of the Lord himself is represented as a 'light to the nations' (42:6; 49:6; cf. 51:4), this is because he mediates light, i.e., the justice which brings salvation."[34]

'Light' in Eccl 11:4-12:8

Direct Reference	*ûmāṯôq hā'ōr* (11:7)	'and sweet is the light'
	haššemeš wəhā'ôr (12:2)	'the sun and the light'
Indirect Reference	*babbōqer* (11:6)	'in the morning'
	la'ênayim lir'ôṯ 'eṯ-haššāmeš (11:7)	'for the eyes to see the sun'
	wəhaššaḥărûṯ (11:10)	'and the dawn'
	haššemeš wəhā'ôr wəhayyārē^{a}ḥ wəhakkôḵāḇîm (12:2)	'the sun, … the moon, the stars'
Contrast Reference	*wəlā'ereḇ* (11:6)	'and in the evening'
	yəmê haḥōšeḵ (11:8)	'the days of darkness'
	ṯeḥšaḵ (12:2)	'be darkened'
	ḥāšḵû (12:3)	'be dimmed'

We find three types of references to 'light' in Eccl 11:4-12:8: (a) direct, (b) indirect, and (c) contrast. In 11:7 and 12:2 the references are direct as we have the word 'light.' The 'morning' in 11:6, the 'sun' in 11:7 and 12:2, the 'dawn' in 11:7 suggest the meaning 'light.' By contrast 'the evening' (11:6), and 'the darkness' (11:8; 12:2, 3) make us understand the presence of 'light.'

'Light' in *Uṭal*

Direct Reference	*oḷinakaiyūṟa* (v. 5)	'teeth sparkling with smile'
	yaḻal (v. 24)	'fire'

32 *TDOT*, I, 162.

33 *TDOT*, I, 163.

34 *TDOT*, I, 163.

Indirect Reference	*pārvai* (v. 2)	'sight'
	uṭaimaṇiyāṭai (v. 6)	'dressed with pearls'
	vaḷarpiṟai (v. 7)	'the crescent'
	maṇipoṉilaṅku (v. 8)	'pearls gold ridden'
	variviḻi (v. 9)	'lining eye'
	kaṇṭiṭum (v. 15)	'see'
	vaḷarpiṟaipōla (v. 19)	'like the crescent'
Contrast Reference	*kaṇkaḷiruṇṭu* (v. 12)	'eyes darkened'
	karuki (v. 24)	'be darkened'

In vv. 5 and 24 the references are direct. The sense experience of 'seeing' (vv. 2, 9, 15), the 'attractive' (vv. 6, 8) and the expression 'crescent' (vv. 7, 9) indirectly suggest the 'light.' The 'darkness' (v. 12, 24) contrastingly makes us realize the presence of 'light.'

3.2. Tasting 'Sweet'

'Sweet' in Hebrew Bible

"The root *mtq* found in the various Semitic languages, may be onomatopoeic in origin, imitating the sound of licking or smacking one's lips. If so, its original meaning would be something like 'to eat with pleasure.'"[35] The word occurs 25x in the HB.[36] When used as a verb it means 'to become sweet' (Exod 15:25) or 'be sweet' (Prov 9:17). "The LXX consistently uses *glykys* in translating the root while Vulg. generally uses *dulcis*."[37]

Since sugar in its various forms is needed to the body and is indispensable for the functioning of the bodily organs the tasting of sweet is pleasant. Figuratively this pleasantness extends to kissing, speaking, and at times seeing. Ugaritic verses speak of El's kissing his wives and describe their "lips as sweet as pomegranates."[38] Homer celebrates the "tongue from which flows speech sweeter (*glykiōn*) than honey." Euripides praises the "sweet light" (*hēdy gar to phōs*).[39] The rhetorician Seneca speaks of a "sweet color" (*color dulcis*), and

35 *TDOT*, IX, 103.

36 As an adjective the word occurs 12x. Judg 14:14; 14:18; Is 5:20 (2x); Ezek 3:3; Ps 19:11; Prov 16:24; 24:13; 27:7; Song 2:3; Eccl 5:11; 11:7.

37 *TDOT*, IX, 104.

38 Cited in *TDOT*, IX, 105.

39 Homer Iliad 1.249; Euripides Iphigeneia at Aulis 1.1218. Cited in *TDOT*, IX, 105.

Goethe of the "sweet light of sounds."[40] For Shakespeare, "sweet are the uses of adversity."[41]

Literally *mātôq* means honey (cf. Judg 14:18; Prov 24:13).[42] From physiological foundation 'sweet' is raised to an emotional dimension when Qohelet synesthetically extends meaning and calls 'light as sweet' (cf. Eccl 11:7).[43] The second use of Qohelet in Eccl 5:11 [Eng v. 10] calls "the refreshing sleep of the labourer as sweet."[44]

'Sweet' in Eccl 11:4-12:8

Direct Reference	*ûmāṯôq hā'ōr* (11:7)	'and sweet is the light'
Indirect Reference	*wə'im-šənêhem kə'eḥāḏ ṭôḇîm* (11:6)	'and both will be good together'
	wəṭôḇ (11:7)	'and it is good or pleasant'
	yiśmāḥ (11:8) // *śemaḥ* (11:9)	'rejoice'
	wîṭîḇḵā (11:9)	'let it cheer you'
Contrast Reference	*ka'as* (11:10)	'vexation'
	rā'āh (11:10)	'pain'
	'ên-lî ḇāhem ḥēpeṣ (12:1)	'I have no pleasure in them'

The word 'sweet' is direct in 11:7. Indirectly the words 'good' (11:6, 7) 'pleasant,' 'rejoice' (11:8, 9) and 'cheer' (11:9) allude to the sensation of 'being or tasting sweet.' The unwanted sensations of 'vexation' (11:10), 'pain' (11:10), and 'no pleasure' (12:1) mark the imperative character of 'sweet.'

---

40 Seneca Controversiae 1.4.7; Goethe, Des Epimenides Erwachen, 1, 17. Cited in *TDOT*, IX, 105.

41 W. Shakespeare, *As You Like It*, Act II, Scene I.

42 Cf. *TDOT*, IX, 106.

43 Cf. *TDOT*, IX, 106. "In this context the sunlight is an image of life, which is perceived as mātôq and is in contrast to the darkness of death." *TDOT*, IX, 106.

44 "The Targum finds here a reference to eternal rest, clearly a mistaken interpretation." The interpretation of Targum turns the meaning of mātôq in Eccl 11:7 upside down. In Judg 14:18, the ecstasy of love is perceived as mātôq. In Prov 16:21, where it reads "sweetness of the lips," mātôq refers to the speech that emerges out of such lips. Based on this the meaning is extended to YHWH's words. For prophet Ezekiel the scroll with the divine message is like honey in his mouth and it is "like honey in its sweetness" (3:3; cf. Rev 10:9). The psalmist exalts the Law of YHWH as "sweeter than honey and drippings from the comb" (19:11, Eng v. 10). Cf. *TDOT*, IX, 107.

'Sweet' in *Uṭal*

Direct Reference	'*inpa*' (v. 1)	'sweet' or 'pleasant'
	'*yuṇarvukalaṅki*' (v. 1)	'mental excitement because of extreme pleasure'
	'*uṇtu*' (v. 6)	'having eaten'
Indirect Reference	'*cukantaru*' (v. 1)	'that gives pleasure'
	'*koṅkaiyamutam*' (v. 4)	'the elixir of the breasts'
	'*yitaḻamutuṇṭu*' (v. 10)	'the elixir of the lips'
Contrast Reference	'*cuṇaiyumaḻintu*' (v. 14)	'losing the tasting buds'

The word '*iṉimai'* ('sweet') is almost literal in v. 1 and figurative in vv. 1, 4, 6, 10. The latter sense of 'taste' is mentioned in v. 14.

3.3. Rhythm of Human Life

The third key motif that unites both the songs is the 'rhythm of human body.' The poets Qohelet and Paṭṭiṉattār, who have observed nature in its harmony and change, apply the same process to the human life cycle. They, who have understood the irreversible process of human life, present the same experience in the form of poetry.

Rhythm of Life in General

Everything in nature has a rhythm. The rising of the sun, its setting, the moon, the stars, the constellations exist and act like a clock work. Seasons change. Nature around us reflects these changes. The tree which is colourful and full of leaves in summer begins to shed its leaves in autumn. It sheds its leaves and fights the killing winter. Then comes the spring where the tree sprouts again. The process is marvellous. But unfortunately, it is not so with human persons. The autumn (of old age) arrives. We too shed our leaves. We too become naked, empty, dry and fragile. But we can never sprout again. The cycle does not continue.

Considering the rhythm of life is important for anyone who wishes to strive forward toward a more fulfilling life in integrity and truth. In the first place, developing a rhythm of life consists of a detailed and careful study of an individual's life. The scope of this individual search emerges from a fundamental belief that God created each one of us and placed within us an inherent potential to become someone we as of now do not know yet. A growing sense of 'there must be something more' helps us have a paradigm shift in our way of looking at ourselves, our world around and God. Understanding the rhythm of life helps us live more fully and to steward more effectively all of the gifts of God in our lives. The understanding of human life cycle presents us with a set of values for our *modus operandi* and *modus vivendi*: celebrating life, blessing and participating in the good, true and beautiful, encouraging others, respecting the image of God in creation, human relationships, living a life of integrity and authenticity, striving for excellence, and defacing superficiality.

Rhythm of Life in Eccl 11:4-12:8

According to Hogan, Qohelet wrote this poem in the time of decline of Jerusalem and its slow rehabilitation.[45] The people thought that God had punished them for their iniquities. Their socio-religious institutions lost their meanings. The rhythm of their lives was lost. Qohelet wants to re-align their harps. As Hogan observes,

> The living order of Israel had been buried beneath a theory of retribution. Qohelet (and Job) burst out of this straitjacket. It is in the struggle to maintain faith in the midst of uncertainty, in the painful struggle for new light in the midst of darkness that they bear clearest witness to the contradictions in our experience of God. Both lived their faith without dishonesty or illusion in the face of senseless chaos. They carry us into the heart of true religiousness, and into the heart of human experience as we are forced to wrestle with hope and despair, light and darkness, order and chaos. Both try to recapture experiences which go beyond the dogma of retribution and have to do with the relationship of the individual to his surrounding reality, including God – *harmonised in a rhythm*.[46]

Rhythm of Life in *Uṭal*

Paṭṭiṉattār, on the other hand, rediscovers the rhythm of human life in the context of the religious domination by Buddhism and Jainism, which considered body as impermanent and illusory.

This understanding is basically the scope of these two poets in their composing of these immortal poems on 'mortality.' The ultimate concern of Qohelet is to offer his readers an invitation to 'rejoice' in the short life 'remembering' the Creator, while for Paṭṭiṉattār it is to liberate the human person from the bondage to his own body. Both these poets want their readers to re-discover the lost symphony and to re-tune their strings to the tone of the Creator. Their presentation of the life stages, though sounds bizarre, bitter, and frightening, is, in fact, the hard-hitting reality we encounter everyday. The poets do not foil their thoughts in a sugar-coated shell but present life in its nakedness, ambiguity, uncertainty, and fragility.

---

45 Cf. M. P. Hogan, *The Biblical Vision of the Human Person. Implications for a Philosophical Anthropology* (Frankfurt am Main 1994) 237.

46 Hogan, *Biblical Vision of Human Person*, 237.

To sum up, there are formal and thematic similarities between these two poems. As far as the form is concerned, (i) Both the poems can be structured based on a four-tier human life cycle; (ii) Both use the similar word-pictures and figurative language – especially 'light' and 'sweet;' and (iii) Both are centred on Human-God relationship. Thematically, the characterisation of God, human person, world, and nature are similar in the poems.

However, there are three major differences between these two poems:[47] (i) Eccl is addressed to the 'young person' while *Uṭal* is addressed to God; (ii) Eccl sees a human person as a mixture of body and spirit while *Uṭal* sees him as a mere body; and (iii) The invitation of Eccl is ethical while that of Paṭṭiṉattār is very spiritual.

B. Status Quaestionis: Contributions and Lacunae

At the outset it is apt to sketch the contemporary studies on Ecclesiastes and Paṭṭinattār. This sketch has two purposes: (i) To survey the most important recent approaches in connection with this research; and (ii) To relate the present study to these different approaches and their results.

We will evaluate the different positions of various authors in current scholarship, the methodologies they have employed, and the conclusions they have arrived at. We will summarise the main contributions achieved by the majority of scholars and the lacunae in connection with our topic. Thus, this research can be taken a step further in the interpretation of the passage.

1. Status Quaestiones of Eccl 11:4-12:8[48]

The vast available scholarship on the book of Ecclesiastes proves the words of Qohelet, "Of making many books there is no end" (Eccl 12:12). The ambiguity of the language of the poem has given rise to a plethora of interpretations and has led scholars to offer significantly different ways of understanding Qohelet's words. The Jewish expositors treat the book of Ecclesiastes by treating the Epicurean messages in them, and by ascribing the book to Solomonic authorship.

The scholars who have analysed the text of Eccl 11:4-12:8 fall under four categories: (i) Those who study this text in parallel to the ANE texts and poems;[49] (ii) Those who read the second half of the poem (12:1-7) figuratively,

---

47 There are few more differences. They will be treated in Chapter Three of our study.

48 Cf. J. S. Wright, "The Interpretation of Ecclesiastes," in Zuck, *Reflecting with Solomon,* 18.

49 For example, Qohelet's pessimism and his advice for the enjoyment of life find their parallels in Egyptian texts. "The most important are 'The Dispute of a Man with His Ba' and the 'Songs of the Harpers.' In the 'Dispute,' a man who has become disillusioned with life contemplates suicide. His ba, or soul, tries to convince him that life is still preferable to death. The 'Harper's Songs' are tomb inscriptions that reflect on death and call for the enjoyment of life. Qohelet also is reminiscent of the Epic of Gilgamesh, in which the hero

while treating the rest of the poem (11:4-10; 12:8) literally; (iii) Those who see a historical representation of Babylonian exile in this poem; and (iv) Those who derive an ethical code suggested by the wisdom teacher.[50] All these scholars arrive at their destination through the means of textual-critical, or historical-critical, form and rhetoric critical tools.

Let us consider them in detail.

1.1. Parallel Literature Approach

Fox identifies some similarities in form between Ecclesiastes and some of the wisdom literature of Egypt, including Kagemeni, Ptahhotep, Neferti, Onchsheshonqy, as well the Sumerian Instructions of Shuruppak, the Aramaic Words of Ahiqar.[51] For example, Qohelet addresses his reader as 'young man' (11:9). In the instruction of Vizier Ptahhotep, the old vizier Ptahhotep offers counsel to his son, calling him 'my child' on a large variety of topics.[52] Among his recommendations one finds an admonition to enjoy one's life, 'follow your heart as long as you live.' Qohelet offers a similar exhortation, "follow the ways of your heart and the desires of your eyes" (11:9).

C. L. Seow who has studied Eccl 11:4-12:8 from the point of philology and linguistics identifies five parallels with ANE literature.

(i) Unpredictability in Nature. Cf. Eccl 11:5 // "Let a living creature, a body-frame, a human form, come forth quickly [from the womb]."[53] Cf. Eccl 11:5 // Job 36:29 // Jn 3:8 ("The wind blows where it chooses, and you hear the sound of it, but you do not know where it comes from or where it goes. So it is with everyone who is born of the Spirit").[54]

(ii) 11:6 ("Sow your seed in the morning and in the evening…") // "Harvest any harvest and do any work."[55]

(iii) 11:7 ("Sweet is the light") // "May my eyes see the sun so that I may have my fill of light" (Gilgamesh Epic) or "Sweet it is to see the light" (Euripides).[56]

---

fails in his quest for everlasting life and is advised to enjoy the life that is given to him." J. J. Collins, *Introduction to the Hebrew Bible* (Minneapolis 2004), 520.

50 A. Bea who names 9:18-12:8 as 'practical advice' is a main proponent of this view. Cf. A Bea, *Liber Ecclesiastae* (Romae, 1950).

51 Cf. M. V. Fox, *Qoheleth and His Contradictions* (Sheffield 1989), 312-15.

52 "The Instruction of the Vizier Ptahhotep," in Pritchard, *Ancient Near Eastern Texts*, 343-46.

53 Cited in C. L. Seow, *Ecclesiastes. A New Translation with Introduction and Commentary* (AB 18C Doubleday 1997), 337.

54 Cf. Seow, *Ecclesiastes*, 344-45.

55 Aramaic Proverb of Ahiqar. Cited in Seow, *Ecclesiastes*, 346.

56 Cited in Seow, *Ecclesiastes*, 347.

(iv) 11:9-10 ("Rejoice…let your heart cheer you") // The Song of the Harpist ("Heap up your joys, let your heart not sink! Follow your heart and your happiness, do your things on earth as your heart commands!").

(v) 12:1b-6 ("The days of evil" or "the effects of old age"). The litany of complaints about old age in *The Instruction of Ptahhotep*:[57]
Agedness is here, old age has befallen,
Feebleness has come, weakness is arriving.
Being in discomfort, one sleeps all day long.
Eyes are dim, ears are deaf.
Strength wanes, for my heart is weary.
The mouth is silent; it cannot speak.
The mind is finished, it cannot remember the past,
The bones hurt all over.
Good has become bad; all taste is gone.
What old age does to all people is a terrible thing.
The nose is blocked up, it cannot breathe.
It is debilitating to stand or to sit.
(Papyrus Prisse, I, lines 3-10)

Let us also recall here a Sumerian text which narrates the effects of the old age in the same vein but figuratively:[58]

The old man answered the king:
My grain roasting fails,
Now my youthful vigour, strength and personal god
have left my loins like an exhausted ass.
My black mountain has produced white gypsum.
My mother has brought in a man from the forest;
he gave me captivity.
My mongoose which used to eat strong smelling things
does not stretch its neck towards beer and butter.
My urine used to flow in a strong torrent,
but now you flee from my wind.
My child whom I used to feed with butter and milk,
I can no more support it.
And I have had to sell my little slave girl;
an evil demon makes me sick.

---

57 Cited in Seow, *Ecclesiastes*, 373. SA. 'The Tale of Sinuhe,' Papyrus Berlin 3022, lines 167-70, Seow, *Ecclesiastes*, 374.

58 B. Alster, *Studies in Sumerian Proverbs* (Copenhagen 1975) 93. Cited in Seow, *Ecclesiastes*, 374. SA. M. V. Fox, "Aging and Death in Qohelet 12," in D. J. A. Clines, *The Poetical Books* (Sheffield 1997), 216.

Also note the *Instruction of Papyrus Insinger*, where one is advised "not to let the body suffer, for there are unpleasant days ahead:"[59]

> He who has passed sixty years, everything has passed for him.
> If his heart loves wine, he cannot drink to drunkenness.
> If he desires food, he cannot eat as he used it. [sic]
> If he desires a woman, her moment does not come.
> (XII, lines 11-14, *AEL* III, p. 199).

The description of the evil days of the old age and the invitation to be joyful when one is young is prevalent in the ANE literature. The scholars such as Whybray, Fox and Seow do claim that Qohelet might have been greatly influenced by these sources and might have composed his poem as a collage collected from different literary pieces to suit his audience.

Lo argues that the theme of death is the overreaching theme in the book of Ecclesiastes that holds Qohelet's argument together from the introductory poem of Eccl 1:4-8 to the concluding poem of Eccl 12:1-7. Lo believes that this theme is needed to set the stage for Qohelet's teaching on the enjoyment of life because in his thought life and death mutually define each other. She advances the discussion further by highlighting the ways in which the theme of death which is first introduced in the opening poem (1:4-8) and then finds its climax in the closing poem (12:1-7) frames Qohelet's message on life.[60]

Closely related to this textual approach is the structural approach. Those who study the structure of Ecclesiastes view the poem differently. Bea considers 11:4-12:8 as a practical advice.[61] Ginsberg divides the entire book into four sections which form a parallel pattern:[62]

A 1:2-2:26 All is vanity and man's only profit is using his goods
B 3:1-4:3 All happenings are foreordained, never foreseeable
A' 4:4-6:9 Complementary to A
B' 6:10-12:8 Complementary to B

A. G. Wright considers 11:7-12:8 as complementary to 1:2-11.[63] These two texts single out and express in an arresting way two main thoughts of the book: what profit is there in toil (the point of four of the six sections on vanity in the first half), and the advice about enjoyment (the only good that Qohelet can find for man to do).

---

59 Seow, *Ecclesiastes*, 375.

60 Cf. A. Lo, "Death in Qohelet," in *Journal of Ancient Near Eastern Studies* 31 (2009) 85-98.

61 Cf. Bea, *Liber Ecclesiastae*, 37.

62 H. L. Ginsberg, *Studies in Koheleth* (New York 1950), 1-11.

63 A. G. Wright, "The Riddle of the Sphinx. The Structure of the Book of Qoheleth," in Zuck, 63-64.

1.2. Figurative-Literal Approach

This approach looks at 11:4-12:1a and 12:8 literally, and 12:1b-7 as figuratively. The section 11:4-12:1a hardly offers problems to the exegetes as its meaning is very straightforward and plain. The scholars are divided in their interpretation of 12:1b-7b. Their views can be grouped under three categories: (i) Literal, (ii) Figurative or metaphorical or symbolic, and (iii) Allegorical.

(i) Literal: Literally these verses refer to the decreasing health of organs of the body. M. Gilbert and O. Loretz offer a literal interpretation of the poem. For Gilbert the poem is the description of "the actual experience of the old: shaking, bending, blindness, obscurity, and isolation."[64] Delitzsch considers 12:2-5a as "a literal description of a Palestinian winter's day or approaching storm, which serves as a metaphor of old age."[65] Following these C. D. Ginsburg reads the poem as a description of a gathering storm and Leahy as a depiction of fearful reactions to a thunderstorm.[66]

(ii) Figurative: "The metaphorical approach claims that the 'evil days' are symbolized by darkness, by the change of seasons (v. 2), by a description of the deterioration of the house and homestead (vv. 3-6)."[67] After stating that "the poem is difficult to understand because of the philological-textual problems, fragmentary understanding of Israelite mourning customs,"[68] Fox attempts to offer a symbolic understanding of the poem. He builds on the literal meaning of Taylor and concludes that the poem is a description of a funeral or communal lamenting.[69] J. F. A. Sawyer finds in the poem "the figure of a ruined house representing the failure of human efforts."[70] Still some other scholars propose an eschatological reading of the poem.[71]

(iii) Allegorical: "The allegorical approach argues that Qohelet is ostensibly describing something such as a house, the objects and actions portrayed represent the effects of old age. The allegory is physiological:

---

64 Cited in Fox, "Aging and Death in Qohelet 12," in Clines, *The Poetical Books,* 202.

65 Cf. F. Delitzsch, *Commentary on the Song of Songs and Ecclesiastes* (Grand Rapids [2]1970), 403-5.

66 C. D. Ginsburg, *The Song of Songs and Coheleth* (New York [2]1970), 458.

67 R. E. Murphy, *Ecclesiastes* (WBC 23A, Dallas 1992) 115. SA. R. Gordis, *Koheleth – The Man and His World* (New York 1968), 329.

68 Fox, "Aging and Death in Qohelet 12," in Clines, *The Poetical Books*, 204.

69 This approach of Fox also brings to light the eschatological symbolism present in the poem. Fox, "Aging and Death in Qohelet 12," in Clines, *The Poetical Books*, 204-19.

70 Cf. Fox, "Aging and Death in Qohelet 12," in Clines, *The Poetical Books,* 203.

71 "It is interesting to compare the imagery of the poem with a passage from an apocalypse, Syriac or 2 Baruch, written about 100 ce: 'For the youth of the world is passed and the strength of the creation is already exhausted…and the pitcher is near to the cistern and the ship to the port, and the course of the journey to the city and life to its consummation' (2 Bar. 85:10)." Collins, *Introduction to the Hebrew Bible*, 525.

specific parts of the body are associated with particular details (e.g., the ladies who look out of the window would refer to eyes that grow dim, v. 4)."[72] The allegorical interpretation of this poem, first found in *Qohelet Rabbah* and *b. Šabbat* 131b-132a, the dominant one, decodes the poem as part of the body, and the whole poem is the description of the physical degeneration of aging.[73] Some scholars see allegory only in vv. 3-5.[74]

1.3. Historical Approach

Jerome "records (commenting on 12:1a) the historical interpretation by which Israel itself is addressed and the exile is referred to."[75] Building on Jerome, J. Barbour's very recent scholarship which reads Ecclesiastes as cultural memory and excavates the story of Israel in the Book finds the city-lament in 12:1-7 and the study considers 11:1-12:8 as the retrospect of the fall of Jerusalem through the eyes of Solomon.[76] In this regard, the poet by making use of the Gen 1-4 materials in Eccl 11:4-12:8, dreams of a reversal of the Garden of Eden.

1.4. Ethical Approach

C. L. Seow is the prime advocate of this view. He calls the unit 9:1-12:8 as "Ethics: Coping with Risks and Death."[77] M. Fox, who divides the poem into two units, brings to light the two ethical instructions of Qohelet to the 'young man.' For Fox "11:7-10 is characterized as *carpe diem* ('enjoy the day'), and 12:1-8 as *memento mori* ('remember you must die')."[78] "Qohelet's ethics has no relationship to divine commandments, for there are none. It arises rather from the necessity of caution and moderation before the inexplicable, on the acceptance of what is fated and cannot be changed, and finally on grasping firmly the only satisfaction open to man – the enjoyment of being alive."[79] Gordis maintains that in this final song "most plausibly, old age is pictured without one line of thought being maintained throughout."[80]

---

72 Murphy, *Ecclesiastes*, 115.

73 Fox, "Aging and Death in Qohelet 12," in Clines, *The Poetical Books*, 201.

74 E.g., A. Lauha and K. Galling. Cf. Murphy, *Ecclesiastes*, 115.

75 Murphy, *Ecclesiastes*, 115.

76 J. Barbour, *The Story of Israel in the Book of Qoheleth. Ecclesiastes as Cultural Memory* (Oxford 2012), 138-67.

77 Cf. Seow, *Ecclesiastes*, 296,

78 Murphy, *Ecclesiastes*, 114.

79 R. B. Y. Scott, Proverbs, *Ecclesiastes* (New York 1965), 191-92.

80 Gordis, *Koheleth – The Man and His World*, 339.

2. Status Quaestiones of Paṭṭiṉattār's *Uṭalkūṟṟuvaṇṇam*

The works done on Paṭṭiṉattār's *Uṭal* are of two types: (i) Study guides; and (ii) Religious interpretation. In the study guide approach,[81] the scholar approaches the text with a scope to simplify it by dividing the *cīr* into meaningful syllabic patterns, and to explain the difficult terms through a supplementary glossary. This type of approach explains the meaning of each individual word but fails to see the presence of the rhythm in the entire poem. This approach does not consider the theme that runs through the poem. Nor does it treat the poetics adequately. In the religious interpretation approach,[82] the poem is seen as part of Śaivite religious tradition and interpreted by pointing out the intertextual links between other Śaivite poems. No single author has ever attempted to scientifically approach the poem.

3. Contributions and Lacunae

This status quaestionis has summed up the different conclusions arrived at so far in the scholarly circles.

As far as the study of Eccl 11:4-12:8 is concerned what is predominant is a diachronic mode and unfortunately no serious study has been done on *Uṭal.* The four approaches – parallel literature, figurative-literal, historical, and ethical – to the study of Eccl 11:4-12:8 are not exhaustive. They in fact give us a piecemeal approach to the text as they do not consider the poem in its entirety. Our research shows that no single scholar has ever treated Eccl 11:4-12:8 as a single literary unit, seeing, appreciating and reviewing its unitary nature. They either treat 11:7-12:8 as a poem on youth and old age and leave out 11:4-6 or they treat 11:4-10 and 12:1-8 as two independent units. We will '*distantiate*' ourselves or '*estrange*' ourselves from the text and see the entire text as a symphony between the divine and the human. This symphony is heard in the different human life stages presented in the poem. Secondly, we look at this text as a narrative poem, where we employ the tools of narrative analysis in the close reading of the text.

The review of the studies on Paṭṭiṉattār's *Uṭal* can be summed up metaphorically: "The harvest truly is plentiful, but the labourers are yet few."

We are here to fill the exegetical lacunae through two approaches which we adopt from the fields of narrative analysis and comparative literature.

3.1. Narrative Analysis

These texts of our study can be studied together, for both of them have the same narrative structure: they consist of an abstract, followed by an orientation (or setting or exposition), followed by the *complication* (also called *problem*

81 Ā. Aṅkamutu, *Paṭṭiṉattār Tiruppāṭalkaḷ* (Chennai 2008).

82 K. Kalyānasundaram, *Siddhar Paadalgal Thoguppu* (Madurai 2003).

or *crisis*), maybe an action or action orientation toward a resolution, resulting in the *resolution* (or occasionally *failure*), which then is ultimately followed by a *coda* (or *closure*). The *orientation* takes the listener into the there-and-then where actions take place, and the *coda* is taking the audience back into the here-and-now of the telling situation. Since they follow the narrative prose pattern in their composition, the possibility to employ the narrative analysis tools is greater. In these narratives the meaning emerges through two doors: (i) Through the door of experience, where the internal addresser addresses the internal addressee; and (ii) Through the door of narrative, where the narrative means such as plot, setting, characterisation, and style are put to use to bring home the sense. When we enter through the first door we are *with* the narrative, while through the second door we are *on* the narrative.

Our study will employ three approaches to work with narratives: (i) A linguistic-based approach that works through the lexical and syntactic configurations of texts and follows their build-up into the topical organisation of the text; (ii) A cognitive-based approach that works from the assumption that the story segments are held together by an overarching structure of the plot organisation; and (iii) An interactive-based approach that views stories (and their meanings) as local accomplishments among participants (in our instance, 'Qohelet and young man,' 'Paṭṭiṉattār and the Lord Śiva'). This interaction is extended to the external addressees, we, the readers. For, poems are mere dead texts when there is no reader who interacts with the text. Our study also takes into consideration the impact that these poems create in the mind of the readers. The aim of these poems is not to entertain but to educate the hearers to transform their lives for the better. At the end of the journey it is not 'what' we have studied that is important, but 'how' we have studied, and 'how' far the study has made an impact on us.

The narrative analytical tools we make use of for our study are:

(a) Structure;[83]

(b) Setting;[84]

(c) Style;[85]

(d) Characterisation;[86] and

---

83 Structuring is done with the formal and the thematic criteria.

84 Setting refers to the time-space, in which the current narrative is set.

85 We use style in a restricted sense. Style generally refers to the way a writer writes. It varies from author to author and depends entirely upon one's use of words, syntax constructions, and tone.

86 This is the way the author presents his characters in a narrative. The characterisation can be either direct and explicit or indirect and implicit. We will study this in detail in the following chapter.

(e) Themes and Motifs.[87]

3.2. Comparative Literature

Elmas Sahin defines comparative literature as "a study of the literary texts written in different languages by the most common and simple meaning, such that this means a study behind linguistic, literary, and cultural boundaries."[88] According to S. Tötösy de Zepetnek, the principles of comparative literature are:[89]

> (i) The comparative literature calls for a dialogue between cultures, languages, literatures, and disciplines; (ii) The one who compares must have an in-depth knowledge of the language in which the concerned literatures are written; (iii) The comparative literature always welcomes insights from other disciplines in the humanities and social sciences; (iv) The comparative literature from the point of view of methodology is an interdisciplinary study with three main types of methodological precision: 'intra-disciplinary' (analysis and research within the text), multi-disciplinary (by employing any other discipline), and pluri-disciplinary (arriving at the conclusions through a team-work); and (v) The comparative literature is a suitable method for two reasons: (a) It means knowledge of more than one language, or literature, knowledge and application of other disciplines; and (b) It works on the principles of the inclusion of the other.

These two approaches fill the exegetical lacunae that exist in the study and interpretation of the poems under discussion. The benefits of these two approaches are: (i) When we apply the tools of exegesis into a study of a Śaivite poem we are already opening up the horizons for the development of a new scientific mode of approaching non-Biblical texts; (ii) The comparative literature approach coupled with narrative analysis provokes affective response from the part of the reader; (iii) When we enter into comparative literature already we delve into comparative cultures. For literature is after all the

---

87 A theme is an idea that an author reiterates in his composition, making it the most important idea in his work. It is the theme that binds together various essential elements of a narrative. For example, 'revenge' is the recurrent theme in Shakespeare's Hamlet or Macbeth. On the other hand, a motif is an image, sound, action, or other figures that have a symbolic significance and contributes toward the development of the theme. For example, in Hamlet we find a recurring motif of incest coupled with incestuous desires of some of the characters.

88 E. Sahin, "On Comparative Litearture," in *International Journal of Literature and Arts* (Special Issue: World Literature, Comparative Literature and Cultural Studies) Vol. 4, No. 1-1, 2016, 5.

89 Steven Tötösy de Zepetnek mentions ten principles of comparative literature. We have adopted five from his study and have adapted them to fit our methodological framework. Cf. S. Tötösy de Zepetnek, *Comparative Literature. Theory, Method, Application* (Amsterdam 1998), 15-19.

product of a particular culture in a given space-time; (iv) A comparative study of different literatures will present us rich knowledge of literatures, languages, cultures and identities of other nations. Hence, looking at the poems as stories of human life stages, touches the core of our existence. The comparison of products gives us a chance to recognize both our values and that of others;[90] and (v) It helps us break down the boundaries we have created. When we compare two pieces of literature we begin to engage in a dialogue across time and space. In other words, "To know how others stand, that we may know how we ourselves stand, that we may correct our mistakes and achieve our deliverance – that is our problem."[91]

Acknowledging all the background studies, our dissertation serves as another link to this chain, seeking to go one step further. Building upon the works of previous scholars, it studies the poems with the tools of narrative analysis, comparative literature, and social-scientific criticism.

C. Human Life-Stages and Life Transition

The notion that human development passes through a series of stages is rooted in antiquity. Roman writers identified three to seven distinct ages of man, proceeding from conception to death. Medieval thinkers and artists formulated a variety of systems of age groups, dividing human life into three-, four-, five-, six-, seven-, ten-, and twelve-part schemata.

In Sophocles' play Oedipus the King, a monster called the Sphinx was killing travelers on the road to Thebes who could not answer its riddle: "What creature walks on four legs in the morning, two legs at noon, and three in the evening?" Finally, the hero of the play, Oedipus, came along and correctly solved the riddle: "Man." In doing so, Oedipus gave us one of our earliest maps of the human life cycle. In the morning of life (childhood), the infant crawls on all fours. In the afternoon of life (adulthood), the human being walks upright on two legs. In the evening of life (elderhood), the senior citizen walks with help from a cane. In Hinduism, human life is believed to comprise four stages. These are called ashramas: (1) '*Brahmacharya*' or the student stage; (2) '*Grahastha*' or the householder stage; (3) '*Vanaprastha*' or the hermit stage; and (4) '*Sannyasa*' or the ascetic stage. The Talmudic writer Rabbi Simon, the Son of Eliezar, divides life into seven stages based on Eccl 12:8, where the word *hebel* occurs 7 times – the two appearances of the word in plural are counted as four and thus seven: (i) Infant; (ii) Child; (iii) Boy; (iv) Young Man; (v) Matrimonial state; (vi) Parental state; and (vii) Old man.[92]

90 Cf. Sahin, "On Comparative Literature," 8.

91 Cited in Sahin, "On Comparative Literature," 8.

92 Cf. W. A. Clouston, *Flowers from a Persian Garden and Other Papers* (London 1890), 257-58.

Jean Piaget conceived of four cognitive stages of human development: (i) Sensory-motor stage [0-2 years]; (ii) Preoperational stage [2-7]; (iii) Concrete operational stage [7-11]; and (iv) Formal operational stage [11+]. Erik Erikson, being influenced by Sigmund Freud, talks about eight psychosocial stages: (i) Infancy [0-18 months]; (ii) Early childhood [2-3 years]; (iii) Play age [3-5]; (iv) School age [5-12]; (v) Adolescence [12-18]; (vi) Young adult [18-40]; (vii) Adulthood [40-65]; and (viii) Maturity [65+].[93]

Thomas Armstrong divides life-stages into twelve: (i) Prebirth; (ii) Birth; (iii) Infancy [Ages 0-3]; (iv) Early childhood [3-6]; (v) Middle childhood [6-8]; (vi) Late childhood [9-11]; (vii) Adolescence [12-20]; (viii) Early adulthood [20-35]; (ix) Midlife [35-50]; (x) Mature adulthood [50-80]; (xi) Late adulthood [80+]; and (xii) Death and dying.[94] Perhaps the best-known periodization of the human life cycle is found in William Shakespeare's play *As You Like It* (Act II, Scene VII), where he describes seven stages of human life, beginning with 'infancy' and ending with 'second childhood.'[95]

Herrin and Kazhdan confirm that the "ancient Greeks and Romans often considered the life of man as consisting of seven periods."[96] Based on Hippocrates' observation on the stages of life Philo writes:

> In man's life there are seven seasons, which they call ages, little boy, boy, lad, young man, man, elderly man, old man. He is a little boy until he reaches seven years, the time of the shedding of his teeth; a boy until he reaches puberty, i.e., up to twice seven years; a lad until his chin grows downy, i.e., up to thrice seven years; a young man until his whole body has grown, till four times seven; a man till forty-nine, till seven times seven; an elderly man till fifty-six, up to seven times eight; after that an old man.[97]

But, Augustine held to "six periods of sacred history, the six days of Creation and the six ages of man" and that on a religious plane a person also

93 Cf. E. Erikson – J. Erikson, *The Life Cycle Completed. Extended Version* (New York 1997).

94 Cf. T. Armstrong, *The Human Odyssey. Navigating the Twelve Stages of Life* (New York 2008).

95 In my research I came across a curious study on 'Seven Stages of Life' and its New Testament significance. See R. L. Overstreet, "The Greek Concept of the 'Seven Stages of Life' and Its New Testament Significance," in *Bulletin for Biblical Research* 19.4 (2009), 537-63.

96 J. Herrin – A. P. Kazhdan, "Age," in *The Oxford Dictionary of Byzantium* (New York 1991), 36.

97 Cited in Overstreet, "Concept of the Seven Stages of Life," 551.

"goes through six spiritual stages."[98] The Pythogoreans "identified four ages of man, namely *pais, neos, anēr,* and *gerōn*, in line with the four seasons."[99]

Carl Jung, the founder of school of analytical psychology, said, 'there is something sun-like within us.' He was talking about how the sun begins to rise at dawn, reaches its summit at noon, and begins to descend in the evening. Human person follows the same movement. For him/her, the descent often means the reversal of the ideals and values that were cherished in the morning. In the first half of life, all our efforts are centred on adapting to our environment. Thus, the person we become in the first 30 – 40 years of life is one that is a result of all the outside forces around us. It is not until the second half of life, at mid-life, that we are able to name ourselves. At mid-life our true identity finally emerges from our own inner world and finds expression in the person we choose to become.

Life transition can be understood in two ways: (i) A life changing event that makes us review our present sense of being. This is predictable insofar as this often happens by choice, such as getting married, having a child, entering into a profession, et al. (ii) A biological, emotional, intellectual, and spiritual change that an individual undergoes as the years pass by. This is not predictable and does not happen by choice. Rather it is forced due to internal and external circumstances. In both cases, transition means change. But, often we consciously or unconsciously become resistant to change. In the process we get stagnated. Whether positive or negative, life transitions make us leave behind the usual and enable us to adjust to new ways of living, at least temporarily. They can leave us feeling completely unprepared and we may be thrown into a personal crisis, feeling shocked, angry, sad, and withdrawn. An individual who faces the transitions comes out as a person who makes a great positive impact on the lives of others. But, the one who does not face the changes becomes a victim of the situation or an environment and pulls on tragically.

D. Conclusion

The first impressions reveal that the texts we have chosen for our study are (i) poems, (ii) narrative poem; and (iii) they share a common ground in three motifs: (a) metaphor of light to refer to life; (b) tasting sweet; and (c) rhythm of human life.

The *status quaestionis* reveals that Eccl 11:4-12:8 has so far been looked through (i) parallel-literature, (ii) figurative-literal, (iii) historical, and (iv) ethical approaches, and *Uṭal* through (i) religious literature, and (ii) spiritual

98 E. Eyben, "Roman Notes on the Course of Life," *Ancient Society* 4 (1973), 224-25.

99 R. Garland, *The Greek Way of Life. From Conception to Old Age* (Ithaca, New York 1990), 2.

commentary approaches. The current study adopts the synchronic method insofar as it employs the tools of narrative analysis and comparative literature and attempts to fill the hermeneutical lacunae.

Having surveyed the various divisions of human-life stages, and having pointed out the reality of life transition with its imperatives, the study opens the doors to enter into the perspectives of Ecclesiastes and Paṭṭiṉattār.

II. ANALYSIS OF ECCLESIASTES 11:4-12:8

Having surveyed the existing literature and having founded the methodological framework, now let us turn our attention to the close reading of the text. The current chapter, after establishing the background and the translation, studies Eccl 11:4-12:8 by employing the narrative analysis tools of setting, style, characterisation, and themes and motifs.

A. Poet: Name and Historical Context

"Qohelet (Ecclesiastes) is not someone's name. The person in question is referred to as 'king over Israel in Jerusalem' (1:12; SA. 1:16; 2:7, 9). No king is known by that name, so we can safely assume that it is a pseudonym."[100] Qohelet is a literary character created by the author to make his theological point,[101] that is, a nickname adopted by the writer to maintain a Solomonic connection for his character while also distancing his character from the actual person.[102] Qohelet may be (a) a fictional character created out of whole cloth, (b) the frame narrator's own alter ego (the vehicle by which he recounts his

100 Enns, *Ecclesiastes*, 17.

101 M. V. Fox, *A Time to Tear Down and a Time to Build Up. A Rereading of Ecclesiastes* (Grand Rapids 1999), 372-73. SA. Fox, *Qoheleth and His Contradictions,* 312. "He may be a fictional persona or the author's mouthpiece." "In Latin, 'persona' originally was the mask through which an actor spoke; it now means a character through whom an author speaks." Fox, *Time to Tear Down*, 372.

102 Cf. T. Longman, *The Book of Ecclesiastes* (The New International Commentary of the Old Testament. Grand Rapids ^{3}1998) 4. The Targum holds Solomon as the author. Cf. P. S. Knobel, *The Targum of Qoheleth* (Edinburgh 1991) 22. SA. E. Levine, *The Aramaic Version of Qoheleth* (New York 1981) 28. For example, in 1:16 we read, "I said to myself, I have surpassed in wisdom everyone who ruled Jerusalem before me." Solomon here claims to own more wisdom than anyone who went before him. But it was David alone who was the king before in Jerusalem. Also, 5:7-8 seem to be a protest against kingship. If Solomon were to be the author of these words he would have avoided this and would escape embarrassment.

own struggles), or (c) a literary product that in some sense had an 'independent' existence before its adaptation by the frame narrator.[103]

Most scholars believe that the book was written around 250 BCE, in Jerusalem.[104] The consensus of contemporary scholars is that the writer of Qohelet was a Jew living in Jerusalem during the period of Greek rule,[105] when the Jewish community was but a small island in the vast sea of the Greek empire.[106]

By the time of the Second Temple period the prophecy was on the decline in Israel. People who witnessed the dominion of Assyria, Babylonia, Persia, Egypt and Greece were disappointed with the social life. A paradigm shift took place in the way they thought. The concern for the nation gave way to a heightened interest in the individual. The key thing now was the individual's happiness. Hence, the focus shifted from the collective to the individual. To help the individual attain happiness had always been the function of wisdom. Such was the case in other places in the ANE Babylonia and Egypt. Transmission of wisdom consisted in the giving of practical counsel; not merely the transmission of technical skills but inculcating the personal qualities required to achieve success and eschew failure in life. Thus, as prophecy waned, wisdom teaching grew stronger. "Wisdom literature reached its apogee during the earlier centuries of the Second Temple, between the fifth and the second centuries BC (sic)."[107] The wisdom teacher creates an imaginary audience and

---

103 Cf. Enns, *Ecclesiastes*, 6.

104 J. Limburg, *Encountering Ecclesiastes. A Book for Our Time* (Grand Rapids 2006), 9. SA. L. Mazzinghi, *Ho cercato e ho esplorato: studi sul Qohelet* (Bologna 2001), 61.

105 "Let us present a brief flashback of Jewish history here. During the days of King David and King Solomon in the 10th century, Israel had been the ranking nation in the eastern Mediterranean world. But then came the split of the kingdom in 922 into Israel and Judah, the fall of Israel to the Assyrians in 722 and of Judah to the Babylonians in 587. A good many of the Jews were deported to Babylon, living there in exile from 587 until 539, when the Persians conquered that city and allowed them to return to Jerusalem and Judah. The Jews lived under Persian rule until 332, when the armies of Alexander the Great moved eastward and 'the world became Greek overnight,' as historians have put it." Limburg, *Encountering Ecclesiastes,* 9.

106 This is the widely accepted view. "Qohelet was written in Hebrew by a Jew in Jerusalem, who knew Aramaic but no Greek, though he was familiar with basic Greek worldview." Cf. Gordis, *Koheleth – the Man and His World*, 7. SA. Limburg, *Encountering Ecclesiastes*, 9. But based on the linguistic and cultural observations made on the Book of Ecclesiastes, some scholars deduce that the book must have been written by a Jew living in a Phoenician city. Cf. M. Dahood, "Canaanite-Phoenician Influence in Qoheleth," Bib 33 (1952), 220. This view is rejected by Seow. Cf. Seow, *Ecclesiastes*, 15. Or in Egypt. This is the view held by Humbert. "The similarities between Egyptian sayings and Qohelet are enticing." H. W. Hertzberg, *Der Predigter – Esther* (Gütersloh 1963), 42.

107 R. Gordis, "The Social Background of Wisdom Literature," *Hebrew Union College Annual* 18 (1944), 81.

addresses his teaching unto him. For, “the final two speeches in 11:1-6 and 11:7-12:8 settle the reader into a long reflective appeal that is delivered almost entirely in second-person narrative.”[108]

For Qohelet, the answer offered by traditional wisdom was no longer sufficient. Therefore, he delves into the discovery of meaning for the fundamental problems of daily life, the purpose of life, man’s destiny, the source of happiness, the basis of morality, and the problem of evil. Traditional wisdom teachers prefer not to inquire into the details of the divine plan (cf. Prov 3:20) while Qohelet makes fearless use of experience and reason when grappling with the fundamental issue concerning humanity’s *summum bonum.* “Qohelet gave dignity and meaning to the identity of being Jewish when Jewish self-identity based on nationhood, Messiah, land, and temple had failed.”[109]

B. Poem: Text[110] and Translation

11:4 *šōmēr rû^{a}ḥ lō’ yizrā‘*
wərō’eh ḇe‘āḇîm lō’ yiqṣôr
He who watches the wind will not sow
and he who sees the clouds will not reap.

11:5 *ka’ăšer ’ênəḵā yôḏē^{a}‘ mah-derek*
hārû^{a}ḥ ka‘ăṣāmîm bəḇeṭen hamməlē’āh
kāḵāh lō’ ṯēḏa‘ ’eṯ-ma‘ăśēh hā’ĕlōhîm
’ăšer ya‘ăśeh ’eṯ-hakkōl
As you do not know what (is) the way of the breath,
how bones in the womb of the full one,
so you do not know the work of God
who makes all.

11:6 *babbōqer zəra‘ ’eṯ-zar‘eḵā*
wəlā‘ereḇ ’al-tannaḥ yāḏeḵā
kî ’ênəḵā yôḏē‘ ’ê zeh yiḵšār
hăzeh ’ô-zeh wə’im-šənêhem kə’eḥāḏ ṭôḇîm

---

108 R. P. O’Dowd, “Epistemology in Ecclesiastes. Remembering what it Means to be Human,” in M. J. Boda - T. Longman III - C. G. Rata, eds., *The Words of the Wise are like Goads. Engaging Qohelet in the 21st Century* (Winona Lake 2013), 215.

109 A. P. Hayman, “Qoheleth and the Book of Creation,” JSOT 50 (1991), 93-111.

110 The text we are using for our study is from K. Elliger – W. Rudolf, *Biblia Hebraica Stuttgartensia* (BHS) Fifth Critical Edition (Stuttgart 2006) 1352-53. The critical apparatus at the bottom of these pages is studied and interpreted in the notes. Additionally, we have consulted A. Schenker – et al, *Biblia Hebraica Quinta* (BHQ) (Stuttgart 2004) 50-52. The BHQ edition interprets the Masorah Magna (MM) or Great Masorah, which is found in the side margins of the manuscript and Masorah Parva (MP) or Small Masorah, which is found between the columns of the manuscript. We have carefully picked up the interpretations, which help us understand the text better.

In the morning sow your seed,
and in the evening do not withdraw your hand,
for you do not know which will succeed –
this or that, or both are good together.

11:7 *ûmāṯôq hā'ōr*
wəṭôḇ la'ênayim lir'ôṯ 'eṯ-haššāmeš
And sweet is the light
and it is good for the eyes to see the sun.

11:8 *kî 'im-šānîm harbēh yiḥyeh hā'āḏām*
bəḵullām yiśmāḥ
wəyizkōr 'eṯ-yəmê haḥōšeḵ kî-harbēh yihyû
kol-šebbā' hāḇel
Even if many years the man lives,
let him rejoice in them all
and let him remember the days of darkness will be many -
All that comes is fleeting.

11:9 *śemaḥ bāḥûr bəyalḏûṯēḵā*
wîṭîḇḵā libbəḵā bîmê ḇəḥûrôṯeḵā wəhallēḵ
bəḏarḵê libbəḵā ûḇəmar'ê 'ênêḵā wəḏā' kî
'al-kol-'ēlleh yəḇî'ăḵā hā'ĕlōhîm bammišpāṭ
Rejoice, O young man, in your childhoods
and let your heart cheer you in the days of your youth
and walk in the ways of your heart and the sights of your eyes
and know that for all these God will bring you to judgment.

11:10 *wəhāsēr ka'as millibbeḵā*
wəha'ăḇēr rā'āh mibbəśāreḵā
kî-hayyalḏûṯ wəhaššaḥărûṯ hāḇel
And turn aside anxiety from your heart
and cause evil to pass from your flesh,
for the childhood and the black hair are fleeting.

12:1 *ûzəḵōr 'eṯ-bor'êḵā bîmê bəḥûrōṯêḵā*
'aḏ 'ăšer lō'-yāḇō'û yəmê hārā'āh
wəhiggî'û šānîm 'ăšer tō'mar 'ên-lî ḇāhem ḥēpeṣ
And remember your creators in the days of your youths –
before the evil days come and
the years arrive, when you will say, "I have no pleasure in them"

12:2 *'aḏ 'ăšer lō'-ṯeḥšaḵ haššemeš*
wəhā'ôr wəhayyārē^{a}ḥ wəhakkôḵāḇîm
wəšāḇû he'āḇîm 'aḥar haggāšem
Before the sun is darkened,

and the light, and the moon, and the stars,
and the clouds return after the rain

12:3 *bayyôm šeyyāzu'û šōmrê habbayiṯ*
wəhiṭ'awwəṯû 'anšê heḥāyil
ûḇāṭlû haṭṭōḥănôṯ kî mī'ēṭû
wəḥāšḵû hārō'ôṯ bā'ărubbôṯ
On the day when the keepers of the house tremble,
and men of strength stoop down,
and the grinders stop because they have become few,
and those looking at the windows have become dim.

12:4 *wəsuggərû ḏəlāṯayim baššuq*
bišpal qôl haṭṭaḥănāh
wəyāqûm ləqôl haṣṣippôr
wəyiššaḥû kol-bənôṯ haššîr
and doors in the street are shut, sound of the grinding subdues,
and (one) rises at the sound of the bird,
and all the daughters of the song are brought low,

12:5 *gam miggāḇōᵃh yīrā'û wəḥaṯḥattîm badderek*
wəyānē'ṣ haššāqēḏ
wəyistabbēl heḥāgāḇ
wəṯāpēr hā'ăḇiyyônāh
kî-hōlēḵ hā'āḏām 'el-bêṯ 'ôlāmô
wəsāḇəḇû ḇaššûq hassōpḏîm
and of that which is high they fear, and the terrors are in the road,
and the almond tree blossoms,
and the grasshopper drags,
and the caper berry shrivels up –
because the man walks to his eternal home,
and the mourners go about in the streets –

12:6 *'aḏ 'ăšer lō'-yērāḥēq ḥeḇel hakkesep*
wəṯārūṣ gullaṯ hazzāhāḇ
wəṯiššāḇer kaḏ 'al-hammabbûᵃ'
wənārōṣ haggalgal 'el-habbôr
before the silver cord is snapped,
and the golden bowl is shattered,
and the pitcher is broken at the fountain,
and the wheel is shattered to the well.

12:7 *wəyāšōḇ he'āpār 'al-hā'āreṣ kəšehāyāh*
wəhārûᵃḥ tāšûḇ 'el-hā'ĕlōhîm 'ăšer nəṯānāh

And the dust returns to the earth as it was
and the breath returns to God who gave it.

12:8 *hăḇēl hăḇālîm 'āmar haqqôheleṯ hakkōl hāḇel*
'Vanity of vanities,' says the teacher, 'all is vanity.'

C. Delimitation and Structure

At the outset let us delimit the poem Eccl 11:4-12:8 as a single literary unit. Thematically, Ogden divides 11:1-12:8 into two sections: 11:1-6 and 11:7-12:8. He gives four reasons to justify the division:[111] (a) There has been a change in subject matter by the time one enters ch. 11, from a concern with wise and foolish conduct in ch. 10 to concerns expressed in terminology depicting the natural world; (b) The role of imperatives in 11:1-6; (c) This section has a series of parallel sentences; and (d) The unifying theme of 'knowing' and 'not knowing.' But we differ from Ogden and establish that the unit begins not in 11:1, but in 11:4. For, (a) The theme of 'sowing the seed' taken metaphorically to mean 'to beget children' is developed in the rest of the poem as how a child grows into an adult and dies. Life moves from 'nothing' to 'nothing;' (b) The two imperatives 'rejoice,' and 'remember' not only knit the poem together but also give momentum to the development of the theme of 'tasting the light / life;' (c) There are similar word-pairs within the poem; (d) The theme of 'knowing' and 'not knowing' is continued until 12:8.

11:4-12:8 stands as an independent literary unit on account of the theme of the rhythm of human life with its four irreversible seasons, conception, childhood, youth, and old age. There are parallelisms, the word-pairs, and the word-plays that are unique to the poem.[112]

The key reasons that would justify our argument that Eccl 11:4 – 12:8 can be considered as a unified literary unit: (i) The words found in this text have an intertextual link with the Creation theology (Gen 1-4). The Creator gives life and takes life in 11:5 and 12:7; (ii) The uncertainties of 11:4-6 are the background for the certainties in 11:7-12:8; and (iii) Imperatives and word-pairs hold the section as a unified whole.

111 Cf. G. S. Ogden, "Qoheleth IX 17 – X 20: Variations on the Theme of Wisdom's Strength and Vulnerability," in *VT* 30 (1980) 27-37. "Qoheleth XI 1-6," in *Vetus Testamentum* 33 (1983), 222-30.

112 The detailed discussion is undertaken in the analysis of the style of the poem.

There are two structural markers: (i) The verb 'to see' which appears as the Qal participle masculine singular in v. 11:4 appears in the entire book 47 times. Of these 47x, 20x it is Qohelet, who is the subject of the verb.[113] The subject reappears in third person singular in 12:8 and forms an *inclusio* with 11:4; (ii) 11:5 speaks about the entry of 'the spirit' into the womb of a pregnant woman to give life to the bones while 12:7 mentions about its exit from the human body.

The word 'spirit' marks the change of argument from what precedes in 11:1-3. In 11:1-3, there is an exhortation to improve one's financial stability (11:1), followed by a counsel (11:2) and a maxim-like declaration (11:3). Though the adverbial phrase 'on the earth,' the verb 'to fill,' and the nouns, 'clouds' and 'rain' are taken up again in our poem in 12:7, 11:5, and 12:2 respectively, the context of these differ from the literary setting of the poem. The section that follows 12:8 is prose in nature and is an epilogue to the book.

The poem can be structured after the theme of rhythm of human life as follows:

Verses	Stage	Theme
11:4-6	Entry Life	Conception (the spirit comes to the bones in the womb)
11:7-8	Stage 1	Birth (it is good for the eyes to see the light)
11:9-10	Stage 2	Childhood (in the days of childhood)
12:1a	Stage 3	Youth (in the days of your youth)
12:1b-5a	Stage 4	Old Age (the evil days)
12:5b-8	Exit Life	Death (the spirit returns to God)

The word 'the spirit' opens the life cycle at 11:5 and closes it at 11:7. In other words 11:5 marks the entry of 'the spirit' while 11:8 marks her exit. The poem moves from 'life' in 11:5 to 'no life' in 12:7.

Now let us analyse the markers that allude to each stage of human life cycle: (i) The expressions, 'the way of the spirit,' 'the womb of the pregnant woman' (11:5), and 'sow your seed' refer to the conception.[114] (ii) The birth is described in a figurative language. The common verb for 'being born' or 'giving birth' is '*yld*' (cf. Eccl 7:1). 'To see the sun' is a common expression

113 Ecc 1:14, 16; 2:3, 12, 13, 24; 3:10, 16, 22; 4:1, 4, 7, 15; 5:12, 17; 6:1; 7:15; 8:9, 10, 17; 9:13; 10:5, 7.

114 The expression is used elsewhere in HB to refer to human conception in Lev 12:2; Num 5:28; and Jer 31:27.

for birth in the ANE tradition.[115] In Eccl 4:3, Qohelet describes a 'yet to be born' or 'one who is not born' as 'not has been who has not seen light.' Therefore, based on these two instances we can deduce that v. 7 connotes to 'birth,' the stage 1 of human life cycle. (iii) The noun in 11:9 *yal*d̲*û*t̲ can be translated as 'childhood' or 'youth. The word appears 3x in the HB (Ps 110:3; Eccl 11:9, 10). In Ps 110:3 *yald̲ût̲* is something that comes off the 'womb.' Therefore, it can be distinguished from 'youth' which is after 'childhood.' 'Childhood' precedes 'youth.' In Eccl 12:1 we have the word *bəḥûrōt̲* which can be rendered only as 'youth.' Moreover, the noun, 'dawn' that appears together with *yald̲ût̲* in 11:10 also confirms this argument, for 'childhood' is the 'dawn' of human life. Hence, we can say that *yald̲ût̲* in 11:9 refers to 'childhood,' the stage 2. (iv) The mention of stage 3 in the poem is straightforward by the word *bəḥûrōt̲*. The verb that precedes this noun, 'to remember' refers to the mental faculty which is fully developed only at this stage of youth or young adulthood. (v) The stage 4, 'old age,' can be inferred from the phrases such as, 'days of evil' and 'years of no pleasure' in 12:1. What follow in 12:2-5 in fact paraphrase these expressions. (vi) Death is expressed both directly - 'the man goes to his eternal home', 'the mourners', 'the dust to the earth,' 'the spirit,' and 'to God' – and indirectly through the funeral rite of breaking of the jar and pitcher in 12:6.

115 This is common in Italian as well. "Maria diede alla luce il suo figlio primogenito..." ("Mary gave to the light – gave birth – to her firstborn son...") (Lk 2:7).

The elements of this thematic structure on the rhythm of human life cycle will fit into the quinary scheme of a plot in narrative analysis.[116]

Abstract	"He who observes the wind will not sow, and he who regards the clouds will not reap"
Initial Situation[117]	'Entry Life'
Complication[118]	'Birth'
	'Childhood'
Transforming action[119]	"Remember your Creator in the days of your youth"
Denouement or Resolution[120]	'Youth'
	'Old Age'
Final Situation[121]	'Exit Life'
Coda	"Vanity of vanities, all is vanity"

116 "The structure of the story is its plot." D. Marguerat - Y. Bourquin, *How to Read Bible Stories. An Introduction to Narrative Criticism* (London 1999) 40. Linearity and relatedness are the hallmarks of a plot. One action must follow the other and the actions must be co-related. Cf. S. Bar-Efrat, *Narrative Art in the Bible* (London 1989) 93. The simplest plot outline comes from Aristotle, who wrote that all plots have a beginning, middle and an end. Patterning after Aristotle, Freytag makes a pyramid structure: rising action, climax and a falling action. Cf. J. L. Ska, *Our Fathers Have Told Us. Introduction to the Analysis of the Hebrew Narratives* (Rome 1990) 30. P. Larivaille has refined the Aristotelian model and has proposed the famous quinary scheme. According to him the plot consists of five stages: (1) Initial situation (or exposition), (2) Complication, (3) Transforming action, (4) Denouement (or resolution) and (5) Final situation. Cf. Marguerat - Bourquin, *How to Read*, 43.

117 Initial situation or exposition is "the circumstances of the action (setting, characters), if need be a shortage of something is indicated (sickness, difficulty, ignorance); the narrative will show an attempt to remove it." Marguerat - Bourquin, *How to Read*, 44.

118 Complication is "an element that sets off the narrative, introducing narrative tension (a lack of equilibrium in the initial state or complication in the quest." Marguerat - Bourquin, *How to Read*, 44.

119 Transforming action is "the outcome of the quest, reversing the initial situation: the transforming action is either at a pragmatic (action) or a cognitive (evaluation) level." Marguerat - Bourquin, *How to Read*, 44.

120 Denouement or resolution is "the removal of the tension by the application of the transforming action to the subject." Marguerat - Bourquin, *How to Read*, 44.

121 Final Situation is the "statement of the new state attained by the subject following the transformation. Structurally this moment corresponds to the reversal of the initial situation by an elimination of the shortage." Marguerat - Bourquin, *How to Read*, 44.

To the quinary scheme we have added two elements from Labov's model adopted by Berlin: 'abstract' and 'coda.'[122] The 'transforming action' is the centre to the structure, where the protagonist of the poem, the young person, is exhorted 'to remember' the Creator, who causes the 'breath' to enter and to exit and who has blessed human life with 'days of pleasure' and 'days of evil.'

The above quinary scheme also can be patterned into a concentric pattern keeping the 'transforming action' as the centre:

A Introduction (11:4)
B 'Entry Life' (11:5-6)
C 'Rejoice when there is light' (11:7-10)
D 'Remember your creator' (12:1a)
C' 'The days of darkness' (12:1b-5a)
B' 'Exit Life' (12:5b-7)
A' Conclusion (12:8)

This structure reflects the three major contradictions present in the poem: (i) Qohelet 'sees' (11:4) 'everything' (11:5) as made by God while in 12:8 he declares everything to be futile; (ii) The life-breath, 'the spirit' enters the human being in 11:5 and exits in 12:7; and (iii) The 'sun' in 11:7 is 'darkened' in 12:2.

D. Setting

As the narrative prose is set in a particular space and time the narrative poem also has a spatial and temporal setting. "Setting is related to plot and character. The characters live and act, with the setting providing the background. The setting provides the physical location of the action, sometimes adds atmosphere, and at other times supports the message of the passage."[123]

Before undertaking the setting analysis let us establish the difference between 'story' and 'discourse' in a poem. The 'story' refers to 'what' is told in the poem, while 'discourse' refers to 'how' it is told what is told in the poem. The 'how' involves the question of who is speaking to whom and how the information is exchanged.

In a poem there is an addresser and an addressee, who can be both internal and external. In our poem, the original writer of the Book of Ecclesiastes is the external addresser while Qohelet mentioned in 12:8 is the internal addresser. Everyone who reads the poem is an external addressee while 'the young man' mentioned in 11:9 is the internal addressee. In the poem, Qohelet, the internal addresser, addresses both the external addressee and the internal addressee.

122 The 'abstract' is a kind of 'title' and 'coda' is a possible conclusion of a story bringing the reader back to his world. Cf. Ska, Our Fathers, 30-31.

123 Longman, *Biblical Interpretation*, 94.

The address to the external addressee, let us call 'indirect' and that to the internal addressee, let us call 'direct.' The 'indirect' and 'direct' addresses in the poem can be tabulated as follows:

<table>
<tr><td>Indirect</td><td rowspan="2">Stanza 1</td><td>11:4</td><td>Prelude</td></tr>
<tr><td>Direct</td><td>11:5-6</td><td>Conception</td></tr>
<tr><td>Indirect</td><td>Stanza 2</td><td>11:7-8</td><td>Interlude - Birth</td></tr>
<tr><td rowspan="4">Direct</td><td>Stanza 3</td><td>11:9-10</td><td>Childhood</td></tr>
<tr><td rowspan="3">Stanza 4</td><td>12:1a</td><td>Youth</td></tr>
<tr><td>12:1b-12:5a</td><td>Old Age</td></tr>
<tr><td>12:5b-7</td><td>Death</td></tr>
<tr><td>Indirect</td><td>Coda</td><td>12:8</td><td>Postlude</td></tr>
</table>

The above table shows the autonomy the poet enjoys in developing the plot of the poem. He constantly shifts his addressee. Shifting of addressee does not mean that the addressee must listen to only what is said to him, but must take everything together. Shifting of addressee extends the suspense.

The poet does not claim omniscience throughout the poem. At the stage of conception of life, even the poet does *not* know how the life-breath enters the bones. But throughout the poem he seems to know the 'complete information.'[124] The description of 'old age' in apocalyptic or eschatological terms shows the extraordinary 'competence' of the poet.

The narrator is dramatized in the poem. He is present as an explicit recognizable 'voice' in the narration.[125] The narrative voice in the poem falls under the categories of 'extradiegetic'[126] and 'homodiegetic.'[127] The narration in the poem is both 'scenic,' 'dramatic' (showing mode) and 'directly addressing' (telling mode).[128] The focalization that the narrator adopts is 'zero focalization,' or 'vision from behind,' as the narrator says more than what the characters can know.[129]

124 'Complete information' is the preferred term to 'omniscient narrator.' Cf. Ska, *Our Fathers*, 45.

125 Cf. Ska, *Our Fathers*, 45.

126 The narrator is outside the story. Cf. Ska, *Our Fathers*, 46.

127 The narrator tells his own story. Cf. Ska, *Our Fathers*, 46.

128 Cf. Ska, *Our Fathers*, 53.

129 Cf. Ska, *Our Fathers*, 67. When we state this we assume that God is not the direct character involved in the poem.

The 'narration time' or the 'discourse time' of the poem is very short, as it requires only a few minutes to read through the poem. On the other hand, the 'narrated time' or the 'story time' spans from conception to death of a human person.[130] The 'story' in the poem covers the entire lifetime of a human person. The 'duration'[131] of the poem is four stanzas and a coda, together having 19 strophes. The poet follows the chronological order. However, when in each stanza he takes up the key expressions from the previous stanza, the key verses act as 'prolepses.'[132]

There are also certain gaps in the stanzas.[133] In stanza 2 (11:7-8) the author introduces two nouns, 'the light' and 'the darkness,' and two verbs, 'let him rejoice' and 'let him remember.' In the following stanza (Stanza 3, 11:9-10), he takes up 'the light' and 'let him rejoice' and omits 'the darkness' and 'let him remember.' The omissions are called back in Stanza 4 (12:1-7).

As far as the order of the time is concerned, the poem is hypotactic as there are logical and temporal connections between the different scenes and episodes and they are expressed by temporal indicators such as 'before' and 'when' or 'at that time.' These seven verses comprise one long sentence in Hebrew: the main clause is 12:1a, while 12:1b-7 consists of five subordinate temporal clauses (before [v.1b] … before [v. 2a] … when [v. 3a] … when [v. 4b] … before [v. 6a]).

In the second direct address (11:9-12:7), i.e., in stanzas 3 and 4, the poet slows down the narrative. The slower the time moves the more important the content because the narrator has decided to select a particular event to highlight apart from the fast-moving panorama of the story.[134] Though the stanzas are in dialogue mode, the ratio between narration time and narrated time is not 1:1 for two reasons:[135] (i) The addressee is not allowed to respond to the addresser. No dialogue; and (ii) The events described reach beyond the moment of addressing.

130 Narration time refers to time in the real world, external to the story. In other words, narration time is concerned with how long it takes a reader to move through the narrative. Narrated time, on the other hand, refers to the time internal to the story world, meaning the minutes, hours, days and years within the story. Cf. Alter, *Biblical Narrative*, 63. Bar-Efrat, *Narrative Art*, 143.

131 The 'duration' is the length of the narrative and is measured in words, sentences, lines, verses, paragraphs, pages, chapters, etc. Cf. Ska, *Our Fathers,* 8.

132 They anticipate what is to come next. Cf. Ska, *Our Fathers*, 8.

133 Gaps are relevant to the narration. Through them the authors create effects of surprise, expectation, suspense. Cf. Ska, *Our Fathers,* 8-9.

134 Cf. Alter, *Biblical Narrative*, 65.

135 "In dialogues narration time is very close to narrative time." Ska, *Our Fathers*, 8.

The time covered in the direct addresses (Stanzas 1, 3, and 4) can be tabulated as follows:

Stanza 1	11:(4)5-6	10 months
Stanza 3	11:9-10	0 – 12 years
Stanza 4	12:1-7	13 – 70 years

In Stanza 2 (11:7-8) and Coda (12:8) the time covered is 0 – 70 years of human life. Thus, in the indirect addresses the time is full while in the direct addresses the time is split.

Closely related to time is space. The main method of developing space is through the movement of characters from one locale to another.[136] In the poem there is no movement in external space. The internal addressee is stable in one place and the internal addresser moves him from 'womb' to 'tomb,' from 'life-breath' to 'no-life breath' in an internal imaginary journey.

E. Style

Besides setting, plot, and characterisation (we do in next section), the Hebrew poet skilfully employs complex literary devices that help him compose a timeless narrative that effectively communicates his ideological point of view.[137] For this reason the methodology to approach a narrative or a narrative poem is often called an art.[138] The enquiry into the style reveals shades of meaning that are subtly expressed by the narrator through not 'what' it is written, but 'how' it is written.[139]

We group our study of the style in Eccl 11:4-12:8 into three categories: (i) Parallelism, which is basically a stylistic feature of repetition of words and thoughts; (ii) Word-play, where through sound techniques such as rhyme, paronomasia, alliteration, and consonance the poet ties words and passages together, thus linking their meanings as either emphasized, paralleled, or contrasted; and (iii) Word-picture such as metaphor, metonymy, synecdoche, simile, allegory, irony, where though words are words, they convey 'more to seeing than what meets the eye.' Identifying and analysing why, when, and how the poet chooses to use these literary devices is an important task that promises to bear fruit, metaphorically speaking.

---

136 Cf. Bar-Efrat, *Narrative Art*, 185.

137 Cf. Bar-Efrat, *Narrative Art*, 198.

138 "Discussions of biblical narrative often have occasion to use the term 'art'...As I have come to understand it, 'art' in this context should not be understood only in the sense of 'skill,' 'craft,' 'technique,' but in the sense of an art-form, like painting and music." A. Berlin, *Poetics and Interpretation of Biblical Narrative* (Winona Lake 1994), 135.

139 Cf. Bar-Efrat, *Narrative Art*, 198.

1. Parallelism

A parallelism is a rhyme of thought. Parallelism implies "a rhythm, a balance, a regularity, not of sound but of thought."[140] Parallelism can be defined as the repetition of the same or related semantic event and / or grammatical structure in consecutive lines or verses.[141] Kugel describes parallelism as follows:

> The basic feature of biblical songs – and, for that matter, of most of the sayings, proverbs, laws, laments, blessings, curses, prayers, and speeches found in the Hebrew Bible – is the recurrent use of a relatively short sentence-form that consists of two brief clauses. The clauses are regularly separated by a pause – slight because the second is ... a continuation of the first and not a wholly new beginning. By contrast, the second ends in a full pause.[142]

In Eccl 11:4-12:8 we find four types of parallelism:

(i) Synonymous;
(ii) Semantic;
(iii) Staircase; and
(iv) Chiastic.

1.1. Synonymous Parallelism

In synonymous parallelism the same sense is expressed in different but equivalent terms.[143] The synonymous parallelism is found in 11:7 and 11:10.

11:7

Colon 1	And sweet	is		the light
	a	b	c	d
	a'	b'	c'	d'
Colon 2	And good	it is	for the eyes	to see the sun

140 Cited in Maria Selvam, *Song of Songs*, 51. Maria Selvam puts forward three approaches to parallelism: (a) Poet-Listener based theory. This approach emphasizes the role of the poet in constructing a parallelism and that of the reader or listener who recognizes and responds to the parallelism; (b) Structural parallelism, which is very rigid and established by examining the grammatical-syntactical structure; and (c) Mathematical concept approach, which is proposed by W. G. E. Watson, is based on the mathematical concepts of symmetry, asymmetry and parallelism. Cf. Maria Selvam, *Song of Songs*, 51-52. Our approach is a mixture of 'a' and 'b.'

141 Cf. A. Berlin, "Parallelism," *ABD*, Vol. 5 (Doubleday 1992), 155-62.

142 Cited in Watson, *Hebrew Poetry*, 120.

143 Cf. Berlin, "Parallelism," 155-62.

11:7 can be divided into two colons consisting of four elements each.[144] However, in colon 1, there is an ellipsis or gapping of 'c.' The adjective 'good' (a') is parallel to 'sweet' (a),[145] and 'to see the sun' (d') is parallel to 'the light' (d). If we read this verse with 12:2, the parallelism may become problematic. For, in 12:2 'the light' is given as a reality independent of 'the sun.' Nevertheless, the problem can be solved. In ancient texts, the expression 'seeing the light' (cf. Job 3:20; 33:30; Ps 58:9) means 'living.'[146] This same expression Qohelet uses as well in 6:5 and 7:11. And if 'seeing the light' means 'living,' 'not seeing the light' would signify 'dying or death' (cf. Ps 58:9). There is an internal evidence to this in 11:8, where the verb used is 'to live' and this verb runs semantically parallel to 'to see the sun' in 11:7 and can be used interchangeably. Hence, the parallelism is justified. Here the parallelism functions as an emphatic affirmation.

11:10

Colon 1	*Turn aside*	*anxiety*	*from your heart*
	a	b	c
	a'	b'	c'
Colon 2	*Cause to pass from*	*evil*	*from your flesh*

The first part of 11:10 consists of two colons with three elements each. The elements a, b, and c are parallel to a', b', and c'. The verb *swr* in Hiphil imperative means 'to remove or to get rid of.' In all the 7 instances[147] it appears as an imperative in the HB the sense is very forceful. It is used to urge on to do away with something completely or to eradicate fully and no more to be entertained.[148] The parallel verb *'br* in Hiphil also means 'to remove or wipe away.' The verb in Hiphil form appears in three other instances in the HB.[149]

144 "A colon is a single line of poetry, either as a semi-independent unit, or as part of a larger strophe." Watson, *Hebrew Poetry*, 12.

145 The Akkadian equivalent of the word, matqu, 'sweet,' is glossed in lexicals texts as ṭābu, 'good, delightful, sweet'. Cf. Seow, *Ecclesiastes*, 347.

146 "May my eyes see the sun so that I may be full of light" (Gilg M 13). Cited in Seow, *Ecclesiastes*, 347.

147 1 Kgs 20:24, Amos 5:23, Ps 39:11, Ps 119:29, Prov 4:24, 27, and Eccl 11:10.

148 For example, "Take away from me your noisy songs; I don't want to hear the music of your stringed instruments" (Amos 5:23). Here the Lord, who proposes "justice flowing like torrents of water and righteous actions like a stream that never dries up," comes heavily upon the people to stop their songs and music that are part of their cultic celebrations. Here the music has to be done away with completely.

149 "...now O Lord, please remove the guilt of your servant" (2 Sam 24:10); "Make my eyes pass by from looking at what is worthless" (Ps 119:37); and "take away the insults that I dread" (Ps 119:39).

The noun, 'vexation or anxiety' appears 6x in Eccl.[150] Of these 6 instances 2 are worth noting: first, in 5:16 Qohelet says that 'vexation or anxiety' is part of the days of darkness;[151] second, in 7:3, where Qohelet prefers 'anxiety' to laughter, where it is 'anxiety' that makes the heart glad. Except in 7:3, in all the instances Qohelet considers 'anxiety' as redundant and evil. The 'heart' (c) and 'flesh' (c') are parallel to one another as they belong to the human body.[152] Hence, anxiety is evil to the heart as pain is evil to the body and both are to be wiped away. The synonymous parallelism also brings to light the holistic view of Qohelet. Qohelet exhorts the young man to remove pain internally and externally. Thus, by removing anxiety from one's heart and by removing evil or unpleasantness from one's body a young person is called to rejoice. The function of this parallelism is to present a global picture or to express a *merismus*.[153]

1.2. Semantic Parallelism

According to the linguistic model of parallelism, the semantic aspect also can create a parallelism. The semantic aspect pertains to the relationship between the meaning of the parallel lines.[154] We have three examples of this parallelism in our poem, in 11:4, 12:1 and 12:6.

11:4

Colon 1	*He who watches*	*the wind*	*will not sow*
	a	b	c
	a'	b'	c'
Colon 2	*He who sees*	*the cloud*	*will not reap*

11:4 divides into two colons with three elements each. The elements a and a' fall under the semantic field of 'seeing,' or 'observing' while c and c' belong to the world of 'agriculture' and 'farming.' The elements b and b' are ethereal elements. The elements a, b, and c are semantically parallel to a', b',

150 "In much wisdom is much vexation" (1:18); "their work is a vexation" (2:23); the days of darkness will contain "much vexation, sickness and anger" (5:16); "sorrow is better than laughter" (7:3); "anger lodges in the bosom of fools" (7:9); and "banish anxiety from your mind" (11:10). NRSV translates the same word into 'vexation,' 'sorrow,' 'anger,' and 'anxiety.'

151 5:16 belongs to the pericope 5:8-20, which talks about futility of worldly life, where appears the word 'sweet' that Qohelet uses in 11:7.

152 These two elements also form a closure with one another: the 'heart' refers to the inner realm of a human person while the 'flesh' stands for the outer.

153 By saying 'heart' and 'flesh' the poet not only says that the young person must banish pain and anxiety from these two elements, but must banish entirely and at all times.

154 Cf. Berlin, "Parallelism," 155-62.

and c'. The elements c and c' are also paralleled to one another by using the negative particle 'not'. The thought presented in colon 1 is repeated in colon 2 in similar semantic word-fields. The word-fields *rhyme* with one another lexically. The meaning conveyed in colon 1 and 2 is the same, i.e., 'those who are over-cautious or who are distracted will neither sow nor reap.' The parallelism expresses a harmony between 'sowing' and 'reaping.'

12:1

Colon 1	come	the days	of evil
	a	b	c
	a'	b'	c'
Colon 2	arrive	the years	'I have no pleasure'

The temporal clause, starting with 'before' is made of two propositions which are in synonymous parallelism. The verbs 'come' (a) and 'arrive' (a') fall within the semantic field of 'nearness' or 'closeness,' while 'the days' (b) and 'the years' (b') are time elements. The 'of evil' (c) is contrasted with a negative in 'no pleasure' (c'). Qohelet, through a repetition of the words in the same semantic field emphasizes the imminent advent of the evil days. Here parallelism expresses inevitability.

12:6

	a	b	c
Colon 1	*snapped*	*the cord*	*of silver*
Colon 2	*shattered*	*the bowl*	*of gold*
Colon 3	*broken*	*the pitcher*	*at the fountain*
Colon 4	*shattered*	*the wheel*	*to the well*

Just as 12:1a, 12:6 is also a temporal clause beginning with 'before' and consists of four colons. This interesting and enigmatic verse demands a lot of attention. Structurally speaking, colon 2 and colon 4 are synonymously parallel to one another as the verbs are from the same root; colons 3 and 4 are synonymously parallel to one another as far as their 'c' elements are considered - colons 1 and 2 refer to the action of 'snapping,' or 'breaking' while colons 3 and 4, not only refer to the actions, but also refer to the place, 'the fountain' and 'the well,' where such action is taking place. And colons 1 and 2 are synonymously parallel to one another as far the material causes, 'silver,' and 'gold' ('c' elements) are considered. The expressions, 'the silver cord,' 'the golden bowl,' 'the pitcher,' and 'the vessel or the water-wheel or the pulley' - all refer to one thing which is used predominantly and is shattered during the funeral literally and symbolically.[155] All these four colons point to the same thing – the death. The function of parallelism in this instance is emphatic.

1.3. Staircase Parallelism

Staircase parallelism is a form of couplet (or tricolon) which proceeds in steps.[156] It is a step-like pattern in which some elements from the first line are repeated verbatim in the second and others are added to complete the thought.[157]

We have its occurrence in **11:9**

Colon 1	Rejoice, O young man, in your childhoods
Colon 2	let your heart cheer you in the days of your youth
Colon 3	walk in the ways of your heart and the sights of your eyes

The noun, 'young man,' in colon 1 is taken up as 'your youth' in colon 2. The noun, 'your heart' of colon 2 reappears verbatim in colon 3. The imperative, 'rejoice' of colon 1 is paraphrased in the imperatives of colons 2 and 3, i.e., 'let your heart cheer' and 'walk in the ways of your heart.' These colons are structured in the pattern of 'three words – four words – five words' in Hebrew. Colon 1 is a general invitation to 'rejoice.' Colon 2 explains colon 1 in terms of 'internal enjoyment,' while colon 3 explicates in terms of 'external enjoyment.' If we take colons 2 and 3 alone, we note a direction in the experience of joy – from within to without. The parallelism is employed through synonymous words.

1.4. Chiastic Parallelism

Fredericks identifies two chiastic parallelisms in the poem:

i. In 11:3 – 12:2, the centre of the chiasm is 'Know that God will bring to judgment' (11:9).[158]

11:3 **A** Clouds and Rain
11:7 **B** Light and Sun
11:8 **C** Consider the days of Darkness
D All that comes is breath
11:9 **E** Enjoy your youth
F Know…the God of Judgment
11:10 **E'** Enjoy your youth
D' All of youth is breath

155 This custom is found in Tamil funeral practice as well.

156 Watson prefers the term 'staircase parallelism' to 'climactic parallelism' or 'repetitive parallelism.' Cf. Watson, *Hebrew Poetry*, 150.

157 Cf. Berlin, "Parallelism," 155-62.

158 Cf. Fredericks, "Life's Storms and Qoheleth 11:1-12:8," 101.

12:1 **C'** Consider God before days of darkness / evil
12:2 **B'** Sun and Light
A' Clouds and Rain

ii. **A** The grinders are ceasing since there are so few
B and those looking through windows darken
A' and the doors of the street are being shut
B' while the sound of grinding diminishes

"In this sentence a chiasm is formed by two comments on the limited milling (either that is ceasing, or that its sound is decreasing) which frame the comments about the openings in the houses of the millers ('windows' and 'doors')."[159]

2. Word-Play

2.1. Word-Pairs

The narrator tends to repeat the words literally within a narrative. The parallel word-pairs can be found either in a colon immediately following or within a single literary unit. A word-pair is a repetition, which is manifested in many forms, including duplication,[160] key words,[161] *leitwort*,[162] and motifs.[163] In our poem we have two types of word-pairs: (i) Identical or repetitive word-pairs where exactly the same word is used in other places.[164] These word-pairs are distant from each other; (ii) Antonymic word-pairs, which are made up of words opposite in meaning.[165]

i. Identical or Repetitive Word-Pairs

In Eccl 11:4-12:8 we have 32 instances, where we find same roots which are being repeated in subsequent or distant lines. For example, 'to keep' is repeated as 'one who watches' (11:4) and 'the keepers of the house' (12:3); 'way' is repeated as 'the way of the spirit' (11:5), 'the ways of your heart' (11:9), and 'the terrors are in the road' (12:5); 'day' is repeated as 'the days of

159 Fredericks, "Life's Storms and Qoheleth 11:1-12:8," 108-09.

160 Duplication is the verbatim or near verbatim repetition of a word or phrase.

161 The repetition of key words or phrases in a narrative provides important hints as to the thematic undergirding of that particular narrative.

162 Leitwort is the repetition of a root-word in a variety of forms.

163 Similar to leitwort is motif, which is the repetition of tangible object, image, or action within a narrative that imports symbolic and thematic significance. Cf. Bar-Efrat, Narrative Art, 211-12. SA Alter, *Biblical Narrative*, 92-95.

164 Cf. Watson, *Hebrew Poetry,* 134.

165 Cf. Watson, *Hebrew Poetry*, 131.

darkness' (11:8), 'the days of your childhood' (11:9), 'the days of your youth' (12:1), and 'on the day' (12:3).[166]

ii. Antonymic Word-Pairs

We have 7 instances of this type of word-pair. These elements though are antonymous to one another, they act as complementary contradiction, which is one of the principal motifs present in the poem.

1.	'morning' (11:6)	'evening' (11:6)
2.	'light' (11:7)	'darkness' (11:8)
3.	'good' (11:7)	'evil' (11:10)
4.	'spirit' (11:4)	'flesh' (11:10)
5.	'to come' (11:8)	'to go' (12:5)
6.	'sun' (11:7; 12:2)	'moon' (12:2)
7.	'God' (11:5, 9; 12:7)	'man' (12:5)

The high density of word-pairs in our text suggests that this poem originated orally.[167] The functions of these word-pairs are the following:[168] (a) The word-pairs assist the poet in composing the poem; (b) The word-pair slows down the flow of verse-making and at the same time reiterates key words in each line, enabling the audience to follow the meaning better; and (c) The word-pairs help the text stand as a single, cohesive, literary unit.

2.2. Assonance

Assonance is vowel repetition. It occurs when there is a series of words containing a distinctive vowel-sound or certain vowel sounds in a specific sequence.[169] "Assonance occurs when two words have the same vowels but different consonants."[170] The assonance is found in 11:4 (repetition of *ō* sound), 11:7 (repetition of *ô* sound), 11:10 (repetition of *ē* and *û* sounds), 12:1 (repetition of *ê̜* and *ā* sounds), 12:3 (Repetition of *i* and *û* sounds). The purpose of assonance here is twofold: (a) aesthetic-emphatic,[171] and (b) to link

166 This section can also be taken as an example of a literary device known as 'tour.' A tour is a series of one or more verses where the poet lists pairs of three to ten words all meaning roughly the same thing, or having something to do with the same subject, or being in some way related. The tour is an extension of the word-pair. Cf. Watson, *Hebrew Poetry*, 350.

167 Cf. Watson, *Hebrew Poetry*, 137.

168 Cf. Watson, *Hebrew Poetry*, 140.

169 Cf. Watson, *Hebrew Poetry*, 223.

170 Cited in Watson, *Hebrew Poetry*, 223.

171 For a detailed study of various purposes of assonance in Hebrew Poetry see, P. P. Saydon, "Assonance in Hebrew as a Means of Expressing Emphasis," *Bib* 36 (1955), 36-50, 287-304.

its component parts together.[172] In our poem, additionally assonance is used for emphasis.

2.3. Alliteration

Alliteration is the effect produced when the same consonant recurs within a unit of verse.[173] It binds the line(s) together in cohesion.[174] The best example for alliteration is in 12:8, where the consonant *h* is repeated 5 times in the same verse.

2.4. Onomatopoeia

Onomatopoeia is the imitation of a sound within the rules of the language concerned.[175] Onomatopoeia and paronomasia belong to linguistic field and can be lexicalized, though both of them operate with sound and bring out to a certain degree the picturesque and plastic element of language.[176] Sound element in onomatopoeia materializes the sense.[177] In 12:5, the verb, 'to fear' is repeated semantically in 'the terrors' or 'the fears.'[178]

2.5. Ellipsis

Ellipsis is the omission of a particle, word, or group of words within a poetic or grammatical unit, where its presence is expected. In other words, ellipsis is the suppression of an element demanded by the context.[179] We have established Eccl 11:4-12:8 as a narrative poem, which narrates human life stages. We have noted the implicit reference to conception, and explicit references to childhood and youth. Curiously the reference to old age is completely omitted. The poet narrates the elements that characterize old age but never uses the word 'old man' explicitly or implicitly. This ellipsis or gapping is assumed to occur intentionally for two reasons: (i) Since the 'old age' is a time of 'loss of memory' or 'forgetting,' the poet symbolically 'forgets' to use the word; (ii) The reader must deduce the word for 'old man' (*zqn*) from a similar sounding root *zkr*, which occurs twice in the poem (11:8; 12:1).

---

172 Cf. Watson, *Hebrew Poetry*, 224.

173 Cf. Watson, *Hebrew Poetry*, 225.

174 Cf. Bar-Efrat, *Narrative Art*, 201-02.

175 Cf. Watson, *Hebrew Poetry*, 234.

176 Cf. Maria Selvam, *Song of Songs*, 64.

177 Maria Selvam gives an example of Song of Songs 1:2a, where the sound effect of the action of kissing is materialized in the pronunciation of yiššāqēnî minnĕšiqôt pîhû, where the root nšq means 'to kiss.' Cf. Maria Selvam, *Song of Songs*, 64.

178 *HALOT* 363; *BDB* 369

179 Cf. Watson, *Hebrew Poetry*, 303-04.

2.6. Merismus

In merismus totality is expressed in an abbreviated form. For example, the expression 'body and soul' refers to the 'whole person.' The significant point is that in merismus, it is not the individual elements themselves that matter but what they amount to together, as a unit.[180] The nouns, 'morning' and 'evening' in 11:6 form a merismus. These two polar extremes include everything that is in between, i.e., 'from morning until evening.' The exhortation here is not to plant only twice in the day (morning and evening), but to be busy planting during the entire day.[181] Also in 12:5, 'when also they fear from on high and terrors are on the path,' it means a merism, i.e., 'terrors on all sides.'[182]

2.7. Hendiadys

Hendiadys is the expression of one single but complex concept by using two separate words, usually nouns. Wright defines it as "the use of two substantives, joined by a conjunction, to express a single but complex idea."[183] The phrase "the light and the moon" is a hendiadys (two separate terms denoting one idea) or perhaps even a *hendiatris* (three separate terms denoting one idea) for "the light of the moon and stars" (e.g., Gen 1:14).[184]

2.8. Double Entendre

Double entendre is a particular way of wording that is devised to be understood in either of two ways, having a double meaning. One meaning is obvious and the other meaning requires more thought. In 12:4, the noun, 'grinding-mill' is here used as a double entendre, figuratively describing the loss of one's teeth at the onset of old age.[185]

2.9. Metonymy

"A metonymy is a word or phrase that is used in a non-literal sense even though the literal meaning is easily discerned."[186] In Gen 29:1, we read, "And Jacob lifted up his feet and walked to the land of the people of the East." Here, 'lifting up one's feet' is a metonymy for 'walking.' In metonymy a thing or concept is called not by its own name but rather by the name of something associated in meaning with that thing or concept: E.g., 'going to bed' = 'going to sleep' or 'raising one's feet' = 'to walk.' In 11:6, "do not let your hand rest" (11:6)

---

180 Watson, *Hebrew Poetry,* 321.

181 Cf. NET Bible, Eccl 11:6, n. 15.

182 Cf. Fox, *Qohelet and His Contradictions,* 12.

183 Cited in Watson, *Hebrew Poetry*, 324-25.

184 Cf. NET Bible, Eccl 12:2, n. 4.

185 Cf. NET Bible, Eccl 12:4, n. 11.

186 Watson, *Hebrew Poetry*, 263.

is an idiom that means "do not stop working" or "do not be idle" (cf. 7:18).[187] Here 'hand' is a metonymy for 'work.' Also in the same verse, the verb, 'to prosper' is used metonymically to denote 'success' or 'skill in work.'[188] The imperative, 'remember' in 12:1 is a metonymy of association for obeying God and acknowledging his lordship over one's life (Cf. Num 15:40; Deut 8:18).[189] In the same way 'the daughters of the song' for 'songs or melodious notes.'[190] Finally, The noun, 'almond nut' in 12:5 stands for 'almond tree' (product for thing producing it).[191]

2.10. Hyperbole

Hyperbole is a way of expressing exaggeration of some kind (regarding size, numbers, danger, prowess, fertility and the like) using common language.[192] In 12:2, the evil days of old age are described as the darkening of the sun, the light, the moon and the stars. The description of old age is exaggerated, for when someone dies the entire universe does not come to a halt.

2.11. Synecdoche

The Greek word 'synecdoche' is a figure of speech where the part stands for the whole or conversely the whole for one of its parts. For example, in Ps 44:6a the Psalmist says, "For I will not trust in my bow." Here 'bow' stands for 'the entire armour.'[193] In 11:7, 'the eyes' stand for the whole person: 'It is good for the eyes to see the sun' = 'It is good for the human person to see the sun.' Also in 11:10, the noun, 'flesh' is a synecdoche of part (i.e., 'flesh') for the whole (i.e., 'whole person').[194]

2.12. Allusion

Allusion is the reference (usually not explicit) within one body of literature to the culture and letters of another body.[195] The noun, 'caper berry, caper fruit' in 12:5 refers to the *Capparis spinosa* fruit which was eaten as an aphrodisiac in the ancient Near East (*HALOT* 5; *BDB* 2–3). The noun alludes to the sexual virility at two levels: (i) At the onset of old age, the sexual virility that marked

187 Cf. NET Bible, Eccl 11:6, n. 14.

188 Cf. NET Bible, Eccl 11:7, n. 17.

189 Cf. NET Bible, Eccl 12:1, n. 1.

190 Cf. NET Bible, Eccl 11:4, n. 14.

191 Cf. NET Bible, Eccl 12:5, n. 17.

192 Cf. Watson, *Hebrew Poetry*, 316-17.

193 Cf. Bar-Efrat, *Narrative Art*, 201-02.

194 E.g., Gen 2:21; 6:12; Ps 56:4; 65:2; 145:21; Isa 40:5, 6. See *HALOT* 164. E. W. Bullinger, *Figures of Speech used in the Bible. Explained and Illustrated* (Grand Rapids 221999) 642. The word appears 5x in the Book as synecdoche (2:3; 4:5; 5:5; 11:10; and 12:12).

195 Cf. Watson, *Hebrew Poetry*, 299.

one's youth is nothing more than a distant memory, and even aphrodisiacs fail to stimulate sexual desire to allow for sexual intercourse; and (ii) The onset of old age is like the shrivelling up of the caper berry fruit; the once virile youth has passed his prime just like a shrivelled caper berry can no longer provide a sexual stimulant.[196]

2.13. Enjambment

The French word enjambment means 'to step over or to put legs across.' It means 'straddling (e.g. of a horse), and is present when a sentence or clause does not end when the colon ends but runs over into the next colon.[197] It refers to the running on of a sense from one line to the next without a major pause or syntactical break. We have an example of this in Eccl 11:9, where the imperative 'to rejoice' does not end in colon 1 but is taken up in similar imperatives in the following colons as, 'let your heart cheer,' 'follow the ways of your heart,' 'walk in the sights of your eyes,' 'banish anxiety from your mind,' and 'put away pain from your body' (cf. 11:9-10).

2.14. Parataxis

"Parataxis is the placing side by side of words, images, clauses, or scenes without connectives that directly and immediately coordinate the parts with one another."[198] In Eccl 12:1b-7 we notice parataxis, as the poet heaps on various elements by linking them through two temporal prepositions 'before' and 'when,' without explaining the connection or explicating the implication.

2.15. Envoy

"Also spelled 'envoi,' the word 'envoy' refers to a postscript added to the end of a prose writing or attached to a poem. This postscript can be of different meter and rhyme."[199] The entire poem Eccl 11:4-12:8 is a postscript consisting of 11 imperatives, which summarise the entire message of the book. Hence, an envoy to the book of Qohelet: 'sow' (11:6), 'don't be idle' (11: 6), 'let him rejoice' (11:8), 'let him remember' (11:8), 'rejoice' (11:9), 'let your heart be pleasant' (11:9), 'follow' (11:9), 'know' (11:9), 'remove' (11:10), 'put away' (11:10), and 'remember' (11:10).

The functions of these literary devices discussed in this section are the following: (a) They help the reader re-hear what has been expressed previously.[200] (b) They serve the author to reinforce his point and to create a

196 Cf. NET Bible, Eccl 12:5, n. 21.

197 Cf. Watson, *Hebrew Poetry*, 333.

198 Cited in Watson, *Hebrew Poetry*, 81.

199 Watson, *Hebrew Poetry*, 331.

200 For example, repetition. Cf. Watson, *Hebrew Poetry*, 278-79.

dramatic effect. (c) They cater to the more learned sections of the audience, help maintain interest and at the same time, enable the poet to display his knowledge.[201] and (d) They break the monotony.[202]

3. Word-Picture

An imagery or a word-picture makes use of words that create visual representation of ideas in our minds. Through cognitive mental process we arrive at the meaning of the imagery. Imageries are concrete and sense-related, not based on abstract concepts or merely ornamental.[203] These images perform two functions in a poem: (a) Presentational. They simply describe what the poet has in his mind; and (b) Representational, when the poet uses them to transfer something familiar to what is less well known, though of more importance.[204]

In Eccl 11:4-12:8 we notice three types of word-pictures: (i) Metaphors; (ii) Allegory; and (iii) Simile.

A metaphor works by transposing qualities from one domain of reality to another. In an allegory the signifier and the signified are kept in two distinct domains and the meaning is arrived at through a decoding or translation between these two domains. Allegory works by substitutions.[205] In a simile both the two distinct domains are compared using explicit particles 'as' and 'like.'[206] The distinction between a metaphor and a simile is that a simile is an intentional comparison that usually employs the words *like* or *as.*[207] The simile is more obvious than metaphor. This is either because it is more explicit, or because the ground of comparison is actually stated. By contrast, metaphor is more concise and at the same time, more vague.[208]

3.1. Metaphor

Let us substitute the word 'metaphor' with 'symbol,' since it is more apt in the context of our poem. As Fox observes,

> Since the symbol carries with it an indefinite penumbra of connotations, paraphrase cannot exhaust its meaning, nor can a symbolic image be directly translated into an entity in another domain, as an allegorical figure can. Rather, in a symbol we observe a reality concentrated and instantiated.

201 For example, allusion. Cf. Watson, *Hebrew Poetry*, 302.

202 For example, enjambment. Cf. Watson, *Hebrew Poetry*, 335.

203 Cf. Watson, *Hebrew Poetry*, 251-52.

204 Cf. Watson, *Hebrew Poetry*, 270-71.

205 Cf. Fox, *Time to Tear Down*, 343.

206 Cf. Berlin, *Poetics and Interpretation*, 136.

207 Cf. Bar-Efrat, *Narrative Art*, 209-10.

208 Cf. Watson, *Hebrew Poetry*, 254-55.

> For example, Adam both is man and represents humanity. Dust symbolizes the body and is its substance… Abel's murder is an instance of brotherly conflict and also represents all human strife.[209]

Let us try and identity the metaphorical actions rather than the metaphorical entities: (i) The verb 'to remove' that we find in 11:10 generally depicts a concrete action of removing a physical object from someone's presence (*HALOT* 748). But, here it is used figuratively (through a metaphorical process of *hypokatastasis*) to denote emotional/psychological action of banishing redundant emotional stress from one's mind. (ii) In 12:2 when the poem says that 'the cosmic elements are darkened,' it symbolically means "universal darkness and silence – that blankets everything from the stars to the mills, from the powerful men to the menials, from the rich women to the maids – thus evoking a prophetic vision of the national and universal desolation."[210] (iii) The ceasing of the grinders (12:3), the shutting down of the market places and the street doors (12:4), and the mourners going about in the street symbolically represent the immediate and unexpected effect that an individual's death creates in a village or neighbourhood.[211]

3.2. Allegory

The word allegory derives from the Greek *allegoria* ('to speak otherwise'). An allegory is an act of interpretation, a way of understanding, rather than a genre in itself. Allegory emerges in the process of an interaction between symbols that creates a coherent meaning beyond that of the literal level of interpretation.[212]

The section 12:2-7 is replete with allegories.[213] Each image presented in the poem is associated with an organ of the body:[214]

12:2	Sun	Face or forehead
	Light	Eyes
	Moon	Cheeks
	Stars	Eyeballs
	Clouds after rain	Eyelids dripping tears

209 Fox, *Time to Tear Down*, 339.

210 Fox, *Time to Tear Down*, 339.

211 Cf. Fox, "Aging and Death," 206-08.

212 Watson, *Hebrew Poetry*, 252.

213 The allegorical interpretation of this section is attested to in Midrash (Qoh. Rab.) and the Talmud (b. Shab. 131b-132a). Cf. Fox, Time to Tear Down, 344. SA. Krüger, *Qoheleth*, 199.

214 Cf. Fox, *Time to Tear Down*, 344.

12:3	Keepers of the house	Knees
	Men of power	Hands
	Grinding women	Teeth
	Those looking through the windows	Eyes looking through the openings in the head
12:4	Doors in the street are shut	The feet are fettered. The body or body openings or ears or lips suffer or close. The anus and bladder suffer retention
	Grinding stops	No more appetite
	Sound of the mill is silenced	The appetite or mouth or digestion or voice diminishes
	Arising to the voice of the bird	Being disturbed in one's sleep. Sleep is interrupted.
	Daughters of the song bow low	Lips. The voice is lowered. Deafness creeps in
12:5	Fears in the way	The old people being afraid to walk
	Almond tree blossoms	The hair grows white
	Grasshopper drags or is heavy	The back of the pelvic cavity becomes sore. Or breathing becomes laboured. Or the joints grow stiff. Or the old man is bent over. Or the ankles swell up. Or the buttocks droop. Or sex becomes difficult. Or the penis fails to become erect.
	Caper berry is brought to a naught	Desire is dulled. Or aphrodisiacs fail.
	Mourners in the street	Angels of death or judgment
12:6	Silver cord is snapped	Tongue is tied
	Golden bowl is shattered	Head dashed in pieces
	Pitcher is broken	Gall at the liver emptied
	Waterwheel at the spring	Body in the grave
12:7	Life-breath returns to God	Spirit returns to God for judgment

3.3. Simile

"In simile when one element is compared to the other, the element compared is particular while the element compared to is general or universal."[215] The particular partakes in the universal category and not vice versa. We have two instances of simile in the poem, in 11:5 and 12:7.

11:5

'Just as the way of the life-breath to the bones in the womb of a full woman cannot be known (colon 1), one cannot ever know the works of God, who does or makes everything (colon 2).' Here the point that is emphasized is human incomprehensibility. Colon 1 is the element to which colon 2 is compared. The particles of comparison are explicit. Colon 1 is a general statement. Colon 2 is a particular statement which is derived from colon 1.

12:7

'And the dust returns to the earth as it was (colon 1), and the breath returns to God who gave it (colon 2).' Compared to the previous example, the simile is reversed here. Colon 2 is the general statement and colon 1 particular. The common verb is 'to return'. There is also a point of dissimilarity implied, as in colon 2 the direction is upward while in colon 1 the direction is downward.

These readings – literal, metaphorical, and allegorical – still leave room for ambiguities. Fox describes the problem in comprehending this text:

> It is not difficult to connect almost any image with something within the multifarious physical and psychological process of aging, and when this cannot be done, the interpreter is free to treat the image as literal or as a metaphor outside the allegorical frame. Difficulties in accommodating the text to the interpretation can be met by invoking the author's oriental richness of imagination and carelessness in exact use of metaphor. Yet even with all this hermeneutic flexibility, the allegorical interpretations leave much unexplained.[216]

F. Characterisation

Characters easily become the focus of the narratee because the interaction, speech, and fate of characters reveal aspects of the ideological point of view of the narrator.[217] Therefore it is important to understand how the narrator establishes and utilizes characters within the narrative poem.

Let us divide the characters into two categories: major and minor. Major characters are often round characters and can be identified by their role within

215 Watson, *Hebrew Poetry*, 255.

216 Fox, "Aging and Death in Qohelet 12," 56.

217 Cf. Bar-Efrat, *Narrative Art*, 47.

the story as 'full-fledged characters.'[218] They are central to the plot.[219] Berlin makes a distinction between two categories of minor characters: flat characters and agents. Flat characters are simple, fleeting, one dimensional archetypes.[220] They usually embody a particular type of person and therefore lack distinctive personal features.[221] Agents, on the other hand, have a purely functionary role within the story to progress the plot, to contribute to the setting, or to highlight aspects of round characters otherwise not revealed.[222] Agents have no value in and of themselves as characters and no personal details are given about them.[223]

All of these character types – round, flat, and agent – can be developed directly and indirectly. Direct characterisation can be accomplished through description and declaration. Indirect characterisation can be achieved through dialogue, action, and comparison between characters.

Direct characterisation is a matter of fact statement or description by the narrator. The description can be either physical or inner-life or personal.[224] Narrator's declaration also falls under description. Direct characterisation by description and declaration advances the plot, provides insight into the personality of a character, and passes judgment on the motivation and action of characters. Indirect characterisation, on the other hand, is developed by observing external aspects of a character, such as dialogue, action, and comparison between characters.[225]

The narrator's ideological point of view is most often communicated through the depiction and interaction of characters. The narrator emphasizes the lives of characters for didactic reasons, using them as examples of how one ought or ought not to live. Thus, characters often embody the meaning of the passage.

In Eccl 11:4-12:8 we have only direct characterisation, i.e., description or declaration by the narrator. As there are no dialogue statements and as the characters do not interact with one another we do not have any instance of indirect characterisation.

Let us group the characters into two broad categories: 'Self' and 'Other.' The 'self' refers to an individual human person, while the 'other' has three

---

218 Cf. Berlin, *Poetics and Interpretation*, 23.

219 Cf. Y. Amit, *Reading Biblical Narratives. Literary Criticism and the Hebrew Bible* (Minneapolis 2001), 71-72.

220 Cf. Berlin, *Poetics and Interpretation*, 23.

221 Cf. Bar-Efrat, *Narrative Art*, 90.

222 Cf. Bar-Efrat, *Narrative Art*, 87-88. SA. Berlin, *Poetics and Interpretation*, 32.

223 Cf. Berlin, *Poetics and Interpretation*, 32.

224 Cf. Berlin, *Poetics and Interpretation*, 36.

225 Cf. Bar-Efrat, *Narrative Art*, 64.

faces, i.e., (a) Transcendental, (b) Social, and (c) Environmental. 'The self' and 'the transcendental other' are the major characters while 'the social other' and 'the environmental other' are minor characters or agents.

1. Self

Qohelet characterizes self, i.e., 'individual human person' at two levels: (a) Ontological – 'who he is'; and (b) Functional – 'what he does.' At times the difference between these two levels is only a hairline, for then the poet seems to unify them into one.

1.1. The Ontological Self

The individual is referred to by four explicit names in the poem: (i) 'observer' (11:4), (ii) 'seer' (11:4), (iii) 'the man' (11:8; 12:5), and (iv) 'young man' (11:9).[226] All these four names are in masculine singular. The names 'observer' and 'seer' are synonymously parallel to one another. The individual is implicitly referred to twice as well: (i) In 11:10 as someone having an internal ('heart') and external realm ('flesh'); (ii) In 12:7 as the composition of 'the dust' and 'the life-breath.' This implicit reference is indirect in 11:5, where it is said that the process of life-breath entering the bones ('the dust') is unknowable and mysterious.

The verbs, 'to observe' and 'to see' are very important to understand the epistemology of Qohelet. For Qohelet knowledge comes to us only through our observation or seeing. On the contrary, whatever is not observable or seeable does not exist or does not make sense. The only assumed exception is 'God.' Therefore, according to Qohelet an individual is someone who observes and makes sense of the reality around. He is an individual endowed with an external faculty to 'see' and an internal faculty to 'comprehend' and 'discern.' The verb, 'to observe' is very significant in covenantal exhortations (cf. Deut 4:2, 6, 9; 6:12; et al). Qohelet takes a verb familiar to the ears of his audience and adds value to it.

The next explicit reference to an individual human person in the poem is 'the man', which Qohelet uses thirty-one times in his book.[227] Though Genesis uses it the most (thirty-six times) the density of the use is higher in

---

226 "Aside from minor Hebrew particles, the word 'tôv' (good) occurs the most in the book (51x) followed by 'ra'ah' ('see,' 47x), and then 'adam' (43x)." Cited in O'Dowd, "Epistemology in Ecclesiastes," 201-02. SA. Seow, *Ecclesiastes*, 67.

227 Qohelet's use of this word can be grouped under three categories: (a) bənē-hā'āḏām ('sons of man') (e.g., 3:18), (b) kōl-hā'āḏām ('all mankind') (e.g., 5:18), and (c) hā'āḏām ('the man') (e.g., 11:8).

Ecclesiastes.[228] Let us analyse the two instances (11:8; 12:5) where the word appears in our poem.[229]

11:8

'Even if many years the man lives, let him rejoice in them all'

The noun, 'the man' is preceded by the verb 'to live' in indicative mood and followed by two verbs, 'to rejoice' and 'to remember' in imperative mood. 'The man' is the subject of these three verbs. The juxtaposition of the verb 'to live' and the noun 'the man' recalls to the reader 'the man became a living soul' (Gen 2:7). The human person who has come into existence because of the life-breath breathed on him by God begins to exist in time ('many years'). As the life-breath is a given thing so also is his lifetime. During this lifetime the task entrusted to him, in jussive mood, is to 'rejoice' and to 'remember.' In the First Creation account (Gen 1:27), 'the human person' is characterized as 'male' and 'female' while it is not so in the Second Creation account or in Qohelet's presentation. In 7:26 and 28 Qohelet is very harsh on woman, as he calls woman 'a trap,' and confesses that in his research he has never 'found' a woman yet. In our poem though the noun used for human person is very exclusive it does convey a collective sense and is to be taken inclusively.

12:5

'because the man walks to his eternal home'

In this verse, 'the man' is the subject of the verb 'to walk.' The verb is used elsewhere by Qohelet in 1:4[230] and 3:20[231] in reference to death. Though the expression, 'his eternal home' is found in Ps 49:12 ("their graves are their homes forever") the meaning is different in 12:5. In Ps 49:12 the referent is 'the grave.' It is very curious to note that 'the man' is only twice in the poem, the first time to introduce the life of human person while in the text it underlines his mortality or death. The human person comes to life and goes. These verbs 'live' and 'die' form an inclusio and the poem covers the entire lifespan of a human person.

The fourth and the final explicit reference to human person is 'the young man.'

---

228 In Genesis the total number of verses is 1533 whereas in Ecclesiastes is 222. Of the 44 instances of adam, 20 of them are found in chs. 2-3. Cf. O'Dowd, "Epistemology in Ecclesiastes," 202.

229 Another name that is used for man is 'īš'. But 'adam' is used four times greater than 'īš'. Cf. O'Dowd, "Epistemology in Ecclesiastes," 202.

230 "A generation goes, and a generation comes, but the earth remains forever."

231 "All go to one place; all are from the dust, and all return to dust again."

11:9

'the young man'

Human person is called and addressed here as a young man. The root *bḥr* is found 4x in Ecclesiastes. Of these 4x, 3x are within the poem. Only once it is used outside, i.e., in 9:4, where "one is counted or chosen among the living… the living dog is better than a dead lion." Thus the 'young man' is someone who has the light of life within. The young man is exhorted to 'rejoice' and to 'remember.'

Now let us turn to consider the implicit references to the human person.

11:10

'And turn aside anxiety from your heart, and cause evil to pass from your flesh'

This verse portrays to us another important dimension of human person, i.e., human person who has two realms – internal ('heart') and external ('flesh'). Human person is essentially corporal. It is through his 'flesh' he is present to the world and to one another. Human person is blessed with five sense perceptions. The verbs 'to observe' (11:4), 'to see' (11:4, 7; 12:3), 'to wake up,' 'hearing' implied' (12:4), 'to tremble,' 'touch' implied (12:5), and in 'desire' 'smell' and 'taste' implied (12:5).

Finally, 12:7 presents human person as a mixture or composition of dust and life-breath. At the moment of his death, the dust returns to the earth and the life-breath returns to God. This too brings to mind the Second Creation narrative where God makes human person out of earth and breathes his life-spirit into him.

1.2. The Functional Self

i. The Knowing

The human person is able to 'observe' and 'see' (11:4). Yet he cannot 'know' really (cf. 11:5). The mysteries of life are hidden to him. His cognitive experience is limited. There are realities such as passing of wind and conception of human life, which are far beyond his comprehension. However, his search for 'knowledge' must not stop. His knowledge is very limited and he cannot 'know' 'how life is born' (11:5a) and 'how God authors everything' (11:5b). Yet his epistemological capacity is acknowledged as he is called 'to know' that 'the Creator will bring him to judgment' (11:9). He is judged for all that he does and knows.

ii. The Ethical

The invitation to 'rejoice' and 'remember' in jussives (11:8) and in imperatives (11:9; 12:1) characterizes a human person as an ethical person. The code of living consists in these imperatives. Moreover, human person is easily carried away by 'the ways of his heart' and 'the sights of his eyes' (11:9). His mind and body are susceptible to vexation, pain and uneasiness (cf. 11:10). Yet he has the capacity to turn them away. The ethics suggested by Qohelet is to 'rejoice.'

iii. The Working

In 11:4 and 6 the poet takes the images from agriculture and employs upon human person. The human person is portrayed as an individual who sows and reaps. Human person is necessarily a worker. Though he may not predict the outcome of his labour he is called to toil and hard work. In 12:2-6, we have other works being referred to – 'watching over,' 'grinding,' 'being powerful and strong,' 'looking over the windows,' and 'mourning.'

iv. The Mutating

The human person is a mutating being. He changes and grows. From mother's womb (11:5) he comes out 'to see the light' (11:8). From his childhood (11:9) he becomes a young person (12:1a) and he ages and dies (12:1b-7). His matter undergoes a radical change: When he stands he trembles. When he walks, he is afraid. His sight is dimmed. His tastes and lusts are lowered. The colour of the hair changes into grey.

v. The Feeling

Human person is blessed with the mental faculties to 'rejoice' and 'remember.' In Hebrew anthropology, the heart refers to the mind of the person. It is the birth place of thoughts and feelings. It is with one's heart one is able to remember and feel the sensation of joy and sorry.

vi. The Dying

Finally, human person is a mortal. He must *return home*. His body disintegrates and becomes part of the earth, from where it came. His spirit returns to God, who gave it.

2. Transcendental Other

Qohelet uses two titles for God in the poem: 'the gods' and 'your creators.'[232] The epithet for God, 'the gods,' which appears thirty-two times in Eccl appears three times (11:5, 9; 12:7) in the poem.[233] Even though Qohelet uses the epithet 'Elohim,' he does not identify him as 'the God of Abraham, Isaac and Jacob' (Exod 3:6, 16). Curiously the poet never uses the personal 'Name' of God, the YHWH.

232 The word 'elohim' appears more frequently than 'hebel.' R. E. Murphy, "Qoheleth and Theology?," in *BTB* 21 (1991), 30-33.

233 The title appears the most in 2 Kgs (35x) and in Gen (24x).

2.1. God who Makes All

11:5

'so you do not know the work of God who makes all'

In this sentence the poet tells that one cannot know the works of God, who makes everything. The expression, 'the works of God,' is unique to Qohelet and is found 3 other times in the book (cf. 7:13; 8:17; 12:14). The verb 'to do' or 'to make' which is used 43x in Eccl has 6x God as the subject (3:11, 14 (2x); 7:14, 29; 11:5). 'God doing everything under the sun' is a common motif in Ecclesiastes.

2.2. God who Judges

11:9

'and know that for all these God will bring you to judgment'

This is the second time the title 'God' appears in the poem. 'God' is the subject of the complementary objective clause of the verb 'know.' The scholars are of two opinions in commenting on this clause:[234] one group considers this as an editorial gloss by the later editors who wanted to subdue the teaching of Qohelet on rejoicing. And those who belong to this group (Galling, Zimmerli, Lauha, Vilchez, Michel and Lohfink) translate the initial *waw* as 'but,' *waw* adversative.[235] The other group (Di Fonzo, Murphy, Fox and Seow) considers this as part of the original text.[236] There are also other instances in the Book where Qohelet engages with the judgment of God.[237] In 3:17 Qohelet tells that "God will judge the righteous and the wicked." Qohelet does not doubt that God will judge the human person (cf. 5:5) but negates that such judgment comes in the other world.

---

234 See the discussion in Mazzinghi, *Ho cercato*, 278.

235 According to Zimmerli, (a) V. 9b interrupts the series of short admonitions in vv. 9a-10a; (b) the expression used here reappears in 12:14, where it is regarded as secondary; and (c) V. 9b reveals the 'intention' to 'tone down the unguarded admonition to enjoyment that Qoheleth addresses to youth" (Zimmerli) or to "protect the text from a libertine interpretation" (Lohfink). Cf. Krüger, *Qoheleth*, 196-97.

236 For Seow, 11:9d "is not incongruous with the author's perspective. For him, the enjoyment of life is both the lot of humanity (2:10) and a gift of God (2:24-26; 3:10-15; 5:17-19). Human beings are supposed to enjoy life to the full because that is their divinely assigned portion, and God calls one into account for failure to enjoy." Seow, *Ecclesiastes*, 371.

237 The word mišpāṭ appears 6x in the Book: 3:16, 5:7, 8:5, 6, 11:9 and 12:14. In 3:16 and 5:7 Qohelet denies any existence of justice. He is very skeptical about human judgment. In 8:5-6 it is in the context of being judged or condemned by the king. 11:9 and 12:14 go together. In 12:14, which is the epilogue of the Book, "God brings every deed into judgment."

Now let us briefly treat the theme of the judgment of God in Qohelet. There is a great difference between how the Jews and the Greeks viewed judgment. Qohelet seems to reflect the worldview of the Greeks.[238]

7:15 "the righteous perish in their righteousness"
7:16 "do not be too righteous"
7:20 "there is no one on earth so righteous as to do good without ever sinning"
9:2 "the same fate comes to all, to the righteous and the wicked."

Here Qohelet goes against the traditional understanding of Judaism, of the Pharisees and the Qumran community. For them, the life lived according to the Law is the just life. Qohelet affirms that no one will ever live a just life. For Qohelet sinning is part of human existence. And even when one is righteous and just he cannot escape the fate of toil, death, and vanity. It is very clear to Qohelet that the good works are not enough to attain salvation; nor is there a God who has predestined the just or the members of a particular group as saved; and there is no life after death.[239]

Qohelet also excludes the fear of God or the observance of the Law from the ethics of human beings. There is no reward for the good or the punishment for the evil. Then what else is the divine judgment according to Qohelet? For Qohelet, it is the power that God exercises on human persons in this life 'under the sun;' all depend on God, whether life of human persons or the gift of joy; perhaps on account of this Qohelet evades to say that God is just or exercises justice.[240] The assignment given to human person is to enjoy as much what is given to him. There is no allusion to a time of judgment in this world or next. The judgment of God over human beings consists in their transitoriness (cf. 11:10b). This happens with a certain irony – especially if in the formulation of v. 9a the author had in mind Num 15:39: the experience of contingency and transitoriness supports the idea of enjoying the 'good days' – and nothing indicates that God judges the matter differently (cf. 9:7b).[241]

238 "The Greeks were concerned about the truth while the Jews were concerned about salvation." P. Sacchi, "Giustizia e giustificazione nel mondo giudaico ellenistico," in A. Paninolle, ed., *Giustizia – Giustificazione nella Bibbia* (Dizionario di Spiritualità Biblico – Patristica 28) (Roma 2001), 107-27.

239 Cf. Mazzinghi, *Ho cercato*, 279.

240 Cf. Mazzinghi, *Ho cercato*, 280.

241 Cf. Krüger, *Qoheleth*, 197.

2.3. God: Giver of Life-Breath

12:7

'and the breath returns to God who gave it'

The background to this clause is the creation narrative in Gen 2-3. It reflects the anthropology presupposed in Genesis narrative. When we compare 12:7 with Gen 2:7 the meaning becomes clearer. In Gen 2:7, we read: "then the Lord God formed man from the dust of the ground, and breathed into his nostrils the breath of life; and the man became a living being." The noun, 'the dust' is also found in the first part of the verse 12:7. The key difference is that Qohelet replaces 'the breath of life' with 'the spirit.'[242] The life-spirit returns to God, 'the Creator' (cf. 12:1). Thus, at the moment of death there is a new beginning. The main verb to note here is the verb 'to give'. God is mostly the object of two verbs in Eccl, 'to do' and 'to give.' The verb appears twenty-five times in Eccl. In eight instances (1:13; 2:26; 3:10; 5:17, 18; 6:2; 8:15; 12:7) the subject of the verb is 'God.'

2.4. God-Creator, Object of Remembering

12:1

'And remember your creators'

The main exegetical problem rests with the form and the meaning of the phrase, 'your creators', which is a *hap. leg.* in the HB, the Qal masculine plural participle form from the verb 'to create' with a second person singular pronominal suffix, the object of the imperative form of the verb 'to remember'. BHS proposes a corrected form 'your creator' in accordance with Isa 43:1.[243] Some explain this form as the 'plural of majesty.[244]

The scholars differ in interpreting this word: (a) *bor'ẹḵā*, 'your creator' (ancient versions, Seow and Mazzinghi); (b) *bĕrû'kā*, 'your well-being' or 'your health' (Ehrlich); (c) *boryāk,* 'your vigour' (Zimmermann); (d) *bē'ērêkā* or *bôrĕkā,* 'your well' (Graetz), a metaphor for one's wife, as in Prov 5:15; and (e) *bôrĕkā,* 'your pit,' a synonym for the grave (Galling).[245] We prefer to rend

242 In Eccl 3:19-21, Qohelet argues that there is no difference between 'the life-spirit' of human person and of animals. Scholars generally agree that both 'breath of life' and 'the spirit' refer to the one and same thing and can be used interchangeably. In the anthropology of Genesis, it means that God is the author of this life principle. God gives at the moment of birth and takes away at the moment of death and the body returns to the earth.

243 Seow negates the proposal as an attempt to correct and prefers the lectio difficilior. Cf. Seow, *Ecclesiastes*, 351.

244 For example, Delitzsch. Seow thinks that this problem emerges as the result of the frequent confusion in late Hebrew of III-Aleph and III-Weak roots (cf. similar form with the participle 'ōśeh ('maker) in Isa 54:5; Ps 149:2; Job 35:10). Cf. Seow, *Ecclesiastes*, 351.

245 Cf. Mazzinghi, *Ho cercato*, 282. Seow, *Ecclesiastes*, 351.

the meaning as 'your creator' for the following reasons: (a) The context of 11:4-12:8 supports this reading. 'God' comes at the beginning (11:5, 9) and at the end (12:7) of the poem.[246] Now 'God' is placed at the centre (12:1) as well. (b) At 12:7, the life returns to God who is the author of it. The giving of life to humans is the creative function of God (12:1) attributed to him in Gen 2:7. (c) There have been allusions to Creation stories in Eccl 11:4-12:8. The words, 'the light,' 'the man' and 'good' in 11:7-8 and the reference to 'the earth' and 'dust' in 12:7 allude to Gen 1:4, 2:7 and 3:19. Moreover the first verb in the HB, 'to create' (Gen 1:1) appears only in Eccl 12:1, which is the unique place in the Wisdom Literature where God is described with the participle of the verb 'to create.'[247] (d) This rendering is in accordance with the ancient versions in MT.[248]

As Qohelet prefers wordplays, through this he might want to puzzle his audience with the homophony and choose to leave the meaning open-ended. Rabbi Akabya ben Mahallel (first century CE), brings to light the different meanings in a single exhortation: "Consider three things and you will not fall into the power of sin: know your source (*be'er*), the place where you go (*bôr*, grave) and to whom you must give account, your Creator."[249]

If we set the word with what goes before in 11:9, 'rejoicing,' the preferred meaning is 'your cistern' or 'your wife' (cf. Prov 5:15) and if we read it with what is yet to come in 12:2-7, the meaning is 'your pit' or 'grave.' When we extend and hold one meaning the other evades. This is the goal of our Qohelet: 'everything is equal to catching the wind.'

Thus, Qohelet presents God as a 'creator' who is in a personal relationship with the 'young man' as 'your creator.'

To sum up, the God of Qohelet is characterised as an unmoved mover of the Scholastic philosophy, who 'does' everything, 'gives' the life-spirit, 'brings' to judgment and who 'creates.' His plans are unpredictable and incomprehensible. Qohelet does not recall the great events of the salvation history – the Exodus event, the covenant or the promised land. God is referred to only in the third person masculine singular. Though God is spoken in terms of personal relationship, He is never addressed directly in the second person singular or plural. Qohelet's God is present, yet is absent; omnipresent and omniscient, yet can never be comprehended. The absence of the word YHWH in Qohelet indicates that his focus is not just the nation of Israel but the entire

246 Qohelet throughout his book names God as 'Elohim.'

247 Of the 12 instances it appears in MT, 11 instances are in Isa 40-66 and Amos 4:13. If from one side 12:1 is a unique text in the world of Wisdom Literature, on the other hand it runs well with the theology of Deutero-Isaiah (cf. Eccl 1:9). Cf. Mazzinghi, *Ho cercato*, 282-83.

248 The new BHQ cancels all the emendations. Cf. Mazzinghi, *Ho cercato*, 282.

249 Pirqé Abôt III, 1. Cited in Mazzinghi, *Ho cercato*, 283. SA. Seow, *Ecclesiastes*, 352.

universe. Qohelet denationalises the concept of God, giving up the divine name YHWH in favour of Elohim.[250]

Qohelet who calls everything under the sun as *hebel* ('vain') lets loose God. God is completely outside *hebel.* Lohfink notes that *hebel* is not mentioned in the theological sections of the book of Qohelet.

3. Social Other

The relationship between the social other and the self is merely functional in the poem. We have two types of social other: (a) Indirect – the woman who is full (11:5); and (b) Direct – the four groups (12:3) and the mourners (11:5)

11:5

'in the womb of the full one'

The feminine adjective suggests the implication of a woman. The woman is full or her womb is full with an infant. The life-breath enters into the infant who is in the womb of the woman. The formation of the infant through a male-female sexual intercourse is presupposed here. Though the sexual union contributes to the formation of the matter or the body of an infant it is God who gives the life-breath (cf. 12:7). The woman becomes a receptacle of human life.

12:3

We have four groups of people mentioned here: (a) The keepers of the house; (b) The grinding women; (c) The men of strength; and (d) The women who look through the windows.

The four types of people are well-chosen. They represent the entire society. From literary point of view, the four types of people mentioned form an AB // A'B' pattern and together embrace the range of social classes in the village.[251] The groups 'a' and 'c' are men while 'b' and 'd' are women. The words 'keeping' or 'watching' and 'grinding' represent the two basic needs of a human society: protection and food. All the people whether rich or poor, strong or weak need these two essential factors. In a society where these two are taken care and promised to its group the society will thrive for the better.

The fifth group, 'the mourners' (12:5) represent the final destiny that a human-in-society would face. The mourners are provided to attend to the funeral lamentation. They know the life-story of the individual who has passed away and they sing the praises in the name of the dead.

---

250 The preference for Elohim, which refers to the God of all peoples, is characteristic of Wisdom Literature. The expression 'sons of man' also connotes universality.

251 Cf. Fox, *Qohelet and His Contradictions*, 302. A similar all-encompassing group appears in Isa 24:2. Cf. Fox, "Aging and Death," 208.

The presentation of the social other represents a movement in the text:

A	Birth	Mother	Female
B	Life	Keepers Grinders Strong Men Resting Women	Male Female Male Female
A'	Death	Mourners	Male

We notice an A B A' pattern in the above table. The 'A' and 'A'' are contrasted thematically (birth, death) and gender-matched (male-female).

4. Environmental Other

We have references to the natural elements in 11:4, 11:7, 12:2, 12:5, 12:6, and 12:7.

11:4

'He who watches the wind will not sow, and
he who sees the clouds will not reap'

The first image presented of a human person in the poem (cf. 11:4) is someone who has two faces – one that looks into the sky to observe wind and clouds and the other that looks down to till the land, to sow the seed, to cultivate and reap fruits. Human person thus is dependent on the environment. Human person is essentially an environmental person. The natural elements 'wind'[252] and 'the clouds' are presented as if these elements can be observed through the physical eyes. The human person has the possibility and potentiality to enter into a relationship with the environment. Here the human person is a servant of the environment. Though he is able to observe the wind and the movement of the clouds he will never be able to control their movements. His role is merely to observe and to make sense of.

11:7

'And sweet is the light and it is good for the eyes to see the sun.'

In 11:7 Qohelet presents the elements of 'the light' and 'the sun.' When read in the background of the First Creation account (cf. Gen 1:3, 14-17)[253] we may say that 'the light' is an independent reality, which exists even before the creation of 'the sun.' Though these elements are metaphorically used to denote life, they do convey that light is essential for human life. The mention of light and the sun serves two points here: (a) To make the audience understand the

252 The noun 'the spirit' reappears with definite article in 11:5 and 12:7 and signifies the 'life-breath' in human beings.

253 The word 'the sun' is not evident in Gen 1.

dependence of humans on these elements for life; and (b) These elements intertextually connect the poem to the First Creation account, where human person is the centre of creation and is invited to be the steward of the earth.

12:2

'the sun is darkened, and the light, and the moon, and the stars,

and the clouds return after the rain'

The scholars often tend to put forward an eschatological or apocalyptic reading of this verse. For example, Seow suggests an eschatological reading of this verse. According to him, "the language of the darkening luminaries belongs to the rhetoric of eschatology and description of the demise of the world (Isa 5:30; 13;10; Amos 5:8; 8:9; Mic 3:6; Job 3:9; 18:6; Joel 2:10; 3:4 [Eng 2:31]; 4:15 [Eng 3:15]; Mt 24:9; Mk 13:24; Lk 23:45; Acts 2:20)."[254]

In our opinion and in the context of our analysing the human life-stages presented in the poem this interpretation does not fit for three reasons: (a) When an individual dies the entire universe does not end. The sun continues to rise. The moon and the stars go on radiating; (b) Qohelet is an evidentialist.[255] He sees the reality, observes it closely, and arrives at truth based on his sense observation. Anything speculative or abstract is beyond his realm. Therefore, it is not possible to render an eschatological reading of the text; and (c) Ironically at the moment of death these elements, from the dying individual's point of view, are of meagre importance.

The words, 'the sun' and 'the light' appear within the poem in 11:7 and 'the clouds' appears in 11:4. Let us begin with the first part of the verse, which mentions about the reality of light and the three luminaries. When we read the verse intertextually with Gen 1, the word order is not the same: the order of 'the sun,' 'the light,' 'the moon,' and 'the stars' in Eccl 12:2 is rendered as 'the light,' 'the sun,' 'the moon,' and 'the stars' in Gen 1. The order of 'the sun' and 'the light' are reversed in 12:2 in accordance with 11:7, where 'the light' comes first and 'the sun' second. This is to symbolically represent the reversal that occurs at the moment of death.[256] The sun never rises again for the dead person. Or the rising and the setting of the sun and the luminaries do not matter to him anymore. All the life-processes and realities are reversed. Moreover, ironically the word reversal suggests the old age, in which one can hardly know the order of events.

254 Seow, *Ecclesiastes*, 376.

255 "Qohelet is an evidentialist whose conclusions about God and the world are drawn not on the basis of revelation but on his own vast ("under the sun") experience." Enns, *Ecclesiastes*, 118.

256 For example, 'the sun' appears thirty-five times in the book. In 1:5, Qohelet writes about the continuous rising and setting of the sun. In 12:2 he takes a different position. The sun never rises again.

The second part of the verse presents 'clouds returning after the rain.' Seow again proposes an eschatological reading of this phrase as the phrase represents a "time of doom" (Ezek 30:3; 32:7).[257]

Thus, this verse presents human person as someone who is part of cosmic and universal realties.

12:5

'and the almond tree blossoms, and the grasshopper drags,
and the caper berry shrivels up'

We have three images from the vegetative world: (a) An almond that blossoms; (b) A locust that drags itself; and (c) The caper berry fruit that breaks.

These three images are more often read allegorically. "At the allegorical level, all three plants may refer to the woes that an old man faces: the hair becomes white, the penis droops, and the caper does not help one's libido."[258] Though these images of almond tree, grasshopper and caper fruit are rendered symbolic meaning as sexual allusions,[259] there is something more said in the text. "They are more likely descriptions of nature which stand in *contrast* to man. Nature, but not man, is reborn in the spring. This thought is expressed in Job 14:7-10: 'A tree has hope; if it is cut off, it may be renewed ... But, man dies and is helpless. A human expires and disappears.'"[260] The tree which is admired for its beauty and elegance becomes ugly now. Moreover, the locust tree literally droops.[261] The caper plant 'comes to naught.' Perhaps it is defoliated. It appears that all three plants are dead or dying. The scene here reminds one of the languishing of nature in the face of impending doom.[262] These images from the vegetative world are characterized in such a way that even nature at times undergoes an irreversible process. The blossom of an almond tree, the bent in the locust tree or in the grasshopper, and the coming-to-naught of the caper berry cannot be undone. One cannot reverse the process and turn the clock backward into de-blossoming, de-bending or de-nullifying. Even at the figurative level these processes are irreversible: one cannot (a) change the grey hair into white, (b) revive the sexual energy that is lost, and (c) enliven the dead taste buds in the tongue.

257 Cf. Seow, *Ecclesiastes*, 353, 376. Lohfink also thinks in the same line: "the language of the darkening luminaries belongs to the rhetoric of eschatology and description of the demise of the world (Isa 5:30; 13:10; Amos 5:8; 8:9; Mic 3:6; Job 3:9; 18:6; Joel 2:10; 3:4 [Eng 2:31]; 4:15 [Eng 3:15]; Mt 24:9; Mk 13:24; Lk 23:45; Acts 2:20)." Cited in Seow, Ecclesiastes, 376.

258 Seow, *Ecclesiastes*, 380.

259 Cf. Fox, *Qohelet and His Contradictions*, 305.

260 Fox, *Qohelet and His Contradictions*, 305-06.

261 Seow calls the locust a tree. This rendering also is possible.

262 Cf. Seow, *Ecclesiastes*, 380.

12:6

In 12:6 we have a series of metaphors which reinforce the finality of death:[263] the silver cord, the golden bowl, the pitcher and the wheel. The location where these things are broken or shattered or snapped is at the spring or at the well. This is done as part of funerary custom.[264] Let us understand this verse in the light of a verse from Śaivite final rite of passage. In Śaiva funeral rite the people sing a following refrain on the following day of a funeral:

taṅkac cuṭukāṭu taṇal pa<u>rr</u>i vēkaiyilē
taṅka vici<u>r</u>i koṇṭu ta<u>n</u>ic cempu tīrttaṅ koṇṭu
taṇalamartta vantēn[265]

The next day after the body is buried or cremated the people visit the burial ground to complete the final rite. The images mentioned here are parallel to what we see in 12:6: 'the golden fan,' and 'the golden bowl with water' to reduce the heat of the burning ground.

12:7

'And the dust returns to the earth'

The word, 'the dust', as referring to the material cause of a thing or person is found twice in the entire HB: Eccl 3:20 and 12:7.[266] The word 'dust' has a religious significance here. The returning of the dust to the earth takes us back to Gen 3:19. Moreover it emphasizes the transitoriness or ephemerality of human life. According to Eccl 3:18-21, humans and animals suffer the same fate: they are made of dust and must return to dust (v. 20). "The statement that humans are dust and will return to dust is probably associated with the burial rites of ancient Palestine."[267]

The environmental other is presented as that which undergoes change. The change follows a certain rhythm which is beyond human comprehension and understanding (11:5-6). God is the author of these things (11:5).

---

263 Cf. Seow, *Ecclesiastes*, 381.

264 "The pots may have been smashed at funerals to symbolize death…In our text, the pots are broken at the fountain, the source of life, and crushed at the pit, perhaps here meaning the grave." Seow, *Ecclesiastes*, 381.

265 "When the golden cremation ground was lit with fire With a golden fan and a bowl of water I came to put off the fire."

266 The word with the article occurs nine times (Lev 14:41; Num 5:17; 1 Kgs 16:2; 18:38; Eccl 3:20; 12:7; Neh 4:2; 4:10). Except in Ecclesiastes in all other places the word refers to the dust which needs to be cleaned. The word without the article appears 110 times in the HB. The meaning of the word ranges from dust, loose earth, soil, ground, ashes, plaster, and rubble. Figuratively it means multitude, worthlessness, devastation, and humiliation. It has also religious significance as we find it appear in the self-abasement (Josh 7:6) rites or formulas (Gen 18:27). Cf. *TDOT*, XI, 257-65.

267 *TDOT*, XI, 264.

G. Themes and Motifs

1. 'Vanity'

The central motif of the book of Ecclesiastes is vanity (*hebel*). The verb in Qal means 'to be or become involved with nothing.'[268] In Babylonian Aramaic it means 'breath' or 'vapour.'[269] The dictionary reading of the word shows,

> The root is used in two ways in the HB, literally and figuratively. The literal, concrete sense is used in reference to the wind, man's transitory breath, evanescent vapor (Isa 57:13; Pss 62:10; 144:4; Prov 21:6; Job 7:16). In this sense, it is often a synonym for 'breath' or 'wind' (Eccl 1:14; Isa 57:13; Jer 10:14). The literal sense lent itself to metaphorical senses: (1) breath / vapor / wind is nonphysical, evanescent, and lacks concrete substance thus, the connotation "unsubstantial" (Jer 10:15; 16:19; 51:18), "profitless" or "fruitless" (Ps 78:33; Prov 13:11), "worthless" (2 Kgs 17:15; Jer 2:5; 10:3), "pointless" (Prov 21:6), "futile" (Lam 4:17; Eccl 1:2, 14; 2:1, 14–15), (2) breath/vapor/wind is transitory and fleeting — thus, the connotation "fleeting" or "transitory" (Prov 31:30; Eccl 6:12; 7:15; 9:9; 11:10; Job 7:16) and (3) breath/vapor/wind cannot be seen thus, the idea of "obscure," "dark," "difficult to understand," "enigmatic" (Eccl 11:10).[270]

The word appears at the beginning (1:2) and at the end of the book (12:8) and serves as a frame narrative to the book. The concordance study shows that the word appears thirty-eight times in Eccl.[271] Often the word acts as a summary point having a climactic force. The word performs two functions: at some places, it sums up what has been said before while in some other places it orients the reader towards what is about to come. Fox argues that 'absurd' would be the most appropriate translation of *hebel.*[272] The word also can be rendered a symbolic meaning as the representation of human experience in its entirety.[273] The word also is used figuratively to denote transience,

268 This root is found in Aramaic and South Semitic languages. Cf. R. Albertz, 'הבל,' *TLOT*, I, 351.

269 Cf. K. Seybold, 'הבל,' *TDOT*, III, 313.

270 See HALOT 236-37; *BDB* 210-11.

271 All the occurrences of הבל are as follows: 1:2, 14; 2:1, 11, 15, 17, 19, 21, 23, 26; 3:19; 4:4, 7, 8, 16; 5:6, 9 (Eng 7, 10); 6:2, 4, 9, 11, 12; 7:6, 15; 8:10, 14 (2x); 9:9 (2x); 11:8, 19; 12:8. But B. K. Waltke is of different opinion: The hebel is "the book's leitwort ('leading word'), occurring thirty-seven times. Not coincidentally thirty-seven is the numerical value of hebel (h=5, b=2, l=30). Recall also that thre are 111 verses in each half, which is three times the numerical value of hebel." B. K. Waltke, *An Old Testament Theology. An Exegetical, Canonical, and Thematic Approach* (Grand Rapids 2007), 955.

272 Cf. M. Fox, "The Meaning of Hebel for Qohelet," *JBL* 105 / 3 (1986), 425.

273 Cf. D. B. Miller, *Symbol and Rhetorics in Ecclesiastes* (Atlanta 2002), 180.

ephemerality, insubstantiality, emptiness and futility.[274] In seven instances[275] *hebel* is followed by 'striving after or chasing the wind.'

When Qohelet says that everything is *hebel*, he is saying, "everything is beyond human apprehension and comprehension."[276] One will never be able to *have* anything, *understand* it, or *control* and *master* it. Whybray, rendering the word as 'vanity,' divides the book into seven sections based on seven types of vanity.[277] According to Whybray's division our poem falls under the seventh section, 'the vanity of the brevity of human life' (11:7-12:7). This section contains the second '*carpe diem*' message in the book.[278]

The *hebel* occurs five times in the poem, 11:8, 11:10, and 12:8 (3x).[279] Let us analyse each instance in detail:

11:8 'All that comes is fleeting'

In the immediate context the adjective 'all' is parallel to 'all of them' in the former colon. The adjective 'all' represents 'the many years of light or life.' Together it means, "all that come to existence" (cf. 5:14-15).[280] The verb 'to come' involves a word-play.[281] Here *hebel* can be rendered as 'fleeting.'[282] All that come into life are ephemeral, transient, and beyond human control.[283]

11:10 'for the childhood and the black hair are fleeting'

274 Cf. V. Onwukeme, *Searching for Meaning with Qoheleth* (Longford 2012) 24. The term is closely linked to the name Abel (Gen 4:2a), which is the pausal form of לבה. Hess translates this name as 'short-lived' or 'fleeting.' Cf. R. S. Hess, *Studies in Personal Names of Genesis* 1-11 (Neukirchen-Vluyn 1993) 27. The transitory sense of the word is rendered in the background of Gen 4:2, where it represents Abel, whose life was fleeting and short-lived.

275 Eccl 1:14; 2:11, 17, 26; 4:4, 6; 6:9. The expression attests the meaning of 'wind.'

276 Seow, *Ecclesiastes*, 59.

277 They are: 1. The vanity of toil and human effort (1:12 – 2:26); 2. The vanity of man's ignorance of the future (3:1-15); 3. The vanity of the presence of injustice in the world (3:16-22); 4. The vanity of the pursuit of wealth (5:9-19); 5. The vanity of unpunished wickedness (8:10-15); 6. The vanity of the fact that all men share a common fate (9:1-10); and 7. The vanity of the brevity of human life (11:7-12:7). Cf. R. N. Whybray, "Qoheleth, Preacher of Joy," in D. J. A. Clines (ed.) *The Poetical Books. A Sheffield Reader* (Sheffield 1997), 195.

278 The first carpe diem message is found in 1:12-2:26. Enns observes that in this section the presence of לבה is very dense, 9x in 31 verses, which is 14 percent of the 222 verses in Eccl. Cf. Enns, *Ecclesiastes*, 9.

279 We also note a paronomasia of the word in 12:6 as ('cord' or 'string' or 'rope').

280 Cf. Seow, *Ecclesiastes*, 348.

281 This word forms an inclusio with the verbs דלה ('to go') in 12:5 and בוש ('to return') in 12:7. All that 'comes' must 'go' and 'return.'

282 Enns translates all the instances of לבה as 'absurd' or 'absurdity.' Cf. Enns, *Ecclesiastes*, 10.

283 Cf. Seow, *Ecclesiastes*, 348.

The initial '*kî*' is causal and can be translated as 'for' or 'because.' The first noun 'the childhood' appears in the previous verse (11:9) closes the section forming an inclusion. The second noun, 'the black hair' is a *hap. leg.*, which can either refer to 'black hair' of a young man (cf. Job 30:30) or most probably and poetically, to 'the dawn.'[284] By leaving the word to mean as 'black hair' and 'dawn,' Qohelet enjoys being enigmatic. In 11:10, *hebel* has a dual meaning: (a) The word sums up what has been said earlier and calls them 'fleeting' or 'transient;' and (b) By implication, as these two realities ('boyhood' and 'black hair') are fleeting, the imperative to 'rejoice' and 'remember' becomes urgent.

12:8 'Vanity of vanities,' says the teacher, 'all is vanity.'

This verse functions in three ways: (a) It closes the poem; (b) It serves as the poet's conclusion or summary statement of the book;[285] and (c) The verse acts as the frame narrative of the book together with 1:2.

Hence in 11:8 and 10 *hebel* can be rendered as 'fleeting' and in 12:8 as 'vanity' or 'absurdity.' Qohelet is creatively employing the term as he tries to say that even attempting to understand 'vanity' also is a 'vanity.'

2. 'All'

The word *kōl* appears sixty-five times in Eccl.[286] Qohelet's outstanding interest to use this word suggests the universal perspective of the author. In our poem the root *kll* appears six times: 11:5; 12:8, 11:8, 9; 12:4, and 11:8). All these instances suggest the universal implication of the message of Qohelet. From the narrative point of view this shows the omniscience of the author, who affirms that he knows everything 'under the sun,' and the truths he proposes are valid universally – at *all* times, and in *all* places.

It can be translated as 'everything' or 'all' or 'all things.' 'Everything' is an idiom for the entire creation (cf. Ps 103:19; 119:91; Jer 10:16) Although, *kōl* is often used in an absolute or comprehensive sense (*BDB* 481), it is frequently used as a synecdoche of the general for the specific, that is, its sense is limited contextually to the topic at hand (*BDB* 482). This is particularly true of *hakkōl* (*BDB* 482) in which the article particularizes or limits the referent to the contextual or previously mentioned topic (e.g., Gen 16:12; 24:1; Exod 29:24; et al). Thus, "all" does not *all times* mean "all" absolutely or universally in

284 The ancient versions did not comprehend the meaning well; the LXX translates as 'folly' (ánoia), while the Vg as voluptas, probably seeing in šaḥărût, the root škr 'to get drunk.' Cf. Mazzinghi, *Ho cercato*, 281.

285 12:9-14 is accepted to be an epilogue to the book, written with an external hand.

286 Cf. Eccl 1:2, 3:7, 8, 9, 13, 14, 16; 2:5, 7, 9, 10, 11, 14, 16, 17, 18, 19, 20, 22, 23; 3:1, 11, 13, 14, 17, 19, 20; 4:1, 4, 8, 15, 16, 17, 18 (Eng 9, 16, 17, 18, 19); 6:2, 6, 7; 7:2, 15, 18, 21, 23, 28; 8:3, 6, 9, 17; 9:1, 2, 3, 4, 6, 8, 9, 10, 11; 10:3, 19; 11:5, 8, 9; 12:4, 8, 13, 14. However, the root ללכ appears ninety times.

comprehension. In several cases the context limits its reference to two classes of objects / issues being discussed, so *hakkōl* means "both" (e.g., 2:14; 3:19: 9:1, 2). Thus, *hakkōl* ('all; everything') refers only to what Qohelet characterizes as "futile" (*hebel*) in the context. This does not mean that everything is futile. For example, fearing God is not "futile" (2:26; 3:14–15; 11:9–10; 12:1, 9, 13–14). Only those objects / issues that are contextually placed under 'all' are designated as 'futile.'

3. 'To Rejoice'

Joy or rejoicing is yet another key theme in the poem. Qohelet who is generally seen as a preacher of a sombre view of life is a strong protagonist of joy.[287] Fox claims that in Qohelet, *śmḥ* means "pleasure, not happiness, and certainly not joy."[288] Fox makes a distinction between happiness, joy and pleasure and says that "pleasure is not an independent emotion or sensation, but an experience or, more precisely, a 'feeling-tone' attached to a more comprehensive experience."[289] The experience of pleasure depends on the individual who experiences it. In other words, the pleasantness does not rest in the external object but in the way in which it affects me, for pleasure is a feeling tone.[290]

The root *śmḥ* ('to rejoice') appears fifteen times in the book.[291] Of these fifteen occurrences, in eight places it is in the verbal form.[292] In seven texts the invitation to rejoice is very firm. They are 2:14a; 3:12; 3:22a; 5:17; 8:15a; 9:7-9a; 11:7-12:1a.[293] Let us consider its two instances in our poem, 11:8 and 9. In both these instances the verb is in imperative mood – 11:8 as a jussive and 11:9 as a direct imperative. The occurrence in 11:9 is unique for three reasons:

287 Cf. Whybray, "Qoheleth, Preacher of Joy,"188.

288 Fox, *Time to Tear Down*, 114.

289 Fox, *Time to Tear Down*, 114.

290 Fox, *Time to Tear Down*, 114.

291 Cf. 2:1, 2, 10, 26; 3:12, 22; 4:16; 5:18, 19 [Eng. 19, 20]; 7:4; 8:15; 9:7; 10:19; 11:8, 9. "Qohelet uses שמח in two ways: (a) enjoyment, the sensation of pleasure (2:10), and (b) a pleasure, a means of pleasure: something that is supposed to induce enjoyment (11:9), such as wine and music. The young man is told to do something, not to feel something." Fox, *Time to Tear Down*, 115.

292 "To be happy and to enjoy themselves" (3:12); "to enjoy their work" (3:22); "those coming after will not rejoice in him" (4:16); "to find enjoyment in one's toil" (5:18); "…to enjoy themselves as they work" (8:15); "wine makes one rejoice in life" (10:19); "let him rejoice in them all" (11:8); and "rejoice, young man" (11:9).

293 "These seven texts are clearly more than mere marginal comments or asides. They punctuate the whole book, forming a kind of Leitmotiv; they increase steadily in emphasis as the book proceeds; and the last, the most elaborate of them all, directly addressed to the reader, introduces and dominates the concluding section of the book in which Qoheleth presents his final thoughts on how life should be lived and why." Whybray, "Qoheleth, Preacher of Joy," 190.

(a) The verb is in the imperative; (b) The addressee is direct; and (c) There is a mention of time element, 'in your youth.'[294]

"The call to enjoyment is reminiscent of an Egyptian tomb inscription, known as *The Song of Antef,* which includes the injunction to 'follow' the heart while one is yet alive."[295] Whybray who studies the joy statements in the book of Ecclesiastes summarizes the conclusions of Qohelet as follows:

a. What good things God has given us are intended for our enjoyment, and in the giving of them he has shown his approval of our actions. To enjoy them is actually to do his will.
b. We must accept our ignorance of God's purposes and of the reasons why he has permitted evil to exist in the world; and we must take life as we find it and enjoy what we can, because
    i. we cannot change the fate that God has chosen for us;
    ii. we cannot know what God has in store for us;
    iii. life is short and death is inevitable.
c. The recognition that toil is part of what God has allotted to us in this life, and that reliance on our own efforts is vain, enables us to find enjoyment even in our toil.[296]

Now let us consider the presence of 'rejoice' and 'remember' together in the poem. In Deut 16:11-12, 'rejoice' and 'remember' are used in such a way as to teach that joy means remembering the salvific works of God. But, in Eccl the invitation to rejoice is linked to the fact that life is short. There are two ambivalent reasons to rejoice: (a) Joy is given to a person by God so that one should not remember how brief one's life is (cf. 5:19 [5:20]); and (b) One needs to remember that his days are short and must recognize the urgency of rejoicing now.

4. 'To Remember'

It is imperative to enjoy life, because that is the way to 'remember your Creator,' that is, to do his will. The verb 'remember' (*zkr*) with God as its object is used in the HB in several somewhat different senses.[297] Here it probably includes obedience to God's will (cf. 11:9b and the references to the 'fear of God' in 3:14; 5:6; 7:18; 8:12, 13; 9:2) and the due performance of religious duties (cf. 4:17 – 5:6); but the context shows that more is meant than this. God is to be remembered specifically as Creator (so only here in the HB); and it is

294 Though it is possible to take the preposition 'bə' as indicating the object of enjoyment, when we read parallel with bîmê bəḥûrōṯẹ̄ḵā in 12:1a, it is better to render a temporal meaning. Cf. Seow, *Ecclesiastes*, 349.

295 Cited in Seow, *Ecclesiastes*, 371.

296 Whybray, "Qoheleth, Preacher of Joy," 195.

297 Cf. B.S. Childs, *Memory and Tradition in Israel* (London 1963), 45-65.

made clear that this 'remembrance' can only be properly carried out in youth, "before the bad days come, and the years draw near when you will say, 'I will get no pleasure in them.'" This suggests that by remembering one's Creator Qohelet means principally the enjoyment of the good things that the Creator has provided.[298]

First let us consider the use of verb *zkr* in Ecclesiastes and in the entire HB. Of the four occurrences[299] of the verb *zkr* in Ecclesiastes, 5:19 is worth noting: "For he does not *remember* the days of his life, for God is answering through the joy of his heart." Here Qohelet tells that it is not expected of humans to *remember*. Moreover, this remembering is distracted by God himself, who makes them "occupied with the joy of their hearts." Thus, *remembering* creates two effects for Qohelet: (a) It will facilitate the rejoicing process (11:8), and (b) It will hinder the joy that one has already (5:19). In the HB, especially in Deuteronomy (e.g., 5:15, 7:18) *remembering* is a key element of life. In Deutero-Isaiah the verb *zkr* is used in two ways: "one must not remember the past because God is doing wondrous new things in the present" (Isa 43:18). On the other hand, one must remember the past, because the past is a testimony to the consistency of God's acts (Isa 46:8).[300] Human memory always has this twofold effect: one that gives you assurance and another that pulls you back.[301] "If memory causes one to be dependent in the present, so that one cannot see new possibilities, one should not remember; but if memory serves the present well and enhances faith, then one should remember. Remembrance of events in the past should help one live in the present."[302]

The object of *zkr* is a complementary clause, "that the days of darkness will be many." "The 'days of darkness' refers not to death or Sheol, but to a time of gloom and misery (cf. 5:16, 12:1)."[303] The act of remembering has 'a future dimension,' for 'the days' refer to the old age and the days of pain which are to come.[304] Physiologically speaking, the Hebrew mind-set associated 'memory' as the faculty of the heart. Memory must not paralyse one from moving ahead in life. When we 'remember' something we are already distant from the reality. Though distant we are able to connect to the reality in our mind. In HB 'memory' is 'to keep something in one's heart.' Thus, *zkr* also anticipates the 'heart', which is the key word in the following verses.

298 Cf. Whybray, "Qoheleth, Preacher of Joy," 194.

299 5:19, 9:15, 11:8, and 12:1.

300 Cf. Seow, *Ecclesiastes*, 370.

301 For example, the memory of India's slavery in the hands of England will make me appreciate the air of freedom or will pull me back as someone who has a wounded past.

302 Cf. Seow, *Ecclesiastes*, 370.

303 Seow, *Ecclesiastes*, 348.

304 Seow, *Ecclesiastes*, 370.

Now let us take the combination of the verbs *śmḥ* and *zkr*. This combination appears only in the context of cultic exhortations.[305] But, in 11:8 there is no reference to God. The invitation to rejoice goes together with remembering the brevity of life. "The source of joy, for Qohelet, is completely different: not the cult, not the Torah, not the memory of the salvific actions of God, but the consciousness of the brevity of life and the indiscernible will of God."[306]

"Remember your creator...before...before...before..." is Qohelet's equivalent to the fear of the Lord as the beginning of the wisdom. It turns his epistemology upside down, starting with God as creator rather than his experience, his reason, his observation. This does not detract from the challenges of life, as the 'before' sections make clear, but it provides a foundation for living amidst the mysteries of life.[307]

In the poem *zkr* is more than memory. It is more than a purely mental faculty involving the storage of information. The 'remembering' leads one to action. Thus, it involves both thought and deed.[308] Another reason perhaps Qohelet uses this word together with *śmḥ* (which assonates with *šmʿ*), *zkr* appears in the prayers or intercessions recorded in the HB.[309] Memory is inculcated through repetition.

5. Complementing Contradictions

Contradictions or play of opposites is yet another theme in the poem of our study. We note seven opposites in the poem:

i. 'Morning' vs. 'Evening'

In 11:6, though these opposites appear as a merismus, the entire poem seems to be a paraphrase of these two words. In the 'morning' of one's life one must 'rejoice' and 'remember' for the 'evening' is to come shortly.

---

305 For example, in Deut 16:11-12 and Ps 97:12. In Deuteronomic test joy is attached to remembering the salvific works of the Lord, which the Israelites celebrate during their feasts. Cf. Mazzinghi, *Ho cercato,* 275.

306 Mazzinghi, *Ho cercato*, 275.

307 C. G. Bartholomew, "The Intertextuality of Ecclesiastes," in K. Dell – W. Kynes, *Reading Ecclesiastes Intertextually* (London 2014), 229.

308 This is also the understanding of the HB. When God remembers the covenant (cf. Gen 9:15-16; Exod 6:5; et al) it means that he calls to mind and intervenes. The link between remembering and intervention is vivid in Num 10:9.

309 In the prayers of Moses (Exod 32:13), Samson (Judg 16:28), Hezekiah (2 Kgs 20:3), Nehemiah (Neh 13:14, 22, 29, 31), Jeremiah (Jer 15:15; Lam 5:1), and Habakkuk (Hab 3:2) we notice this.

ii. 'You do Not Know' vs. 'You do Know'

The verb 'know' appears in 11:5, 6, and 9.[310] In the first two instances the verb is preceded by a negative particle while in the third instance it is in the affirmative. The first two instances speak about the incomprehensibility of certain realities while the third is a proof that human person can still know and make sense of. In the third instance the word also means, 'be reminded,' or 'recall' or 'remember.' In some areas (i.e., planting and harvesting times) humans can learn by observation and tradition, but in other areas (mysteries of nature and mysteries of God's activities) humans cannot know. Wisdom, though good, helpful, and desirable cannot solve all of life's unknowns. 'You cannot know the activity of God' - This has been a common theme (cf. 1:13; 3:10, 11; 8:17). God and his works and ways cannot be completely known.

iii. 'God' vs. 'Man'

God is someone who creates (12:1), makes all things (11:5), causes everything to existence (11:5), brings people to judgment (11:9), and gives the life-breath (and takes it back) (12:7). Man does not know (11:5), is blessed with a span of life (11:8), is a composite of body and spirit (11:10), is dust and returns to the dust (12:7). Human person's life is very unpredictable. "In view of the basic unpredictability of the future (cf. 11:4), human action always remains risky."[311]

iv. 'Light' vs. 'Darkness'

By making 'light' an independent existential reality, Qohelet draws a contrast with darkness.

v. 'Good' vs. 'Evil'

The cognate of the root 'good' appears twice[312] (11:2, 10) and that of 'evil' once (11:10) in the poem.

vi. 'Spirit' vs. 'Flesh'

But for the 'life-breath' that is given by God human person is nothing but dust. This dust makes the flesh. The flesh is prone to pain and suffering.

---

310 In the entire book the word appears 30x. Cf. 1:17; 2:14, 19; 3:12, 14, 21; 4:13, 17; 6:5, 8, 10, 12; 7:22, 25; 8:1, 5, 7, 12, 16, 17; 9:1, 5, 11, 12; 10:14, 15; 11:2, 5, 6, 9.

311 Krüger, *Qoheleth*, 194.

312 But in the book 41x. Cf. 2:1, 3, 24, 26; 3:12, 13, 22; 4:3, 6, 8, 9, 13; 5:4, 10, 17; 6:3, 6, 9, 12; 7:1, 2, 3, 5, 8, 10, 11, 14, 18, 20, 26; 8:12, 13, 15; 9:2, 4, 7, 16, 18; 11:6, 7; 12:14.

vii. 'Coming' vs. 'Going'

The verb 'come' appears as Qal in 11:8 and Hiphil in 11:9.[313] The verb 'go' appears in 11:9 in imperative and 12:5 in indicative.[314] In 11:8, Qohelet says that all that *comes* is fleeting, because all that *comes* must *go*. In the context of our poem, 'come' signifies 'entry of human life,' while 'go' signifies 'its exit.'[315]

Fox who studies the contradictions in the book of Ecclesiastes notes,

> Qohelet's contradictions are the starting point but not the message of the book. He marshals them to tear down meaning, but he does not stop there. He is not a nihilist. He also builds up meaning, discovering ways of creating clarity and gratification in a confusing and indifferent world. Nor does Qohelet employ paradox, Zen-like, as a means to enlightenment. He discovers paradoxical truths, but the paradoxes give no flashes of insight into some greater, ineffable meaning.[316]

He continues,

> To be precise, Qohelet is not so much contradicting himself as observing contradictions in the world. To him they seem to be antinomies, two equally valid but contradictory principles. He does not resolve these antinomies, but only describes them, bemoans them, and suggests how to live in such a refractory world. The contradictions do not make the book incoherent. On the contrary, Qohelet's persistent observation of contradictions is a powerful cohesive force, and an awareness of it brings into focus the book's central concern: the problem of meaning in life. The book of Qohelet is about meaning: its loss and its (partial) discovery.[317]

Thus, the close reading of Eccl 11:4-12:8.

H. Conclusion

The close reading of Eccl 11:4-12:8 brings to light the following: (i) Qohelet, who is the author the text, in his historical and theological context, shifts his attention from external to internal dimension of a human person as the external identities became extinct. (ii) The text, which is at the concluding section of the Book of Ecclesiastes, sums up the key themes of the book in a beautiful collage of human life-stages; (iii) The author, through various poetic devices

313 In the entire book the verb 'come' appears 15x. Cf. 1:4, 5; 2:12, 16; 3:22; 5:2, 14, 15; 6:4; 8:10; 9:14; 11:8, 9; 12:1; and 12:14.

314 The verb 'walk' or 'go' appears 30x. Cf. 1:4, 6 (2x), 7 (3x); 2:1, 14; 3:20; 4:15, 17; 5:14 (2x), 15; 6:4, 6, 8, 9; 7:2 (2x); 8:3, 10; 9:7, 10; 10:3, 7, 15, 20; 11:9; 12:5.

315 In this context, the verb 'return' also is significant.

316 Fox, *Time to Tear Down*, 3.

317 Fox, *Time to Tear Down,* 3.

and techniques, characterises the human person, God, and the world in a mutual relationship. The invidividual is taken along his life-stages, the centre of which is God, the Creator.

III. ANALYSIS OF PAṬṬIṈATTĀR'S UṬALKŪṞṞUVAṆṆAM

In this chapter, at the outset, let us define the author of the text, his historical context. Then, we shall transliterate and translate the Tamil poem. Finally, as we did in the previous chapter let us employ the narrative analysis tools of setting, style, characterisation, and themes and motifs to read the text closely.

A. Poet: Name and Historical Context

There has been three Paṭṭiṉattār in the history of Tamiḻ literature.[318] The first one is known as Tirumuṟai Paṭṭiṉattār XI, who belongs to the 10th cent. CE. The third one is also known by the same name Paṭṭiṉattār, but has not made any memorable contribution to literature. The text of our study belongs to the in-between Paṭṭiṉattār or the Second Paṭṭiṉattār. Scholars by and large agree that he belongs to the 14th cent. CE.[319] According to V. Ramaswami, "the first important poets who tried to write in a language comprehensible to the people were Paṭṭiṉattār and Tāyumāṉavar."[320] The Second Paṭṭiṉattār is "represented in the anthology of siddha literature and must have been a contemporary and master of Pattirakiri who has also his contribution in the anthology."[321] He is also considered one among the cittās.[322] There are only two instances where

318 P. Karuppaiyā, *Paṭṭiṉattār Oru Pārvai* (Chennai 2012), 22.

319 Aṅkamuttu holds that Paṭṭiṉattār belongs to the 10th cent. ce. Cf. A. Aṅkamuthu, *Paṭṭiṉattār Tiruppāṭalkal* (Chennai 2008), xvii.

320 Cf. K. V. Zvelebil, *Tamil Literature*, 221.

321 Mohan Lal, ed., *Encyclopedia of Indian Literature*, Vol. V (New Delhi 2001), 4293.

322 The cittās belong to the 14th-15th cent. ce. Though the cittās belonged to different groups in the ladder of caste stratification, the majority hailed from the lower strata. Their songs were a literary protest to the higher strata, to the institutionalized religion. They critiqued the religious rituals, recommendations and traditions and condemned the Vēdās. They were rebels. "Vērttu iraippu vantapōtu vēdam vantu vutavumō?" ("Will the Veda come and help a man who is perspiring and longing for breathing?"). "Tāvāram illai. Tanikkoru vīdillai. Tēvāram ētukkaṭi kutampāi" (We don't have a courtyard. We don't have a single house. What is the use of Tēvāram?). Cf. Karuppaiyā, 23.

the Second Paṭṭiṉattār seems to reflect the cittā mindset in his poems.[323] Since he lived close to the cittā period these two songs reflect the rebellious tone of the cittās.[324] Otherwise he adheres to the tradition very strongly. His songs reflect the Śaiva Bhakti tradition.[325]

Paṭṭiṉattār's original name is Cuvētāraṇyar alias Tiruveṇkāṭar.[326] He hails from Kāvēripūmpaṭṭinam (Pūmpukār), a famous port-town of the Cōḻā dynasty. His parents are Civanēcan and Ñānakkalai. His father Civanēcan, a sea-trader, was a devout devotee to the Lord Śiva. Tiruveṇkāṭar had an elder sister. When he was five years old his father passed away. After a very brief schooling he undertook his father's sea-trade and faired good at the trade. He was married to Civakalai, the daughter of Civacitamparam and Civakāmi of the same town. Their family grew in prosperity, hospitality and magnanimity. They welcomed the servants of the Lord at home and served them. At the bottom of their hearts lay their anxiety to have a child. They prayed to the Lord Śiva. Meanwhile a poor couple, Civacarumar – Cucilai, found a male child under a vilva tree. Upon the Lord Śiva's command, they took the child and gave to Tiruveṇkāṭar. Tiruveṇkāṭar who was happy to own

323 *Nīṟṟai puṉainteṉṉa nīrāṭap pōyeṉṉa nīmaṉamē*
māṟṟip piṟakka vakaiyaṟin tāyillai māmaṟainūl
ēṟṟik kiṭakku meḻukōṭi mantira meṉṉa kaṇṭāi
āṟṟiṟ kiṭantun tuṟaiyaṟi yāma lalaikiṉṟatē.
(Maturai Potu, 40).

[What is the use of applying the ashes on the entire body? What is the use of immersing in the holy waters? O mind, you do not know the way to exit this birth. What do you find in the seven crores prayers that you find in the Vedas? You are like someone in the river who does not know to board the boat.] In this song, Paṭṭiṉattār criticizes the traditional piety of applying the ashes on the body, getting into the tīrtās, and reciting the Vedic mantras. SA.

Nēmaṅkaḷ niṭṭaikal vētaṅkal ākama nītineṟi
ōmaṅkal tarppaṇam canti cepamantra yōkanilai
nāmaṅkal cantaṉam veṇṇīṟu pūci nalamuṭanē
cāmaṅkal tōṟum ivarceyyum pūcaikaḷ carppaṉaiye.
(Maturai Potu, 44).

[The ordinances, the beliefs, the principles of the Vedas, the pronouncements, the sprinkling of water, saluting the Sun, prayers, meditation postures, utterings of the holy name, applying the sandal paste and the ashes, the offerings at night – all these are empty]. Cf. Karuppaiyā, 23-24.

324 For historical and textual problems pertaining to Tamil Siddha works, cf. K. Zvelebil, *The Smile of Murugan*, 1973, 218-20. K. V. Zvelebil, *The Poets of the Powers* (London 1973) 15-24. Also, A. V. Subramania Aiyar, The Poetry and the Philosophy of the Tamil Siddhars (Tirunelveli 1957).

325 Karuppaiyā, 23.

326 Tiruveṇkāṭar is the name of the Lord Šiva dwelling in Kāvēripūmpaṭṭinam.

a child gave them in return the child's weight of gold. They named the child Marutavāṇan. When he grew up he was educated under a village teacher. He too was interested in sea-trade like his father. With his companions he went on a sea-trade to foreign countries. While his companions returned with sacks of gold and silver, Marutavāṇan returned with two sacks of dry dung and hay. The companions made fun of him and on their return complained to his father that his son had lost his mind. Tiruveṇkāṭar yelled at his son for his irresponsible behaviour. But, when he opened his son's sack and poured out the dung on the floor, to his surprise, there were precious gems and gold hidden inside. He was dumb-bound and awe-struck. He wanted to embrace his son and ask pardon. But, his son disappeared. He went out to search for his son. Upon his returning home in vain, his wife gave him a small box which Marutavāṇan wanted to be given to his father. When he opened the box he saw an earless needle and a piece of palm-leaf with an inscription. It read, "*kātaṟṟa ūciyum vārātukāṇ kaṭaivaḻikku*" ("Not even an earless needle will accompany you on your final way").

At these words Tiruveṇkāṭar was enlightened. He took these words to be the words of the Lord Śiva. "Because *kaṭai* can mean both 'store, bazaar,' or 'end,' the line can be read in two ways: Broken needles (lit. needles without ears) will not come on the way to the market place. Or Broken needles will not be found on the final way (i.e., the way to salvation). Thus, in the Siddha context, the reference to broken needles alludes to the uselessness material wealth to sannyasi, the renunciant who has abandoned everything upon entering on the 'final' way."[327] He realized that the Lord Śiva had sent Marutavāṇan to enlighten him. At once he renounced everything – his mother, his wife, his trade, his property, his house, his friends – and with a loincloth he left his home. He dwelt in the village inn. His elder sister wanted to poison him with an *āppam* ('bread'). Uttering, "*uṉ viṉai uṉṉai cuṭum ōṭṭappam vīṭṭai cudum*" ("Your action will burn you and round-bread will burn the house") he threw the *āppam* on the roof of the house and the roof lit with fire. Then he went to Tiruveṇkāṭu. When his mother's death was noticed to him he returned to Kāvēripūmpaṭṭinam to perform last rites for his mother. From then on he was called Paṭṭiṉattār, after the name of his hometown. His way of life inspired the King of Pattirakiri, who also renounced everything and followed him. When he reached Tiruvoṟṟiyūr, the pēikkarumpu ('devil-sugarcane'), which he had been holding since he left Kāvēripūmpaṭṭiṉam began to taste sweet. This was the revelation to him that this was the place where he would attain union with God. He saw there some village boys playing with the sea sand. He joined to play with them and told them to bury him under the sand. When they buried

327 E. F. Kent, *Converting Women. Gender and Protestant Christianity in Colonial South India,* (New York 2004), 148.

him he rose up. And they did so the second time. When the third time they buried him, he never rose up. When they uncovered the sand they found him being turned into a *Śivalinga*. Upon hearing the news, the villagers rushed to the spot. They offered flowers in honour and venerated him. His five songs "Kōil Nāṉmaṇimālai," 'Tirukkaḻumalai Mummaṇikkōvai," "Tiruviṭaimarutūr Mummaṇikkōvai," "Tiruēkapamuṭaiyār Tiruvantāti," and "Tiruvoṟṟiyūr Orupā Orupaṯu" are added to the Patinōrām Tirumuṟai. The song of our study, *Uṭal,* might have been one of his last compositions.

B. Poem:[328] Text[329] and Translation[330]

1 *orumaṭamātu moruvanumāki*
yiṉpacukantaru maṉpuporunti
yuṇarvukalaṅki yoḻukiyavintu
ūṟucurōṇita mītukalantu

An ignorant woman and a man
together in sweet pleasure coupled with love,
semen spurt in passionate emotion
mixing with her sticky flow,

2 *paṉiyilorpāti ciṟutuḷimātu*
panṭiyilvantupu kuntutiranṭu
patumavarumpu kamaṭamiteṉṟu
pārvaimeivāicevi kālkaikaḷeṉṟa

328 We have three versions of the poem at hand: (a) Tiru. V. Kalyāṇasuntaraṉār, *Paṭṭiṉattār Pāṭalkaḷ* (Chennai 32010) 168-78. This edition has adopted relatively the most ancient version we have access to. This edition divides each stanza into three aṭi; (b) Ā. Aṅkamuttu, *Paṭṭiṉattār Tiṟuppāṭalkaḷ* (Chennai 2008) 305-17. Aṅkamuttu has borrowed the text from the former edition. He while retaining the aṭi structure of the former, has re-written the poem by dividing the lines into comprehensible syllables; (c) The electronic edition of Tamil Virtual Library. This online edition takes us back to the original composition of the poem in four aṭi. But falls short because it has failed to retain the original cīr division. For our study we take the text of (a) and adopt the line pattern of (c).

329 The text we are taking for our study of Udaṟkūṟṟuvaṇṇam is from the text used by Tiru. Vi. Kalyāṇasuntaraṉār. The reason is this is the more difficult text. Lectio difficilior potior ('the more difficult reading is stronger') is a main principle of textual criticism. This principle is an internal criterion. Though there are other texts available we are taking this text based on the principle of difficilior. The difficulty that the text renders to the reader.

330 Some authors like Ā. Aṅkamuttu, M. Nārāyaṇappillai, Vē. Kōpālaṉ divide the original cīr of the Song into easily comprehensible words. But this does not permit one to appreciate the rhythm with which the poet has composed this song. The Tamiḻ Virtual University edition not only divides the cīr but also writes the stanzas in four lines. Excluding the prelude or musical note, the poem divides into 24 stanzas. The stanzas 6, 12, 18 and 24 have four lines, the fourth line of which acts as a virtual full-stop. All other stanzas consist of 3 lines each. The numbering is ours and numbering the stanzas is for practical reasons and it help us be more specific when we have a close reading of the poem.

A little drop - as big as a semi-dew –
entering the womb gyrating and gathering
as a lotus-bud, tiny tortoise,
having eyes, body, mouth, ears, legs and arms,

3 *uruvamumāki yuyirvaḷarmāta*
moṉpatumoṉṟuni raintumaṭantai
yutaramakaṉṟu puviyilviḻuntu
yōkamuvāramu nāḷumaṟintu

Taking shape, life growing nine and
one month completing, lass'
womb opening, falls on the earth,
seeking luck, week and day,

4 *makaḷirkacenai taravaṇaiyādai*
maṇpaṭavuntiyu taintakaviḻntu
maṭamayilkoṅkai yamutamarunti
yōraṟivīraṟi vākivaḷarntu

An army of women dressing in furls,
curling on sands, kicking and turning,
sucks nectar from peachick like breasts,
first sense, second sense growing,

5 *oḷinakaiyūṟa litaḻmaṭavāru*
vantumukantiṭa vantutavaḻntu
maṭiyiliruntu maḻalaimoḻintu
vāvirupōveṉa nāmamviḷampa

Dazzling smile in wet lips,
fondly kissed by lasses crawling, coming and
sitting on the lap, babbling names
like 'come' 'stay' 'go,'

6 *uṭaimaṇiyāṭai yaraivaṭamāṭa*
vuṉpavartiṉpava taṅkaḷoṭuṇṭu
teruviliruntu puḻutiyaḷaintu
tēṭiyapālaro ṭōṭinaṭantu -
añcuvayatāki viḷaiyāṭiyē

Pearl-embedded dresses dancing on the hip-belt,
feeding from everyone's plate,
in the street amidst the dust
running and walking with the playmates –
fun and frolic ages five.

7 *uyartaruñaṉa kuruvupateca*
muntamiḻiṉkalai yuṅkaraikaṇṭu
valarpiṟaiyeṉṟu palarumviḷampa
vāḻpatiṉārupi rāyamumvantu

Exhorted with wise sage's
teaching and the arts of Tamil,
exalted into a crescent moon by many,
lively sixteen arriving,

8 *mayirmuṭikōti yaṟupatanīla*
vaṇṭimir taṇṭoṭai koṇṭaipuṉaintu
maṇipoṉilaṅku paṇikaḷaṇintu
mākatarpōkata kūṭivaṇaṅka

Combing the long-hair and wearing
a garland attracting the honey bees,
adorned with pearls-embedded golden jewels,
respected by all who praise

9 *mataṉacorūpa ṉivaṉeṉamōka*
maṅkaiyarkaṇṭuma ruṇṭutiraṇṭu
variviḻikoṇṭu kaḻiyaveṟintu
māmayilpōlava pōvatukaṇṭu

Calling out, 'behold the love-god,'
women enamoured of him and wink,
with their lined-eyes devouring,
seeing them passing like peahens,

10 *maṉatupoṟāma lavarpiṟakōṭi*
maṅkalaceṅkala cantikaḻkoṅkai
maruvamayaṅki yitaḻamutuṇṭu
tēṭiyamāmutal cēravaḻaṅki

Not able to control the mind, running behind
pressing their round-tight breasts
losing himself sucking nectar off their lips,
giving them all his hard-earned capital,

11 *orumutalāki mutuporuḷāyi*
runtataṉaṅkaḷu vampiliḻantu
mataṉacukanta vitaṉamiteṉṟu
vālipakōlamu vēṟupirintu

The inheritance and the capital
being lost in suits and quarrels,
lamenting the dissipated youth,
the youthful charm, the passionate fires freezing,

12 *vaḷamaiyumāṟi yiḷamaiyumāṟi*
vaṉpalviḻuntiru kaṇkaḷiruṇṭu
vayatumutirntu naraitiraivantu
vātavirōtaku rōtamaṭaintu
ceṅkaiyinilōrta ṭiyumākiyē

Richness ending, youth ending,
strong teeth falling off eyes darkening,
aging old, hair greying,
dispute, hatred, anger accompanying -
holding a stick in his cold-red hands.

13 *varuvatupova torumutukūnu*
mantiyeṉumpaṭi kuntinaṭantu
matiyumaḻintu cevitimirvantu
vāyaṟiyāmalvi ṭāmamoḻintu

Coming and going is like a bent
monkey steps slowing down,
mind diminishing, ears stiffened,
blabbering incongruous words,

14 *tuyilvarunēra mirumalpoṟātu*
toṇṭaiyuneñcumu larntuvaṟaṇṭu
tukilumiḻantu cuṇaiyumaḻintu
tōkaiyarpālarka kōraṇikoṇṭu

When falling asleep unceasing cough,
throat and chest dried up and parched,
clothes slipping off, sensations lost,
being mocked at by women and children,

15 *kaliyukamīti livarmariyātai*
kaṇṭiṭumenpava cañcalamiñca
kalakalaveṉṟu malacalamvantu
kālvaḻimēlvaḻi cāranaṭantu

Disturbed by the respect received in this
trouble-filled age, perplexity abounds,
stools and urine passing uncontrolled,
drenching legs and groins, crawling around,

16 *teḷivumirāma luraitaṭumāṟi*
cintaiyuneñcumu laintumaruṇṭu
tiṭamumulaintu mikavumalaintu
tēṟinalātara vēteṉanontu

Confused and staggering in speech,
thoughts and feelings landslide,
being terrified and strength dissipated,
realizing that there is none to care,

17 *maṟaiyavaṉveta ṉeḷutiyavāru*
vantatukaṇṭamu meṉṟuteḷintu
iṉiyeṉakaṇṭa miṉiyeṉatonta
mētiṉivāḻvuni lātiṉiniṉṟa

as written by God in the book,
that the calamity has arrived
what else is there? what else is the relation?
the life on earth does not last long,

18 *kaṭaṉmuṟaipēcu meṉavuraināvu*
ṟaṅkiviḻuntukai koṇṭumoḻintu
kaṭaivaḻikañci yoḻukiṭavantu
pūtamunālucu vācamuniṉṟu
neñcutaṭumāṟi varunēramē
Tongue that commanded, 'speak about the duties,'
falls asleep, talking with his hand's gestures,
unable to swallow, food drips out,
the four elements and the breath stopping –
arrives the hour that shakes his heart.

19 *vaḷarpiṟaipōla veyiṟumurōma*
muñcaṭaiyuñciṟu kuñciyuviñcu
maṉatumiruṇṭa vaṭivumilaṅka
māmalaipōlyama tūtarkaḷ vantu
With the crescent teeth, hairy and knotted chunk,
merciless heart, dark-complexioned,
like huge mountains
arrive the messengers of death,

20 *valaikoṭuvīci yuyirkoṭupōka*
maintaruvantuku ṉintaḻanontu
maṭiyilviḻuntu maṉaivipulampa
mālkiṉarēyiva kālamaṟintu
Throwing the net, taking away the life,
children coming to bow are vexed,
wife wailing falls on the lap,
'behold he is dead' thus written in the sand of time,

21 *paḻaiyavarkāṇu meṉumayalārka*
pañcupaṟantiṭa ninṟavarpanta
riṭumeṉavantu paṟaiyiṭamunta
vēpiṇamvēka vicāriyumeṉṟu
The neighbours calling him 'a known man'
come around and disperse as cotton-flakes,
those command to make a shed, drummers coming,
'enquire about cremation' a voice shouting

22 *palaraiyumēvi mutiyavartāmi*
runtacavaṅkaḻu vuñcilareṉṟu
paṇitukiltoṅka kaḷapamaṇintu
pāvakamēceitu nāṟumuṭampai

Many others loaded with mini tasks,
the elders command 'wash the corpse,'
with dresses, hangings, garlands and
scents engulfing the stinking body,

23 *varicaiketāma leṭumenvōṭi*
vantiḷamaintarku ṉintucumantu
kaṭukinaṭantu cuṭalaiyaṭaintu
mānuṭavāḻvena vāḻvenanontu

Take it off safe and steady –
the youngsters coming, bending,
rushing to the burial ground,
lamenting 'what a human life'

24 *viṟakiṭamūṭi yaḻalkoṭupōṭa*
ventuviḻuntumu ṟintuniṇaṅka
ḷurukiyelumpu karukiyaṭaṅki
yōrpiṭiṉīṟumi lātavuṭampai
nampumaṭiyēṉai yiṉiyāḷumē.

Covered with the firewood, lit with a torch,
boiled and fallen, limbs broken,
ones melt, burnt and scorched
ot even a handful of ash remains of body –
rule over me the servant who trusts this (body)!

C. Delimitation and Structure

There are several factors that support the literary unity of *Uṭal*: (i) This poem alone among the Paṭṭiṉattār corpus is preceded by *cantam* or rhythmic guideline at the beginning of the poem; (ii) The rhythmic guideline followed strictly in the poem makes the poem stand as a unified whole syntactically. Even a removal or addition of a stanza will break the pattern of *cantam* ('rhythm') and *poruḷ* ('meaning'); (iii) There are as many as 32 word-pairs which bind the poem together; (iv) The poem thematically moves from lifelessness to lifelessness; (v) The entire poem is an argument on the human body. The other elements that are discussed are mere supportive to this argument.

The poem *Uṭal* excluding the prelude consists of 24 stanzas. At the end of stanzas 6, 12, 18 and 24 there is an '*ēkāram*,' which marks the ending of the section. Based on this structural marker Kamil Zvelebil has divided the poem into four parts:[331] (i) Stanzas 1-6 (life); (ii) Stanzas 7-12 (youth); (iii) Stanzas 13-18 (old age); and (iv) Stanzas 19-24 (death). Zvelebil's fourfold division of the poem takes into consideration the formal criterion of *ēkāram*

331 His written works are inaccessible. But his written works are encoded electronically and are made available at: http://karkanirka.org/2008/09/26/utarkurruvanam_patinathar1/. Accessed on 01 December 2015.

and the dramatic criterion of change of theme. The structure brings to light the movement in the poem from birth to death. By naming the first stage as 'life,' Zvelebil draws a parallel between '1' and '4,' '2' and '3.' Life progresses until stanza 12 and then begins to deteriorate. We agree with Zvelebil in taking stanzas 7-12, 13-18 and 19-24 as descriptions of 'youth,' 'old age' and 'death' respectively. Since the stage 1, life, extends even until old age, Zvelebil's grouping of stanzas 1-6 is partial. We digress from him as we divide his stage 1, 'life' into three stages: 'conception' (stanzas 1-2), 'birth' (3-4), and 'childhood' (5-6).

Our division of the poem can be tabulated as follows:

Stanzas	Stage	Theme
1-2	Entry Life	Conception (semen spurt in passionate emotion mixing with her sticky flow)
3-4	Stage 1	Birth (lass' womb opening, falls on the earth)
5-6	Stage 2	Childhood (babbling names)
7-12	Stage 3	Youth (exalted into a crescent moon by many, lively sixteen arriving)
13-18	Stage 4	Old Age (Coming and going is like a bent monkey steps slowing down)
19-24	Exit Life	Death (Throwing the net, taking away the life)

This structure takes into consideration the movement of life from 'conception' to 'death.' At the moment of 'conception,' 'semen' and 'ovary' come in contact with one another. In Tamil mind, *cukkilam* is male semen, which is white in colour, while *curoṇitam* is female semen, which is red in colour. The *cukkilam* is that which is responsible for the development of hard part of the body such as bones and the *curoṇitam* for the development of the soft part of the body which is flesh. At v. 24, Paṭṭiṉattār beautifully shows the reversal of the union of these two elements: '*ventu viḻuntu muṟintu niṇaṅkaḷ uruki elumpu karuki aṭanki*' ('the flesh boils and drops while the bone is burnt down'). As the body *integrates* in v. 1, it *disintegrates* in v. 24.

Another thing to be noted is that the transition from one stage to another is written in the form of 'already' and 'not yet,' i.e., the end of a stage already presupposes the beginning of the next stage. V. 2 already presents the formation of the foetus in the womb, which is to be born in v. 3. V. 4 already presents the infant which is about to enter into childhood. V. 6 shows the readiness of the child to excel as a young person in v. 7. V. 12 already presents the transition from youth to old age. V. 18 metaphorically speaks about the death.

As far as the 'story' of this narrative poem is concerned the plot develops in a pyramidal pattern. According to Freytag's theory of pyramid, "a typical plot begins with a rising action, reaches a climax, and ends with a falling action."[332] (i) 'Semen mixing with her sticky flow' (v. 1); (ii) 'richness ending, youth ending' (v. 12); and (iii) 'limbs broken, bones melt, burnt and scorched' (v. 24). In all these three stages, the yearning of the poet is that he wants to be ruled by God alone. Ironically in all these three stages the poet has forgotten this central element of life.

If we structure the 'discourse' of the poem, the quinary scheme is fitting. Added to the quinary scheme is an element from Labov's model, 'coda.' At the end of the stanza 24 the poet makes a prayer to God:

Initial Situation	'No Life' (vv. 1-2)
Complication	'Birth' (vv. 3-4)
	'Childhood' (vv. 5-6)
	'Youth' (vv. 7-12)
Transforming Action	'richness ending, youth ending' (v. 12)
Denouement or Resolution	'Old Age' (vv. 12-18)
Final Situation	'No Life' (vv. 18-24)
Coda	'rule over me the servant who trusts this' (v. 24)

D. Setting

If we were to fit this poem *Uṭal* into a theatrical mode, the poem seems to occur at three stages, one after another.

Stage 1	v. 1	'A' (a lad) and 'B' (a lass)
Stage 2	v. 2-24b	'C' (the person who is born, grows, ages and dies)
Stage 3	v. 24c	'D' (Paṭṭiṉattār) and 'E' (God)

Stage 1 is very brief. The actors of stage 1, the lad and the lass, are not the characters which are in focus. The child which is the fruit of their love-union is the protagonist and the central character of the narrative poem. Stage 3 sets the poet virtually in front of God, to whom the entire poem is addressed. Stage 2, the central stage, acts as the point of arrival for stage 1 and point for departure for stage 3. Stage 2 is very long spanning from birth to death of a human person. The stage 2 can be further divided into three stages based on the structural markers *vaḷarpiṟai* ('crescent') and *mati* ('moon') in vv. 7, 13

332 It corresponds to Aristotle's three parts of a drama (beginning, middle, and end or complication, climax, and unravelling). Cf. Ska, *Our Fathers*, 20. Cf. n. 163.

and 19. At these three instances the theme of the poem changes as there is a transition in the life-stage of the human person:

v. 7	*vaḷarpiṟai*	From childhood to youth
v. 13	*mati*	From youth to old age
v. 19	*vaḷarpiṟai*	From old age to death

The major theme that runs through the poem is 'union' of the human and the divine. Based on the theme of union we can distinguish these stages as follows:

Stage 1	Human-Human Union
Stage 2	Human-Human Union. Human-Divine Disunion
Stage 3	Human-Divine Union

Having structured the poem formally and thematically, let us now turn on to consider the spatial setting in the poem.

Stage 1	v. 1	Bedroom
Stage 2	v. 2	Womb of a mother
	v. 3	Cot and cradle
	vv. 4-5	House
	v. 6	Neighbourhood
	v. 7	School
	vv. 8-12	Public life
	vv. 13-18	House
	v. 19	House of *Yamā*
	v. 20	House, neighbourhood
	vv. 21-22	Courtyard
	v. 23	Street
	v. 24ab	Cremation ground
Stage 3	v. 24c	Inner voice of the poet

The space setting helps us understand and appreciate the omniscience and omnipresence of the poet. The poet knows what happens in the bedroom. He observes the development of life in the womb of a mother. He sees through what is happening within a house. He follows the character along the street, in the neighbourhood and back to the house. He is in the know of what is happening in the world above, in the world of *Yamā*, who sends his messengers to take away human life. He describes the qualities of these messengers. He explicates what happens to a person at the moment of death. Finally, he accompanies the dead person in the courtyard, in the street, and until the cremation ground. At the cremation site the poet utters a very brief interior monologue through which he surrenders to God, the Lord Śiva, considering all these stages of life as vain and absurd.

"The narrative is a sequence which is doubly temporal: there is the time of the thing told and the time of the narrative (time of the signified and the time of the signifier)."[333] The narration time, the time that one takes to read through the poem, is about 10 minutes. The narrated time is about seventy years. The story begins from 0 and reaches to 70 years of a human person. However, the reader is not told at what age the protagonist of the story dies.

The narrated time in the story can be sketched as follows:

v. 1 (1 day)

This event of male-female sexual union narrated in this verse does not last the entire day. The time covered is only the time that it takes for a man and a woman to indulge in intercourse and the time it takes for the semen to travel the vaginal tube to reach the ovaries.

vv. 2-3 (0 – 10 months)

The time element is vividly accented in the expression, '*Uyirvaḷar mātam oṉpatum oṉṟu*' ('Taking shape, life growing nine and one month completing'). The time covered is ten months that it takes for a foetus to develop in the womb of a woman. This development occurs in three successive stages: (a) Entry of the semen into the ovaries; (b) Formation of the primary zygote; and (c) The development of the eyes, body, mouth, ears, and limbs.

The foetus which is only a pound of flesh now becomes alive (*uruvamum āki uyirvaḷar*). The time that takes for life-spirit to enter into the foetus or the process of such entry is not narrated. One may deduce that the entire process takes nine and one months.[334] Towards the end of this section the birth of the baby is narrated. The baby is welcomed in an auspicious moment or the moment of the birth of the child is analysed to find out the astral locations, that would help predicting the future of the child. This auspicious moment is learnt through a careful study of stars and their movements (*yōkamum vāramum nāḷum aṟintu*). The time taken for this astrological enquiry is implied in this section.

333 C. Metz, Essais sur la signification au cinéma (Paris 1968) 27. Cited in Marguerat - Bourquin, *How to Read*, 86.

334 The poet discriminates nine and one for two reasons: (a) to retain the rhythm in the poem; and (b) traditionally it is held that it takes nine lunar months (9 x 29.5 days = 265.5) for a baby to develop in the womb.

vv. 4-6 (0 – 5 years)

This section sets the new-born baby in the context of its neighbourhood. We notice the narration of five events in this section:

(a) The womenfolk of the neighbourhood are presented as if they are the ones who adorn and dress the child (*makaḷirkaḷ cēnai tara aṇai āṭai*);
(b) Meanwhile the new-born develops his motor muscles (*maṇpaṭa unti utaintu kaviḻntu*);
(c) He is dependent on his mother for his survival;
(d) The development of the speech (*maḻalai moḻintu vā iru pō ena nāmam viḷampa*); and
(e) The child becomes part of the neighbourhood in mimicking the dress code, the food habit, and being socialized. The temporal phrase '*añcu vayatāki viḷaiyāṭiye*' ('fun and frolic ages five') acts as a summary statement of all the years that have gone before.

v. 7 (6 – 16 years)

The time covered in this verse is boyhood and early youth. This phase is the learning period. The child is introduced to (a) Wisdom learning or religious catechesis (*uyartaru ñaṉa upatesamum*), and (b) The Tamiḻ literary art (*Tamiḻiṉ kalaiyum karaikaṇṭu*). Those who see the boy excelling in wisdom, religious knowledge and literature admire and call him a *vaḷarpiṟari,* the crescent or the moon, which is ever-growing. In one verse the poet covers eleven years of boyhood and sums up with a temporal phrase, '*vāḻpatiṉāṟu pirāyamum vantu*' ('lively sixteen arriving').

vv. 8 – 11 (17 – 25 years)

This section describes the youth in full blossom, 17 – 25 years. The self-discovered youth (a) adopts to the learnt dress code (*koṇṭai puṉaintu…aṇintu*); (b) is highly looked upon by the elders (*mākatar pōkatar kūṭi vaṇaṅka*); and (c) loses his earnings yearning for the women (*māmayilpōl avar…vampil iḻantu*).

v. 12 (41 – 60 years)

Though there is an immediate and unannounced transition from youth to old age reflected in the poem, the process is not immediate. In this verse the poet shows how the richness and the youth disappear (*vaḷamaiyum māri iḷamaiyum māri*) and the symptoms of old age, such as loss of vision and hairs turning grey creep in (*iru kaṇkaḷ iruṇṭu vayatu mutirntu naraitirai vantu*). The time frame covered in this section is roughly about 41 – 60 years. The physiological deterioration of eyesight, loss of hair or black hair turning grey, and loss of vigour is a slow and steady process and the process differs from individual to individual.

vv. 13 – 18 (61 – 70 years)

The narrated time is very slow in vv. 13 – 18. The section narrates (a) the physical ailments that surround an old man, (b) the emotional impacts that are accompanied, and (c) the reception of this old man into the neighbourhood. The old man is at the point of death.

vv. 19 – 20 (70 – 0 years)

The vv. 19 – 20 describe the moment of death in a dramatic way. Death is described as the removal of the life-spirit from the man by the messengers of *Yamā*, the god of death. We may compare this with vv. 2-3, where life-spirit is not mentioned as given by god. The exit of the life-spirit is mentioned as an act of god.

vv. 21 – 24 (1 day)

The narrated time is almost stilled to one day – the day of funeral. Though the time is stilled, the activities are brisk and fast. The entire neighbourhood, which welcomed the man into the world (cf. vv. 4 – 6) now surrounds again to bid farewell. The after-events of death in a society – lamentation, funeral customs and the final rite – are cited in this section.

The final phrase of the poem, *nampum adiyēṉai iṉi āḷumē* ('rule over me the servant who trusts this – O Lord!') is the turning point as it takes the reader from terrestrial world to extra-terrestrial realm. The narrated time of this final phrase is in the ratio of 1:1 with narration time. Each reader of the poem is called to uplift one's self in the presence of the Lord realizing the impermanence of the body.

1. Summary Statements

The narrator develops the narration through the following summary statements:

i. '*life growing nine and one month completing*' (v. 3)
ii. '*fun and frolic ages five*' (v. 6)
iii. '*lively sixteen arriving*' (v. 7)
iv. '*holding a stick in his cold-red hands*' (v. 12)
v. '*arrives the hour that shakes his heart*' (v. 18)
vi. '*rule over me the servant who trusts this (body)!*' (v. 24)

The summary statements in vv. 3, 6, 7, 12, and 18 act as climactic statements of description of all the events narrated before them.[335] V. 24 sums up the entire poem insofar as it states the impermanence and the futility of the entire body process described throughout the poem.

335 The summary functions as a synthesis or recapitulation. Cf. Marguerat - Bourquin, *How to Read*, 87.

2. Pause

"The pause functions to insert a descriptive element. At this moment, the time of the story is zero, while the narrative continues."[336] We notice a pause in the narrative poem in vv. 21-24. Here the protagonist of the story is dead and still. The events narrated in these verses are mere descriptions of what the neighbours do to the dead person. The poet makes use of this pause to heighten the narrative tension. This pause ironically makes the reader aware of the nullification of independence that the death brings along. At death, the person, who has been active and independent, becomes totally inactive and dependent. The climax of the poem is the mourning of the poet over his own independence and dependence.

3. Ellipsis

In ellipsis or gapping, an event is passed over. The narrative is silent about certain events, which the readers have to suppose.[337] There is a narrative gap between vv. 11 and 12. V. 11 says that 'the appearance of youth wades' (*vālipa kōlamum vēṟu pirintu*). V. 12 describes an entire different stage where the symptoms of old age become manifest (*vaḷamaiyum māṟi iḷamaiyum māṟi*). Here the reader is not told about what is the life-stage in between. There is an ellipsis of almost 26 – 40 years. From vv. 18 – 22 one may deduce what a person must have done during these silent years – must have had many works to command and to do (*kaṭaṉmuṟai pēcum*) ('Tongue that commanded') [v. 18], (*palaraiyum ēvi*) ('the elders command') [v. 22]), must have married and begotten children (*maintarum vantu, maṉaivi pulampa*) (children coming to bow are vexed, wife wailing falls on the lap) [v. 20].

4. Order and Frequency

Another element to consider in time is the order of events. The narrator can choose either to opt for a synchronous narrative (keeping pace with the chronology of the story – beginning with the beginning and ending with the end) or an anachronous narrative (moving backward and forward).[338] Our poet opts for a synchronous narrative. He does not change the chronology of the events. However, there are few phrases that act as analepses (flashbacks): (a) *kaṭaṉmuṟai pecum eṉaurai nā* (*Tongue that commanded, 'speak about the duties'*) (v. 18). (b) *paḻaiyavar kāṇum* (The neighbours calling him 'a known man') (v. 21). And (c) *palaraiyum ēvi mutiyavar tām irunta cavam kaḻuvum*

336 Marguerat - Bourquin, *How to Read*, 88.

337 Cf. Marguerat - Bourquin, *How to Read*, 88.

338 Cf. Marguerat - Bourquin, *How to Read*, 89.

(the elders command 'wash the corpse') (v. 22) As far as the frequency is concerned, the poem is a singulative narrative.[339]

To sum up, the setting is the container of the story. The analysis of the spatial and temporal setting becomes increasingly significant as we evaluate the characterisation and the motifs of the poem.

E. Style

The mechanisms of Tamil poetry are spoken of in two terms, *yāppu* and *tūkku. Yāppu* refers to the process of composition using letters (*eḻuttu*), basic metrical units (*acai*), metrical feet (*cīr*), and lines (*aṭi*), whereas *tūkku* refers to the process of assessment or evaluation like weighing (*niṟuttal*), dividing (*aṟuttal*), and singing (*pāṭal*).[340]

Tamil poetry grammar or prosody (*ceyyuḷ ilakkaṇam*) is known as *yāppu* (literally means, 'to tie,' that which tie the song together). The six basic components of *yāppu*[341] are:

(i) *Eḻuttu*, the letter;
(ii) *Acai*, the basic metrical unit;
(iii) *Cīr*, the foot which is composed of one or more *acais*;
(iv) *Taḷai*, the manner in which different feet are connected;
(v) *Aṭi*, the line; and
(vi) *Toṭai*, the fastening. It is also translated as 'rhyme.'[342]

339 In a singulative narrative the narrative tells only once what has happened. On the contrary, in a repetitive narrative, the narrator returns several times to a single event in the story, and in iterative narrative, he mentions only once that has happened several times in the story. Cf. Marguerat - Bourquin, *How to Read*, 96-97.

340 Cf. V. S. Rajam, *A Reference Grammar of Classical Tamil Poetry* (Philadelphia 1992), 187-88.

341 Tolkāppiyam Poruḷatikāram Ceyyuḷiyal deals with Tamil prosody. The first cūtram of Ceyyuḷiyal enumerates thirty-four component parts of poetry. They are: 1) Māttirai, 2) Eḻuttu, 3) Acai, 4) Cīr, 5) Aṭi, 6) Yāppu, 7) Marapu, 8) Tūkku, 9) Toṭai, 10) Nōkku, 11) Pā, 12) Aḷavu, 13) Tiṇai, 14) Kaikōl, 15) Kūṟṟu, 16) Kēṭpōr, 17) Kaḷaṉ, 18) Kālam, 19) Payaṉ, 20) Meyppāṭu, 21) Eccam, 22) Muṉṉam, 23) Poruḷ, 24) Tuṟai, 25) Māṭṭu, 26) Vaṇṇam, 27) Ammai, 28) Aḻaku, 29) Toṉmai, 30) Tōl, 31) Viruntu, 32) Iyaipu, 33) Pulaṉ, and 34) Iḻaipu. Cf. Maria Selvam, *Song of Songs*, 124.

342 Toṭai is in fact the art of stringing together lines into a poem, like flowers into a garland. In Cey. cūt. 400, Tolkāppiyar mentions four major types of rhyme or toṭai:

(1) Mōṉai: a rhyme where initial letters agree.

(2) Etukai: a rhyme where the second letters agree (cf. alliteration and assonance).

(3) Muraṇ: the contrary either in mere word or in its meaning (cf. word antithesis and semantic antithesis).

(4) Iyaipu: a rhyme where the last letters or syllables or feet agree. This is similar to end-rhyme. Cf. Maria Selvam, *Song of Songs*, 124.

Let us also add a seventh element, *nōkku* - Tol. Por. Cye. 416 states: "The *nōkku* is said to be the way of viewing the composition from the unit of time to the perfection of line." In other words, *nōkku* is that which gives orientation, cohesion and unity to the various constituents to make one single whole. The *cūtram* implies that each line in a poem is, as a rule, a meaningful whole.[343]

Now let us apply these elements to our poem:

i. *El̲uttu* (Letters). The letters are of three types: *kur̲il* (short), *neṭil* (long), and *or̲r̲u* (with a dot above). The prelude of the poem not only serves as a musical notation, but also acts as the formula based on which the entire song is composed. The first four lines of this formula runs through all the 24 stanzas while the fifth line is applied only in the stanzas 6, 12, 18, and 24.

Let us note the beauty of the composition as far as the choice of the letters is concerned: (a) In line '1' there is no *mellin̲a or̲r̲u*;[344] (b) There is no *neṭil* in lines '2' and '3;' (c) Except in line '3' all the *cīr* begin with a *kur̲il*; (d) Except in line '5' all the *cīr* end with a *kur̲il*; and (e) The lines '2,' '3,' and '4' end with a *cantam*.[345]

The stanzas 6, 12, 18 and 24 are to be noted specially. They have an extra line at the end of each and this extra line serves as the climactic statement of the stanzas that go before. These lines have the final '*ēkaram*,' where the singer takes a breathing pause before resuming the song.

The stanzas 6 and 18, 12 and 24:

añcuvayatāki viḷaiyāṭiyē (v. 6)

---

343 Cf. Maria Selvam, *Song of Songs*, 127-28.

344 The letter ந் in the formula can be replaced with any soft consonant (mellin̲am). There are also other dotted letters in between, for example v. 24. Here, the consonant is a medial consonant. In Tamil there are three types of consonants: (a) hard consonants (ka, ca, ṭa, ta, pa, r̲a); (b) soft consonants (ṅa, ña, ṇa, na, ma, n̲a); and (c) Medial consonants (ya, ra, la, va, l̲a, ḷa).

345 Cantam (< Skt. chandas) is relatively a late-comer in Tamil literature. Kamil Zvelebil calls this, "historically a massive assault of syllable-based metrics on the indigenous Tamil system which had been originally quite different." Cantam is a pattern of rhythm based on syllabic quantity. The indigenous Tamil prosadic pattern is

= = -- / -- -- / = = -- / -- --

= = -- / -- -- / = -- / --

In addition, the lines have the following cantam: tana tana tanana / tana tana tanāna / tana tana tanāna, i.e., ~~ ~~ ~--~ / ~~ ~~~--~ / ~~ ~~ ~--~ / ~~ -- --. Each line has a double organisation: in terms of acai organised into feet (cīr), which is the original Tamil metrical structure; and in terms of syllables organized into regular rhythmic groups purely on the basis of quantity, whether short or long, which represents the impact of the Sanksrit metrical structure. All this is part of the process whereby the connection between poetry and music, which began with the adoption of fixed melody-types (paṇ) for poetry identified with devotional singing of Śaiva and Vaiṣṇava bhakti hymns, which later evolved into kīrttan̲ai. Cf. K. V. Zvelebil, *Tamil Literature* (Wiesbaden 1974), 109-10.

neñcutaṭumāṟi varuṉēramē (v. 18)
ceṅkaiyinilōrta ṭiyumākiyē (v. 12)
nampumaṭiyēnai yiṉiyāḷumē (v. 24)

The first *cīr* of these two verses are in rhythm with one another by an *etukai* – *añcu* and *neñcu*. The *aṭiyumākiyē* (v. 12) and *aṭiyēṉai* (v. 24) rhyme with one another by a *mōṉai*, and *yiṉi* of the first word in v. 12 is taken up in the second word in v. 24. The final *yē* of v. 6 rhymes with that of v. 12, and the final *mē* of v. 18 rhymes with that of v. 24. Hence, vv. 6, 12, 18, and 24 are rhythmically connected to one another. The final coda of these stanzas thus are stylistically and thematically significant in the poem.

ii. *Acai.*

The basic metrical unit in Tamil prosody is called the *acai*, 'movement' ('to move, sway'), which is mostly based on vowel length. There are two basic types of *acai*: *nēr* ('to be straight; straightness') and *nirai* ('to be in a row; array'). In other words, *nēr* is a fine *acai* ('*nēriya* acai') as it is formed by a single letter while *nirai* is a movement of a pair – one letter following in row with another.[346] Certain combinations of these four *acai* give rise to a metrical foot, which is known by the generic term '*cīr*' ('order, beauty').[347] An *acai* cannot be identified to a syllable. Nor does an *acai* contain a meaningful unit. The number of *acai* in a metrical foot is not always equal to the number of letters in it.

To cite an example, let us analyse the v. 6:
uṭai-maṇi-yā-ṭai yarai-vaṭa-mā-ṭa (Line 1)
nirai-nirai-nēr-nēr nirai-nirai-nēr-nēr
vuṉ-pavar-tiṉ-pavar taṅ-kaḷo-ṭuṇ-ṭu (2)
nēr-nirai-nēr-nirai nēr-nirai-nēr-nēr
teru-vili-run-tu puḻu-tiya-ḷain-tu (3)
nirai-nirai-nēr-nēr nirai-nirai-nēr-nēr
tē-ṭiya-pā-laro ṭō-ṭina-ṭan-tu (4) –
nēr-nirai-nēr-nirai nēr-nirai-nēr-nēr
añ-cuva-yatā-ki viḷai-yā-ṭiyē (5)
nēr-nirai-nirai-nēr nirai-nēr-nirai
This stanza begins and ends with nirai.

iii. *Cīr*

'*Acaiyiyaintu cīrkoḷa niṟṟaliṉ cīrē.*' In our poem all the *cīr*, except the final *cīr* in line '5' are *nāvacaiccīr* (composed of four *cīrs*). The *nāvacaiccīr* consists of 16 possibilities and each possibility has a name. The above stanza in the formulaic form can be written as follows:

---

346 Rajam, *Reference Grammar*, 116.

347 Cf. Rajam, *Reference Grammar*, 118.

karu-viḷan-taṇ-pū karu-viḷan-taṇ-pū (Line 1)
kū-viḷan-taṇ-ṇiḻal kū-viḷan-taṇ-pū (2)
karu-viḷan-taṇ-pū karu-viḷan-taṇ-pū (3)
kū-viḷan-taṇ-ṇiḻal kū-viḷan-taṇ-pū (4)
kū-viḷa-naṟum-pū puḷi-māṅ-kaṉi (5)

Let us note that lines '1' and '3,' '2' and '4' are parallel to one another in following the *cīr* pattern. The line '5' has a unique *cīr* pattern of the combination of *nāvacaiccīr* and *mūvacaiccīr*.

iv. *Aṭi*

A standard *aṭi* ('line') consists of four metrical foot. An *aṭi* can be evaluated either (a) on the basis of letter, *eḻuttu* ('*kaṭṭalai aṭi*') or (b) on the basis of metrical foot, *cīr* (*vakai aṭi*). We evaluate the poem on the basis of metrical foot, *cīr.* A line which is made of two metrical feet is called *kuṟaḷ aṭi*; that of three metrical feet is *cintaṭi*; of four feet, an *aḷavaṭi*; and of five feet, a *neṭil aṭi*. A line made up of more than five feet is a *kaḻineṭilaṭi*.[348] In our poem each stanza consists of two *cīrs*. Therefore, it is *kuṟaḷ aṭi*. Our poem can also be called a *vañci aṭi* because it has two metrical feet and the maximum number of six letters in each metrical foot.[349]

From *aṭi* one may deduce what type of *pā* ('song') the poem is. The term *pā* refers to meter per se and only by metonymy refers to a poem.[350] Our poem is a *vañcippā*. When we take the *pā* as meter, the meter *vañci* has been recognized as the one with the *naṭai* ('behaviour') of the *āciriyam*.[351] The behaviour of the *āciriyam* is found in the poem in the stanzas 6, 12, 18, and 24. In the final *aṭi* of these stanzas, the ultimate *cīr* ends with an *ēkāram,* which is the key characteristic of the *āciriyappā*. Each *pā* produces an *ōcai* ('sound'). The sound created by the *vañci* meter is *tūṅkal* ('sleep or suspending'). The *ōcai* is restricted by an individual metrical foot.

v. *Taḷai*

The way in which two adjacent metrical feet in a line hang together is crucial to a Tamil poem. The last *acai* of a metrical foot and the first *acai* of the following metrical foot are supposed to form a metrical binding which ultimately produces what is equivalent to rhythm. This binding is known as *taḷai* ('to bind or fasten').[352] The adjacent metrical foot in our poem is either in nēr-nirai pattern or nirai-nēr pattern. Hence, *oṉṟā vañcittaḷai*.

---

348 Cf. Rajam, *Reference Grammar*, 142.

349 Cf. Rajam, *Reference Grammar*, 149.

350 Rajam, *Reference Grammar*, 167. There are four types of meter or pā: (a) āciriyappā; (b) vañcippā; (c) veṇpā; and (d) kalippā.

351 Ends like an āciriyam. Cf. the final lines in vv. 6, 12, 18, and 24.

352 Cf. Rajam, *Reference Grammar*, 155.

vi. *Toṭai*

Toṭai is an aesthetic component. It is said, '*toṭai aṟṟa kavitai naṭai aṟṟu pōkum*' ('a poem without binding is without order'). It literally means 'stringing' (< *toṭu* = 'to string'). It refers to the way in which successive feet or lines are strung in a poem.[353] Four types of *toṭai* are found in our poem: *mōṉai*, *etukai*, *iyaipu*, and *muraṇ*. Among these the first three are phonological, based on the shape of the words, and the last one is semantic, based on the meaning of the words that may or may not rhyme with one another. This can be found either within a line (*aṭi*) across the metrical feet (*cīr*) or across the lines.[354]

Mōṉai Toṭai

a. Within the Same *Aṭi*

v. 1 ***yu****ṇarvukalaṅki* ***yo****ḻukiyavintu*
v. 3 ***uru****vamumāki* ***yuyir****vaḷarmāta*
v. 5 ***van****tumukantiṭa* ***van****tutavaḻntu*
ma*ṭiyiliruntu* ***ma****ḻalaimoḻintu*
v. 6 ***tē****ṭiyapālaro* ***ṭō****ṭinaṭantu*
v. 10 ***tē****ṭiyamāmutal* ***cē****ravaḻaṅki*[355]
v. 11 ***vā****lipakōlamum* ***vē****ṟupirintu*
v. 19 ***va****ḷarpiṟaipōla* ***ve****yiṟumurōma*
v. 20 ***ma****ṭiyilviḻuntu* ***ma****ṉaivipulampa*
v. 21 ***vē****piṇamvēka* ***vi****cāriyumeṉṟu*

b. Across the Lines

v. 1 ***mo****ruvanumāki* (Line 1) // ***ma****ṉpuporunti* (2)
yiṉ*pacukantaru* (2) // ***yuṇ****arvukalaṅki yoḻukiyavintu* (3) //
ūṟu*curōṇita* (4)
v. 2 ***pa****ṉiyilorpāti* (1) // ***pa****ṇṭiyilvantupu* (2) // ***pa****tumavarumpu* (3) //
pā*rvaimeivāicevi* (4)
ku*ntutiraṇṭu* (2) // ***ka****maṭamiteṉṟu* (3) // ***kā****lkaikaḷeṉṟa* (4)
v. 3 ***uru****vamumāki yuyirvaḷarmāta* (1) // *y****uta****ramakaṉṟu* (3) //
yō*kamuvāramu* (4)
v. 4 ***ma****kaḷirkacenai* (1) // ***ma****ṇpaṭavuntiyu* (2) // ***ma****ṭamayilkonkai* (3)
ta*ravaṇaiyādai* (1) // ***ta****intakaviḻntu* (2)
ya*mutamarunti* (3) // ***yō****raṟivīraṟi* (4)
v. 5 ***va****ntumukantiṭa vantutavaḻntu* (2) // ***vā****virupōveṉa* (4)
v. 6 ***u****ṭaimaṇiyāṭai* (1) // ***vu****ṉpavartiṉpava* (2) // ***vi****ḷaiyāṭiyē* (5)
taṅ*kaḷoṭuṇṭu* (2) // ***te****ruviliruntu* (3) // ***tē****ṭiyapālaro* (4)
v. 7 ***uyar****taruñaṉa* (1) // ***yuṅ****karaikaṇṭu* (2)

353 Cf. Rajam, *Reference Grammar*, 190.

354 Rajam, *Reference Grammar*, 191.

355 Ta and Ca belong to the same group.

***va**larpiṟaiyeṉṟu* (3) // ***vā**ḻpatiṉārupi* (4)
v. 8 ***ma**yirmuṭikōti* (1) // ***ma**ṇipoṉilaṅku* (3) // ***mā**katarpōtakar* (4)
***ko**ṇṭaipuṉaintu* (2) // ***kū**ṭivaṇaṅka* (4)
v. 9 ***ma**taṉacorūpa* (1) // ***ma**ṅkaiyarkaṇṭuma* (2) // ***mā**mayilpōlavar* (4)
v. 10 ***ma**ṉatupoṟāma* (1) // ***ma**ṅkalaceṅkala* (2) // ***ma**ruvamayaṅki* (3)
***ca**ntikaḻkoṅkai* (2) // ***cē**ravaḻaṅki* (4)
v. 11 ***mu**tuporuḷāyi* (1) // ***ma**taṉacukanta* (3)
***va**mpiliḻantu* (2) // ***vi**taṉamiteṉṟu* (3) // ***vā**lipakōlamum*
***vē**ṟupirintu* (4)
v. 12 ***va**ḷamaiyumāṟi* (1) // ***va**ṉpalviḻuntiru* (2) // ***va**yatumutirntu* (3) //
***vā**tavirōtaku* (4)
v. 13 ***va**ruvatupova* (1) // ***vā**yaṟiyāmalvi* (4)
***to**rumutukūnu* (1) // ***ṭā**mamoḻintu* (4)
v. 14 ***tu**yilvarunēra* (1) // ***to**ṇṭaiyuneñcumu* (2) // ***tu**kilumiḻantu* (3) //
***tō**kaiyarpālakar* (4)
v. 15 ***ka**liyukamīti* (1) // ***ka**ṇṭiṭumenpavar* (2) // ***ka**lakalaveṉṟu* (3) //
***kā**lvaḻimēlvaḻi* (4)
***ca**ñcalamiñca* (2) // ***cā**ranaṭantu* (4)
v. 16 ***te**ḷivumirāma* (1) // ***ti**ṭamumulaintu* (3) // ***tē**ṟinalātara* (4)
v. 17 ***ma**ṟaiyavaṉveta* (1) // ***me**ṉṟuteḷintu* (2) // ***mi**ṉiyeṉatonta* (3) //
***mē**tiṉivāḻvuni* (4)
v. 18 ***ka**ṭaṉmuṟaipēcu* (1) // ***ko**ṇṭumoḻintu* (2) // ***ka**ṭaivaḻikañci* (3)
***vā**camuniṉṟu* (4) // ***va**runēramē* (5)
v. 19 ***va**ḷarpiṟaipōla **ve**yiṟumurōma* (1) // ***va**ṭivumilaṅka* (4)
***mu**ñcaṭaiyuñciṟu* (2) // ***ma**ṉatumiruṇṭa* (3) // ***mā**malaipōlyama* (4)
v. 20 ***mai**ntarumvantuku* (2) // ***ma**ṭiyilviḻuntu maṉaivipulampa* (3)
***mā**lkiṉarēyivar* (4)
v. 21 ***pa**ḻaiyavarkāṇu* (1) // ***pañ**cupaṟantiṭa* (2) // ***pa**ṟaiyiṭamunta* (3)
v. 22 ***pa**laraiyumēvi* (1) // ***pa**ṇitukiltoṅkal* (3) // ***pā**vakamēceitu* (4)
v. 23 ***va**ricaikeṭāma* (1) // ***va**ntiḷamaintarku* (2) // ***vā**ḻvenanontu* (4)
v. 24 ***vi**ṟakiṭamūṭi* (1) // ***ve**ntuviḻuntumu* (2)
***ya**ḻalkoṭupōṭa* (1) // ***yō**rpiṭinīṟumi* (4) // ***yi**ṉiyāḷumē* (5)

Etukai Toṭai

a. Within the Same *Aṭi*

v. 1 *o**ru**maṭamātu m**oru**vanumāki* (Line 1)
*yi**ṉpa**cukantaru ma**ṉpu**porunti* (2)
v. 2 *pa**ṇṭi**yilvantupu kun**tu**tiraṇṭu* (2)
v. 3 *mo**ṉpa**tumoṉṟuni rai**ntu**maṭantai* (2)
v. 4 *ma**ṇpa**ṭavuntiyu tai**nta**kaviḻntu* (2)
v. 5 *van**tu**mukantiṭa va**ntu**tavaḻntu* (2)
v. 6 *uṭ**ai**maṇiyāṭai ya**rai**vaṭamāṭa* (1)

*vuṉ**pa**vartiṉpavar taṅ**ka**ḷoṭuṇṭu* (2)
*tē**ṭi**yapālaro ṭō**ṭi**naṭantu* (4)
v. 7 *mun**tami**ḻiṉkalai yuṅ**ka**raikaṇṭu* (2)
*va**lar**piṟaiyeṉṟu pa**lar**umviḷampa* (3)
v. 8 *vaṇ**ṭi**mirtaṇṭoṭai koṇ**ṭai**puṉaintu* (2)
*ma**ṇi**poṉilaṅku pa**ṇi**kaḷaṇintu* (3)
v. 9 *ma**ṅ**kaiyarkaṇṭuma ru**ṇ**ṭutiraṇṭu* (2)
v. 10 *ma**ṅ**kalaceṅkala ca**n**tikaḻkoṅkai* (2)
v. 11 *ru**n**tataṉaṅkaḷum va**m**piliḻantu* (2)
*ma**ta**ṉacukanta vi**ta**ṉamiteṉṟu* (3)
v. 12 *va**ḷa**maiyumāṟi yi**ḷa**maiyumāṟi* (1)
*va**ṉ**palviḻuntiru ka**ṇ**kaḷiruṇṭu* (2)
*vā**ta**virōtaku rō**ta**maṭaintu* (4)
v. 13 *va**ru**vatupova to**ru**mutukūnu* (1)
*ma**n**tiyeṉumpaṭi ku**n**tinaṭantu* (2)
v. 14 *tō**kai**yarpālakar kō**raṇ**ikoṇṭu* (4)
v. 15 *ka**ṇ**ṭiṭumenpavar ca**ñ**calamiñca* (2)
*ka**la**kalaveṉṟu ma**la**calamvantu* (3)
v. 16 *ci**n**taiyuneñcamu lai**n**tumaruṇṭu* (2)
v. 17 *va**n**tatukaṇṭamu me**ṉ**ṟuteḷintu* (2)
*i**ṉ**iyeṉakaṇṭa mi**ṉ**iyeṉatonta* (3)
*mē**ti**ṉivāḻvuni lā**ti**ṉiniṉṟa* (4)
v. 18 *ṟa**ṅ**kiviḻuntukai ko**ṇ**ṭumoḻintu* (2)
v. 19 *mu**ñ**caṭaiyuñciṟu ku**ñ**ciyumviñca* (2)
v. 20 *mai**n**tarumvantuku ṉi**n**taḻanontu* (2)
v. 21 *pa**ñ**cupaṟantiṭa ni**ṉ**ṟavarpanta* (2)
v. 22 *ru**n**tacavaṅkaḻu vu**ñ**cilareṉṟu* (2)
v. 23 *va**n**tiḷamaintarku ṉi**n**tucumantu* (2)
*ka**ṭu**kinaṭantu cu**ṭa**laiyaṭaintu* (3)
v. 24 *ve**n**tuviḻuntumu ṟi**n**tuniṇaṅka* (2)
*ḷu**ru**kiyelumpu ka**ru**kiyaṭaṅki* (3)

b. Across the Lines

v. 4 *ma**ka**ḷirkaḷcenai* (1) // *vā**ki**vaḷarntu* (4)
*ta**ra**vaṇaiyādai* (1) // *yō**ra**ṟivīraṟi* (4)
v. 6 *pu**ḻu**tiyaḷaintu* (3) // *vi**ḷai**yāṭiyē* (5)
v. 7 *u**ya**rtaruñaṉa* (1) // *rā**ya**mumvantu* (4)
v. 11 *o**ru**mutalāki* (1) // *vē**ṟu**pirintu* (4)
v. 14 *mi**ru**malpoṟātu* (1) // *kō**ra**ṇikoṇṭu* (4)
v. 20 *va**lai**koṭuvīci* (1) // *kā**la**maṟintu* (4)
v. 24 *vi**ṟa**kiṭamūṭi* (1) // *ḷu**ru**kiyelumpu karukiyaṭaṅki* (3)

Iyaipu Toṭai

v. 1 *orumaṭamā**tu*** (1) // *yoḻukiyavin**tu*** (3) // *mītukalan**tu*** (4)
*moruvanumā**ki*** (1) // *yuṇarvukalaṅ**ki*** (4)
v. 2 *paṇṭiyilvantu**pu*** (2) // *patumavarum**pu*** (3)
v. 3 *puviyilviḻun**tu*** (3) // *nāḷumaṟin**tu*** (4)
v. 4 *taintakaviḻn**tu*** (2) // *vākivaḷarn**tu*** (4)
v. 5 *vantutavaḻn**tu*** (2) // *maṭiyilirun**tu*** *maḻalaimoḻin**tu*** (3)
v. 6 *teruvilirun**tu*** *puḻutiyaḷain**tu*** (3) // *ṭōṭinaṭan**tu*** (6)
v. 8 *koṇṭaipuṉain**tu*** (2) // *paṇikaḷaṇin**tu*** (3)
v. 9 *ruṇṭutiraṇ**ṭu*** (2) // *variviḻikoṇ**ṭu*** (3) // *pōvatukaṇ**ṭu*** (4)
v. 11 *runtataṉaṅka**ḷum*** (2) // *vālipakōla**mum*** (4)
*vampiliḻan**tu*** (2) // *vēṟupirin**tu*** (4)
v. 12 *vaḷamaiyumā**ṟi*** *yiḷamaiyumā**ṟi*** (1)
*vayatumutirn**tu*** *naraitiraivan**tu*** (3) // *rōtamaṭain**tu*** (4)
v. 13 *kuntinaṭan**tu*** (2) // *matiyumaḻin**tu*** *cevitimirvan**tu*** (3) //
*ṭāmanmoḻin**tu*** (4)
v. 14 *tukilumiḻan**tu*** *cuṇaiyumaḻin**tu*** (3)
*larntuvaṟaṇ**ṭu*** (2) // *kōraṇikoṇ**ṭu*** (4)
v. 15 *malacalamvan**tu*** (3) // *cāranaṭan**tu*** (4)
v. 16 *tiṭamumulain**tu*** *mikavumalain**tu*** (3) // *vēteṉanon**tu*** (4)
v. 17 *iṉiyeṉakaṇ**ṭa*** *miṉiyeṉaton**ta*** (3) // *lātiṉiṉiṉ**ṟa*** (4)
v. 18 *koṇṭumoḻin**tu*** (2) // *yoḻukiṭavan**tu*** (3)
v. 20 *ṉintaḻanon**tu*** (2) // *maṭiyilviḻun**tu*** (3) // *kālamaṟin**tu*** (4)
v. 21 *ninṟavarpan**ta*** (2) // *paṟaiyiṭamun**ta*** (3)
v. 23 *ṉintucuman**tu*** (2) // *kaṭukinaṭan**tu*** *cuṭalaiyaṭain**tu*** (3) //
*vāḻvenanon**tu*** (4)

Now let us consider the aesthetic character of our poem. As far as the *vaṇṇam* (literally, 'colour') is known as 'rhythmic variation.'[356] Our poem has two types of *vaṇṇam*: (a) *Mellicai vaṇṇam* or *iyaipu vaṇṇam* (produced by soft consonants);[357] and (b) *Tūṅkal vaṇṇam* (using *vañci uriccīr*).[358]

Our poem also reflects a didactic composition (*paṉuval*) mixed with gentle utterances (*moḻi*).[359] *Aḻaku* is attained in our poetry through the metrical feet (*cīr*) and the choice of appropriate words in the composition (*ceyyuḷ*).[360] The word '*uṭampu*' (cf. vv. 2, 3, 4, 12, 16, 22, and 24) points to the *māṭṭu* ('fastening, wrapping') in the poem. The prosodic element *māṭṭu* refers to the

356 There are 20 types of vaṇṇam. Cf. Rajam, *Reference Grammar*, 209-11.

357 Cf. Rajam, *Reference Grammar*, 208.

358 Rajam, *Reference Grammar*, 212.

359 Only exception to this feature is the length of the poem. Usually the paṉuval is a precise composition. The classical anthology of patiṉeṇkīḻkkaṇakku is a good example for paṉuval. Cf. Rajam, *Reference Grammar*, 215.

360 Cf. Rajam, *Reference Grammar*, 216.

technique of properly joining the words, which are separated by many other words occurring between them in a composition, so as to bring coherence to the subject matter of the composition.[361]

1. Linguistic Characteristics

i. The poem consists of 24 stanzas. The stanzas 6, 12, 18, and 24 have the final *ēkaram* (cf. *viḷaiyāṭiyē, taṭiyumākiyē, varunēramē, yiṉiyāḷumē*), which act as a virtual full stop and marks the change of argument.
ii. The final syllable of all the three lines of each stanza have a *melliṉam* within (cf. v. 1: *poruṉti, vintu, kalantu*), which sets the song in rhythm.
iii. Each stanza ends with an adjectival participle. The adjectival participle modifies the verb of action (cf. v. 1: *kalantu* modifies the action of mingling of semen and vaginal liquid), stands as a continuative having a retrospective or prospective function (v. 1: *kalantu.* It sums up what is said in v. 1 and initiates what is to yet to be said in v. 2), or marks simultaneity or causality (cf. v. 4: *vaḷarntu.* It describes simultaneity).[362]
iv. The poem is filled with adjectival participles or phrases. This is because of the principle of economy of words in classical Tamil poetry.[363]
v. The poem is a good example for *inner-textuality.* I define this term in two ways:
   (a) From author's point of view, the poet constantly repeats the words, e.g. the word '*neñcu*' appears in vv. 14, 16, and 18 and its synonyms *koṅkai* is found in vv. 4 and 10, and *maṉatu* in v. 19;
   (b) From reader's point of view, the poem acts as a mirror. In the process of reading the reader finds himself in a position described in the poem and begins to read himself in the light of the poem and hopefully vice versa.
vi. The poet chooses to use the short and precise sentences of two *cīrs* to make the poem easily memorable.

2. Metrical Factors

i. The poem is composed after *tullal* meter. The presence of *āciriyam* in vv. 6, 12, 18, and 24 ring in the ears a *ceppal*, through which the poet instructs his hearers. The metre is very precise and straightforward. The choice of this metre helps the poet present his poem with rhythm, alliterations, and assonances.[364]

---

361 Rajam, *Reference Grammar*, 214.

362 Cf. Maria Selvam, *Song of Songs*, 129.

363 Maria Selvam, *Song of Songs*, 129.

364 Maria Selvam, *Song of Songs*, 129-30.

ii. The poem consists of 100 lines. If we include the prelude the poem has 105 lines. This size is very symbolic. In the number 105, '1' stands for 'The *Mutalvan̲*' (God), '0' stands for the human person, and the mantra that unites '1' and '0' consists of five syllables, *na ma ci vā ya.* The remembering or uttering the mantra of *na ma ci vā ya,* is a constant theme in the Śaivite Bhakti tradition.[365]

iii. The reduplication of the hard consonants (*ka, ca, ṭa, ta, pa, ṟa*) and medial consonants (*ṅa, ña, ṇa, na, ma, n̲a*) within the *aṭis* and across the *aṭis* has threefold function: (a) They create rhyme and act as ornamentations; (b) The combinations or repetitions of soft consonants (*melliṇam*) or medial consonants (*iṭaiyin̲am*) signify softness and gentleness, while the repetition of hard consonants (*vallin̲am*) is a sign of quickness and toughness; and (c) The recurrence of long vowels would indicate an atmosphere of joy or sorrow or sobriety (cf. the first acai of the *cīrs* in the fourth line is long).[366]

iv. Unlike the *akam* poems, this poem is born of the poet's daily observation of his own life and the life of his contemporaries. The poem is not a result of poet's imagination. The poet, who has observed and lived out the hard realities of life, assimilates his own experiences, organizes them and presents them in temporal linearity.

3. Imagery

Imagery is the life principle of poetry and it is imagery that distinguishes poetry from prose.[367] The poet dialogues with the hearers or readers through images and word-pictures. Imagery consists in the way in which the poet successfully communicates his emotions to the listener or reader as if the poem were a picture. Tolkāppiyar uses the term *meyppāṭu* and says that *meyppāṭu* is to compose a poem in such a way as to make the reader feel and exhibit his emotions by physical changes on reading or hearing the poem.[368] Let us group all the terms – metaphors, metonymy, simile, analogy – into a single term, 'word-picture.' The function of all these is to set 'the scene before the eyes.'[369] In our study we adopt the conceptual blending model approach to understand

365 Cf. S. Kapoor, *A Short Introduction to Śaivism* (New Delhi 2002), 51.

366 Maria Selvam, *Song of Songs*, 129-30.

367 Maria Selvam, *Song of Songs*, 131. Maria Selvam cites a beatiful metaphor from Aṟavānan̲: "A poem to a human being. The metre of the poem is the frame or skeleton, the words and phrases are flesh and blood, the content is mind, and the way in which it is communicated is the life principle of the poem."

368 Maria Selvam, *Song of Songs*, 131.

369 This is how Aristotle makes sense of a word-picture. Cf. A. R. Gray, *Psalm 18 in Words and Pictures*. A Reading Through Metaphor (Leiden 2014), 10.

the word-pictures present in our poem. The working model of interpretation of the word-pictures can be presented as follows:[370]

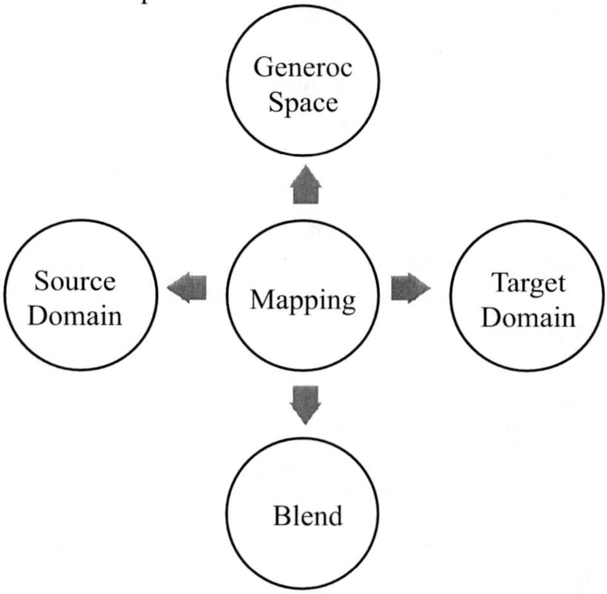

The core feature of this model is 'mapping'. It is the mind that makes the connection.[371] Gray expands the 'Generic Space' into 'Context,' where she focuses on the internal and external literary frames, historical, cultural and geographical information.[372] In Tamil, metonymy is known as *ākupeyar* and *aṉmoḻittokai*, while metaphor is *uruvakam*.[373] Metonymy and metaphor are formed in two ways: (a) By extension – using a word that is related to the intended referent in terms of its source, place, time, part, attribute, or action or using a nominal compound; (b) By periphrasis – placing two nouns in apposition which are at times followed by the particle '*āka*' ('as it is').[374]

4. Word-Pictures

i. *paṉiyilōrpāti* (v. 2)
Source: the half particle or a semi-dewdrop

370 Gray, *Psalm 18*, 26.

371 This belongs to the cognitive linguistics, which treats metaphor not primarily as words or expressions, but as mental process. The mapping moves from 'source to 'target'. 'Generic space' acts as the common ground and 'blend' summarizes the entire mental process.

372 Gray, *Psalm 18*, 33.

373 Ākupeyar literally means 'a name which has become (the name for another)' and aṉmoḻittokai, 'a compound of other words.' Uruvakam means 'a house for a form' (< Sansk. rūpaka). Cf. Rajam, *Reference Grammar*, 922.

374 Cf. Rajam, *Reference Grammar*, 922-23.

Target: male semen

Generic Space: smallness, insignificance and fluidity

Blend: though small and insignificant, the presence of a semi-dewdrop does make a difference in the life of vegetation. So does a semen fertilize an ovum in the womb of a woman upon entering it.

ii. *patumavarumpu kamaṭam* (v. 2)

Source: lotus bud, tortoise

Target: the shape of the foetus in its initial stage

Generic Space: the rounded and fluid shape

Blending: as the lotus bud is round and fluid before blossoming into a full flower, so is a human foetus in the womb of a woman.

iii. *oḷinakai* (v. 5)

Source: light

Target: smile

Generic Space: light attracts

Blending: as the light attracts attention, the smile of a newborn attracts the neighbours.

iv. *valarpiṟai* (vv. 7, 19)

Source: crescent

Target: the growing young man

Generic Space: the moon which is growing begins to spread its light. It illuminates others.

Blending: as the moon is growing and spreading its light so does a young person grows. As the crescent moon is a sign of hope so is the young person.

v. *mati* (v. 13)

Source: moon

Target: mind

Generic Space: the functioning of mind is connected to the moon. The growing and dying moon does affect a person's thinking.

Blending: as the moon which disappears cancels the light, the disappearance or dying of a person's mind makes him dark within. The person can no more be enlightened.

vi. *māmayilpōl* (v. 9) (SA. *maṭamayil* in v. 4)

Source: peacock

Target: young girl

Generic Space: a peacock is attractive. It attracts the peahens with its elegant feathers which it spreads like a hood.

Blending: as the peacock attracts a peahen, the young girl attracts the young boy.

vii. *māmalaipōl* (v. 19)

Source: mountain or hill

Target: the messenger of Yamā, the Lord of Death

Generic Space: the mountain is enormous in size. It is dark and destructive. No life can escape when it falls upon.

Blending: the messengers of Yamā are enormous in size, dark and bring about destruction. Nobody can escape from their fists.

5. Direct Addresses

This is the second stylistic feature which reveals the narrative character of the poem. In a narrative, the narrator makes the characters converse with one another. In this poem, the poet does not allow the characters to speak to one another. But he quotes their words in direct speech. This style makes the reader of the poem get reminded of the moment in which he too addressed or was addressed in the yester years of his life.

i. *vāvirupō* (v. 5)

The first speech that originates in the mouth of an infant, the poet says, are '*vā*' ('come'), '*iru*' ('stay'), and '*pō*' ('go'). The first ever utterances from the infants are usually '*mā*' or '*pā*' – addressed to the mother or the father. But, the poet chooses three verbs as the representations of the babbles from the baby. These three verbs summarize the theme of the poem. We all 'come' into the world, 'stay' here for a while, and (must) 'go' when the stay is over. This message, the poet, puts in the mouth of the infant and makes his reader hear it and be reminded of the shortness of life.

ii. *vaḷarpiṟai* (v. 7)

The word *vaḷarpiṟai* reappears in v. 19 as a metaphor denoting the messenger of death. In v. 7, this is in the mouth of the neighbours or townsfolk, who looking at the young person growing in stature, wisdom, knowledge and arts, exclaim and say, 'This man is an epitome of growth and success!' and 'As the moon grows into full shape and shine in darkness may this young man be a light to his own self, his family and the world!'

iii. *mataṉacorūpaṉ ivaṉ* (v. 9)

'*Mataṉ*' is a god or deity of love and sex. '*Mataṉacorūpaṉ*' means 'one who is moulded after the god of love and sex.' The young girls who gaze at the young man adorned with well-knit hair, flowers, scents, pearls, and ornaments, are enamoured of him and utter this expression. The attractive physique or physical built also is a reason for their exclamation.

iv. *varuvatupōva torumutukūṉu manti* (v. 13)

The expression builds on the verbs '*vā*' ('come') and '*pō*' ('go') taken from v. 5. Now the person has aged. He has lost his strength. He is not able to stand erect. He walks with the help of a stick. His appearance is now made fun of by the neighbours, who call him a *manti* ('monkey'). The phrase also can be set against the previous direct address in v. 9, where the young girls call the young man, 'a rebirth of love god.'

v. *kaliyukamīti livarmariyātai kaṇṭiṭum* (v. 15)

The *kaliyukā* is characterized by evil ruling over good. This *yukā* changes the values upside down. The person who was respected for his beauty, vigour, wealth, and fame is now looked down upon. The word *mariyātai* ('respect') is used ironically.

vi. *kaṭan̠mur̠aipēcum* (v. 18)

'Talk about the daily tasks' – the young man when he was able to take up responsibilities commanded his people who were under him to take care of daily chores. Now the tongue which commanded is made silent and it can never utter a word. The person is now communicating through motioning of the fingers.

vii. *paḻaiyavarkāṇum* (v. 21)

'*Paḻaiyavar*' can either refer to the man who is old or the man is known and familiar to all. The person who has been old and has been familiar to everyone is dead. The neighbours are in haste to see this person who has now frozen to be nothing but a dead body.

viii. *pantariṭum* (v. 21)

The neighbours who are at the dead man's house to attend to the funeral and the last rite of passage command to one another to make a shed in front of the house. This can also mean the custom of spreading a white cloth over the dead body or held over the corpse. This word summarizes all the rites that are associated with the funeral.

ix. *varicaikeṭāmal eṭum* (v. 23)

The expression can either mean (a) to refer to the conformity to the burial tradition; or (b) to the carefulness with which the persons must attend to the body. When the person is formed in the womb of a woman, the formation of body takes a particular order: *pārvai, vāi, cevi, kai, kāl* ('eye,' 'mouth,' 'ear,' 'hand,' and 'leg'). After death the body becomes susceptible to falling apart. Hence, careful attention is to be shown while removing the body from its present place.

x. *in̠iyāḷumē* (v. 24)

This is the climactic line of the poem, where the poet makes a plea to the Lord Śiva to liberate him from the false hope that he has tied with the body till now. Only at this point the reader recognizes that the entire poem is addressed to the Lord Śiva.

6. Word-Plays

The poet employs a word-play at the level of rhyme and meaning. Let us tabulate the findings as follows:

	Element A	Element B	Type & Comment
1.	*o̲lukiya vintu ūṟu curōṇitam mītu kalantu* (v. 1)	*ventu vi̲luntu muṟintu niṇaṅkaḷ uruki yelumpu karuki* (v. 23)	Contrast by rhyme. 'A' describes the process of integration while 'B' describes the process of disintegration.
2.	*pārvaimeivāicevi kālkaikaḷeṉṟa* (v. 2)	*varicaikeṭāma leṭum* (v. 23)	Contrast by meaning. During conception the body-formation happens in a linear process (*varicai*), where elements cannot be anticipated or postponed. After death the body is so vulnerable that failing to keep up the *varicai* will render the body lose its proper shape.
3.	*māmayilpōl* (v. 9)	*māmalaipōl* (v. 19)	Contrast by rhyme. The young person is not able to escape the attracting girls who are like peahens. In the same way the old man is not able to escape the messengers of death who fall upon him unawares like huge mountain.
4.	*oḷi* (v. 5)	*a̲lal* (v. 23)	Contrast by meaning. The first light is the beginning of life. The last light signals the end of life.
5.	*koṅkai* (vv. 4, 10)	*ceṅkai* (v. 12)	Contrast by rhyme. At birth the man was after the mother's breasts. At youth he was after the young girl's breasts. As the life sets, the breasts disappear. What the man has to hold on to is a stick.
6.	*uṭampu* (vv. 22, 24)	*nampu* (v. 24)	Contrast by rhyme. The poet has so far set his hope on a wrong thing.

7.	*yokamuvāramu nāḷumaṟintu* (v. 3)	*kālamaṟintu* (v. 20)	Contrast by rhyme and meaning. At both the moments of birth and death the time is very important. This shows the boundary within which a human life travels from birth to death.
8.	*oḻukiya vintu* (v. 1)	*oḻukiṭa vantu* (v. 18)	Contrast by rhyme. Both the processes in 'A' and 'B' are uncontrollable.
9.	*kaḷapamaṇintu pāvakamē ceitu* (v. 22)	*nāṟum uṭampai* (v. 22)	Contrast by meaning. The body stinks even if it is poured with perfumes.
10.	*nīr* (v. 1-2) (*paṇiyilōrpāti*)	*nīru* (v. 24)	Contrast by rhyme. The element 'A' is not even a finger tip, while the element 'B' is not even a handful.
11.	*kaiyiṉilōr taṭiyumākiyē* (v. 12)	*virakiṭai mūṭi* (v. 24)	Contrast by meaning. The firewood which burns the body is anticipated in the old man's hand in the form of a walking stick.

7. Iṭakkaraṭakkal

It refers to the euphemism, i.e., saying a thing in such a way as not to embarrass the listeners or readers. In v. 1, *aṉpu porunti* is an *iṭakkaraṭakkal* for 'having a sexual intercourse.'[375] In v. 10, *mayanki* also is an *iṭakkaraṭakkal* for sexual intercourse.

F. Characterisation

In *Uṭal* we have both direct and indirect characterisation, i.e., description or declaration by the narrator and the interlocution of the characters to one another. The characters depicted in the poem can be broadly categorized into two: (a) Self (individual human person), and (b) Other (Transcendental, social,[376] and environmental).[377]

375 Kalyāṇasuntaraṉār, 169.

376 By 'nature' we refer to the flora, the fauna and the elements of nature.

377 The 'world' represents the persons and processes that a human person has to interact with.

1. Self

The poet who is external to the poem observes a lass (A) and a lad (B) in sexual union, the fruit of which is 'light' (C).[378] The 'light' is disintegrated at death. The 'life-breath' is taken back by the messengers of *Yamā* and the body is given to fire. Now the poet (D) sees all these realities from close to far, concludes that he has been disillusioned and prays that the Lord may rule over him.

Thus, human person is characterized at four levels: (a) Lass (A); (b) Lad (B); Light (C); and the Poet (D). Let us have a close look at each of these characters.

a. Lass (A)

Paṭṭiṉattār uses seven words to refer to woman / women in the poem:

(i) *maṭamātu* (v. 1);
(ii) *maṭantai* (v. 3);
(iii) *makaḷirkaḷ* (v. 4);
(iv) *maṭamayil* (v. 4) (SA. *māmayil* in v. 9);
(v) *maṅkaiyar* (v. 9);
(vi) *tōkaiyar* (v. 14); and
(vii) *maṉaivi* (v. 20).[379]

Nāccinārkkiṇiyar in his commentary on Sangam Literature classifies life-stages of a woman into seven. According to him the stages are: (i) *pētai* (5 – 7 years); (ii) *petumpai* (8 – 11 years); (iii) *maṅkai* (12 – 13 years); (iv) *maṭantai* (14 – 19 years); (v) *arivai* (20 – 25 years); (vi) *terivai* (26 – 31 years); and (vii) *pēriḷampen* (32 – 40 years).[380] His classification starts when the female child is at the age of 5. At the stage 0 – 5 years, there is usually no distinction. Both the male and the female child are called *kuḻantai.* When Paṭṭiṉattār calls the character 'A,' he probably has in mind the fourth stage of '*maṭantai.*' This stage is being referred directly in v. 3 (*maṭantai*), and implicit in v. 4 (*maṭamayil*). The word *maṅkaiyar* in v. 9 refers to the third stage. The '*makaḷirkaḷ*' (v. 4) and

378 Let us assume 'Light' to be the metonymy for a human person who is born of the sexual union between 'A' and 'B.' This can be justified on the following grounds: (a) The first organ that is developed in a foetus is 'eyes.' The poet refers to this as '*pārvai*' (cf. v. 2); (b) The newborn baby's smile is equated to 'light' (*oḷi*) in v. 5; (c) At the onset of childhood and at the prime of youth, the person is referred to as a crescent (*vaḷarpiṟai*) in v. 7. (d) As he ages his internal light is shut down (cf. v. 13, *maṭiyumaḻintu*, the moon or the light dying); and (e) at his death the final farewell is given to him with light (cf. v. 24, *yaḻalkoṭupōṭa*, setting the fire).

379 Cf. http://karkanirka.org/2009/08/24/tamil_wordlist_11/. Accessed on 10 January 2016, 14:10.

380 The life-stage finishes at the age of 40. The reason is either (a) the lifespan of the women was very short or (b) the stage extends from 32 to 0 years, i.e., 32 to death.

tōkaiyar (v. 14) can be called a generic term for 'womenfolk' and *maṉaivi* (v. 20) might belong to the seventh stage '*pēriḷampen.*'

The '*maṭamātu*' (A) is the first word in the poem. By choosing to keep this word at the beginning the poet wants to convey to the reader that (i) the woman is the originator of life, and (ii) it is the woman who is at the centre of a man's life as someone who cares for and suckles (v. 4), who attracting distracts (v. 9), who looks down upon (v. 14), and who mourns the loss (v. 20). At both these levels the poet implies that a woman is *incomplete* without a man: the woman needs the company of a man for her sexual union (v. 1), she needs an object to express her care (v. 4), she needs to attract men (v. 9) and her life is almost impossible without his man (v. 20).

Elsewhere in the corpus the poet uses the words *illāḷ* ('one who rules over the house,' 'housewife'),[381] *vēlviḻiyār* ('eyes as spear'),[382] *peṇṭīr* ('women'),[383] *aṉṉai*,[384] and *kaṉṉiyar* ('virgins').[385]

Let us also note two poems entirely on woman: (i) *Nāṉkāvatu Kaccit Tiruvkaval*; and (ii) Paṭṭiṉattār's eulogy to his mother at her funeral pyre. Though often times the poet is very hard when describing women, he is often misquoted for his misogynist tone in *Nāṉkāvatu Kaccit Tiruvkaval.* This poem is addressed to all human persons who celebrate women and are enamoured of them ('*mātarai makiḻntu kātaṟ koṇṭātum māṉiṭark kellām yāṉeṭut turaippēn,*' lines 5-6). In this poem, the poet quotes the words with which the humans admire women and reveals the other part of the beauty of which they are enamoured. For example, the teeth of women, which the humans praise as pearls, are nothing but the teeth that smell of rice and meat (*aṉṉamuṅ kaṟiyu macaivit tiṟakkum muṉṉiya pallai mutteṉa moḻintum,* lines 31-32). In the final line he invites these men to shed off these praises of women and to return to the One Lord. Or, in other words, to shed off such a flirting attitude one must surrender to the feet of the Lord (*ēkanātaṉai iṇaiyaṭi iṟaincumin pōka mātaraip pōṟṟuta loḻintē,* lines 69-70). Here one must not quote the poet out of the context as a misogynist. For the poet does not degrade the woman or her physique. In fact, by showing the other side of the reality, of which the men are ignorant of and degrade women later, he gives a warning also to women.[386] The poet in fact exalts the status of women, as we see from his eulogy to his dead mother. He praises for bearing him in her womb for three hundred days,

381 *Illāḷum cuṟṟamum maintarum vāḻvum eḻiluṭampum, Tiruvēkampālai,* v. 5.

382 *Varikkōla vēlviḻiyār anurāka mayakkiṟceṉṟu, Tiruvēkampālai*, v. 11.

383 *Tiruvēkampālai*, v. 13. SA., *Tiruviṭaimarutūr*, v. 2.

384 *Tiruvēkampaviruttam*, line 1. SA., *Aruṭpulampal – Mutalvaṉ Muṟaiyīṭu,* v. 24.

385 *Iraṇṭāvatukoyiṟṟiruvakaval*, line 2.

386 Cf. Karuppaiyā, 59-60.

for nursing him, for pampering him, for rearing him up, for guiding him and for being everything to him.

b. Lad (B)

The '*oruvaṉ'* does not tell us whether this one is a boy, a youth, or an adult. The word stands for someone who can initiate and culminate a sexual union with a young girl. This '*oruvaṉ*' does not reappear in the rest of the poem. The semen that is emitted by this *oruvaṉ* is responsible for the development of the foetus in the womb of the *orumaṭamātu.*

c. Light (C)

The light, i.e., the human person, who is the fruit of the sexual union between 'A' and 'B,' is someone who is the process. The human person (C) is a male (cf. *mataṉacorūpan* in v. 9). This human person is basically a by-product of a male-female loving, pleasurable, sexual union. His body contains both hard (such as bones) and soft parts (such as flesh and blood). The hard part he receives from the semen of the '*oruvaṉ'* while the soft part he receives from the ovum of the '*orumaṭamātu.*'

Person in Process

The human person is presented more as a 'becoming' than a 'being.' This process or becoming occurs at 8 stages:[387]

i. Prebirth (vv. 1-2). The child is an effect of a cause. The cause is the physical and emotional love-bond between his parents. The growth of the foetus in the womb is a slow, steady, and systematic process following a linearity. The child has the potentiality and possibility to become someone.
ii. Birth (v. 3). The child is born when the days are complete.[388] The child born in the poem is not a premature baby or a baby born through a Caesarean. The process is natural. The feeling of hope that the child induces is not mentioned in the poem.
iii. Infancy (v. 4) [0-3 years]. The infant is full of energy, vibrant, and brisk. It is dependent on its mother for its food and sustenance. Its senses are developed.[389] Vitality is the hallmark in this stage.
iv. Childhood (vv. 5-6) [3-5 years]. The sparkling smile of the child is attractive. It reaches to all and tries to hold everyone. It begins to

387 But let us not confuse it with the four-stage pattern found in the poems of our study. Here I use 'stage' to explain the development of physical body as described in *Uṭal*.

388 The completion of days as nine and one is given as *aiyiraṇṭu tiṅkal* (5x2 moons) and *munnūru nāḷ* (three hundred days) in Paṭṭiṉattār's eulogy at his mother's funeral pyre. Cf. vv. 1-2.

389 Cf. Tolkappiam, the classification of senses. One, two, three, etc.

enjoy being adorned and ornamented. It learns to eat. Playfulness is the key characteristic mark in this stage. It leaves the house for the first time to look for the playmates who are of its age and taste.

iv. Boyhood (v. 7) [6-14 years]. The child through a rite of initiation becomes part of the faith, culture and memory of the society. The role of the teachers is very important here. The child becomes skilled in language and arts. Moreover, this is the prime of one's life. At this stage the boy develops an inner subjective self. The boy already turns out to be a teen or an adolescent. The principles of imagination, ingenuity and passion mark this stage.

v. Adulthood (vv. 8-12) [15-50 years]. The young person takes up an enterprise through which he begins to contribute to the society. At this stage he turns out to be an independent individual who can make decisions on his own and abide by them. He accomplishes many responsibilities, including finding a home and partner, establishing a circle of friends, and getting a good job. Towards the end of this stage he begins to contemplate his past to cherish and to rectify the errors. The poet also adds a dimension where the young person flirts after the women to the extent of losing his savings and inheritance (v. 11). This stage also marks the climax point after which life begins to dwindle. The growth stops and the process begins to be reversed. The person loses his riches, his youth, his teeth, his sight, his vigour, and his black hair. He also engages himself in petty quarrels, develops a sense of fear and guilt.

vi. Late Adulthood (vv. 13-18) [51-70 years]. The light of life begins to be dim and the person begins to be confined to remain in his home. The acts of benevolence that he did bring the neighbours to him. The person loses his health.

vii. Dying and Death (vv. 19-24) [70-0 years]. The person who was integrated at the moment of conception from two elements of father and mother, now begins to disintegrate into body and spirit. The spirit is taken back by God, who gave it and the body returns to the earth as ashes and fire. The poet does not describe how the life-breath enters into the foetus. But he describes its contrary movement, i.e., how the life is taken away from a body (cf. v. 20, '*valaikoṭuvīci uyirkoṭupōka*').

Each stage of life has a lot to offer to the human person. The person enjoys every stage fully before passing to the other.

Person as Matter

The human person, though made up of *uyir* and *uṭal*, is primarily a matter, which comes into existence as a physical process begins to be extinct at the moment of death. The body comes to life through the life-breath.

2. The Transcendental Other

Only at the end of the poem the reader realizes that the entire poem is a hymn to the Lord Śiva by the poet. In the presence of the Lord, the poet laments over the impermanence of human life, body and world.

a. *maṟaiyavaṉ* (the hidden one)

It is very curious to note that the name of the Lord Śiva is omitted in the poem.[390] Only internal evidence to an epithet to God is the word *maṟaiyavaṉ* found in v. 17. Initially the title *maṟaiyavaṉ* stood for the Lord Brahma.[391] Years later the title was taken into Śaivism and began to be attributed to the Lord Śiva. Śiva is often described as the spirit of the Vedas (*kuṟaiyā maṟaiyam...pirāṉ*)[392] and as the essence of the Vedas (*Arumaṟai poruḷē*),[393] as the teacher of the Vedas (*ceḻumaṟai pakarnta pāṭṭaṉē*)[394] or as the expert reciter of the Vedas (*nāṉmaṟai pāṭavallāṉ*).[395] The word Veda in its Sanskrit form is also used: e.g., *Vetattin poruḷāṉāi*,[396] 'you became the substance of the Vedas' (VII 86.1.) or *Veta mutalāṉāi*,[397] 'you became the first among the Vedas' (VII 40.10) as simply by referring to Śiva as the vedin or *Maṟaiyaṉ* or *Maṟaiyavaṉ*. Campantar has several references to this Vedic association of Śiva. The Periya Purāṇam also refers to god as the object of the Vedas.[398]

Tirumūlar gives a new interpretation of the epithet. The Lord Śiva, the Uncreated (*Svayampu* – Self-created) stands as the cool rays of light; the

390 In *Tiruvēkampalai*, Paṭṭiṉattār uses the title *kacciyēkampanē* (42x). In this song the title *Iṟaivā* also is used 25x. In *Tiruttillai* he uses the titles *Tillaiccaṅkaranē* (cf. v. 1), *citamparatēcikanē* (cf. v. 4), and *āṇṭavanē* (cf. v. 14). In *Mutalāvatu Koyiṟṟiruvakaval* the name Śiva is explicit (cf. line 46). In other songs there are epithets used for the Lord Śiva referring to his as a Dancer or the Lord of the Universe.

391 This name is attested by Āḻwārs. Cf. *Pūtattāḻvār's Pācuram* (cf. *Nālāyira Divya Prabandham*, 2277) which is sung during Vaikāsi Brahmotsavam.

392 *Tirumuṟai* VII. 10. 1.

393 *Tirumuṟai* VII. 69. 2.

394 *Tirumuṟai* VII. 69.9.

395 *Tirumuṟai* VII. 57.10.

396 *Tirumuṟai* VII. 86.1.

397 *Tirumuṟai* VII. 40.10.

398 R. Ghose, *The Tyāgarāja Cult in Tamilnāḍu. A Study in Conflict and Accomodation* (New Delhi 1996) 137. SA. *maṟaiyavaṉ makiḻntu nōkki*, in *Tiruttoṇtar Purāṇam, Tirumuṟai* XII. 431.

Uncreated stands as the Vedas. If you chant the attributes of the Uncreated, He will appear as the unborn *maṟaiyavaṉ*. As *maṟaiyavaṉ* He gave us birth, honouring us, so that we would ourselves become adept in Vedas. As *maṟaiyavaṉ* stands within the five letters (*Na-Ma-Ci-Va-Ya*), He Himself is the five letters:[399]

tāṉē eḻukuṇam taṇcuṭa rāiniṟkum
tāṉē eḻukuṇam vetamu māiniṟkum
tāṉē eḻukuṇam āvatum ōtiṭil
tāṉē eḻunta maṟaiyavan āmē. (Tirumantiram, 939)
maṟaiya vanāka matitta piṟavi
maṟaiya vanāka matittiṭak kāṇpar
maṟaiyavan añceḻuttu uḷniṟkap peṟṟa
maṟaiyavan añceḻuttu tāmatu vākumē. (Tirumantiram, 940).

Paṭṭiṉattār elsewhere uses this title in his corpus in *Tiruttillai*, v. 17, as *nālin maṟaipporuḷ ampalavāṇarai* (the Dancer, the Mystery or the Hidden of the Four [Vedas]) and in *Mūṉṟāvatu Kōyiṟṟiruvakaval,* line 47, as *maṟaiyavar tillai* (the Hidden One or the Lord of the Scriptures in Tillai).

b. *āḷumē* (rule over me)

The second reference to God in the poem is the final word in the poem, '*āḷumē*' (= 'to rule,' from the root originates the word *āṇṭavaṇ* ('one who ruled/s'). Here the verb is in the vocative case, through which the poet pleads the Lord so that He might *rule over* him or take possession of him. Paṭṭiṉattār makes use of the cognate of this verb in the vocative elsewhere in *Tiruttillai,* v. 8,

kālaiyupāti malañcala māmaṉṟik kaṭṭucciyiṟ
cālavupāti pacitāka mākumuṉ cañcitamām
mālaiyupāti tuyilkāma māmivai māṟṟiviṭṭē
ālamukantaru ḷampalavā ennai yāṇṭaruḷē.

In this verb the poet invites God to come to him to take possession of him. Elsewhere in *Mūṉṟāvatu Kōyiṟṟiruvakaval,* lines 44, 45, 46, 48, and 51, the poet comes to take refuge ('*aṭaikkalam*') in the Lord.

3. The Social Other

Human persons or the others, that are characterized in the poem are essentially 'social.' They relate themselves to other humans by a relation of objectivity, inter-subjectivity, and functionality. The other is necessary and taken for

399 Paṭṭiṉattār also attests these five letters in *Tiruvēkampālai*, v. 9:
Kallāp piḻaiyum karutāp piḻaiyum kacinturuki
Nillāp piḻaiyum niṉaiyāp piḻaiyum niṉṉaṉceḻuttaic
Collāp piḻaiyun tutiyāp piḻaiyun toḻāppiḻaiyum
Ellāp piḻaiyum poṟuttaruḻvāi kacciyēkampaṇē.

granted in the poem. Since his inception the human person is in touch with, or caused by others. He is birthed by his parents. The poem makes 13 references to the existence of others.

Relation of *objectivity*: In this level of relationship, the other is treated as an 'it,' or as an 'object.' The relationship of *makaḷirkacenai* (v. 4), who dress the newborn, *uṇpavartiṉpavar* and *tēṭiyapālar* (v. 6), the playmates, *mākatarpōkatar* (v. 8), who admire and adore the beauty and wisdom of the young person, *maṅkaiyar* (v. 9), who are attracted by the young man's well-built physique, and *tōkaiyarpālarkaḷ* (v. 14), who make fun of the old man who finds it hard to move.

Relation of *inter-subjectivity*: In this type of relationship the other is a holy 'thou,' where one is related to each other through the bond of love characterized by immediacy, reciprocity and availability. Though these persons are distant from one another still the relationship can be maintained. This type of relation emerges through blood, matrimonial or covenantal relationship. There is always an element of choice, freedom and promise in this type of relation. The *ñaṉakuru* (v. 7), the teacher or the maestro, *maintar* (v. 20) and *maṉaivi* (v. 20), who mourn the death are the examples of this type of relationship.

Relation of *functionality*: In this relationship the other is seen as an indifferent functionary. In this relationship one *handles* the other as a tool in hand. Humans set up this type of relationship which is characterized by order, security, causality and calculation. The *ayalārkaḷ* (v. 21), who attend to the funeral rites, and *iḷamaintar* (v. 23), who carry the dead to the cremation ground can be given as examples for this type of relationship in the poem. Their role is merely functionary. The neighbours of a village have a moral or functional responsibility to help one another at all times, in weather fair (cf. v. 4) and foul (v. 21).

4. The Environmental Other

The natural elements that are mentioned in the poem are three: (a) The wood (as 'walking stick' in v. 12, as 'firewood' in v. 24); (b) The messengers of *Yamā* (v. 19); and (c) The *nālu pūtam* (v. 18, cf. *aḻal* ['fire'] in v. 24).

a. The Wood

The wood is explicit in v. 12 as a '*taṭi*' ('cane') and in v. 24 as '*viṟaku*' ('firewood') and is implicit in v. 1 (as 'cot') and in v. 4 (as 'cradle'). Elsewhere in the corpus, the poet uses the wood as a metaphor for the human body. For example, *kālattaccan veṭṭimuṟikkum marampōr carīrattai* ('the carpenter of time cuts down the tree of the body') in *Tiruvēkampālai,* v. 2, *ācaik kayiṟṟilāṭum pamparam, ōyā nōikkiṭam, oru marakkalam* ('a toy that is controlled by a string of desire, a place where the diseases are endless, and a boat') in *Iraṇṭāvatu Koyiṟṟiruvakaval,* lines 14-15.

In v. 24 of our poem, the wood acts as a metonymy for the human body. The human body that is burnt not even amounts for a handful of ashes.

b. The Messengers of Yamā

God of death, Yamā is presented as someone who is part of the nature. They are compared to *māmalai* ('huge mountain'). They are black in colour and they are inescapable. They arrive at the end of one's life with their net or *pāca kayiṟu* in hands to take hold of life. Tiruñaṉacampantar also attests this imagery in his poem adding an element of fire to the character of the messengers:

Matinutaṉ maṅkaiyoṭu vaṭapā liruntu maṟaiyotu meṅkaḷ paramaṉ
Natiyoṭu koṉṟaimālai muṭimē laṇinten uḷamē pukunta ataṉāl
Kotiyuṟu kālaṉaṅki naṉṉōṭu tūtar koṭunōika ḷāna palavum
Atikuṇam nallanalla vavainalla nalla aṭiyā ravarkku mikavē.
(*Tēvāram*, 2nd Tirumuṟai, 085, 4).

c. The *nālu pūtam*

Śaivism understands the nature as the mixture of the *pañcapūtās,* ('five elements,' earth, water, fire, air, and ether) and human person as a combination of the four elements (earth, water, fire, and air). Elsewhere in *Aruṭpulampal – Mutalvaṉ Muṟaiyītu,* v. 7, Paṭṭiṉattār, human body which consists of five elements (cf. *maṇmutalām aimpūtam māṇṭuviḻak kaṇḍēnaṭi*). Based on this we can re-read the line (v. 18) in our poem as *pūtamunālu* (earth, water, fire, ether) and *cuvācamum* (air).

G. Themes and Motifs

1. Body

As the title of the poem suggests the major theme that runs through the poem is 'human body.' Paṭṭiṉattār presents body as an outcome of a sexual act that happens between a lad and a lass. Body comes into being through the mixture of semen and ovary. This mixture is triggered by the love-making act of two individuals, male and female.

The poem is centered on the word 'body' – the development of the body (cf. vv. 1-3), the functioning of the body (vv. 4-6), the attraction of the body (vv. 7-11), the degradation of the body (vv. 12-23) and the disintegration of the body (v. 24).

The words used to refer to the body are '*mei*'[400] (literally 'true,' also means 'body') in v. 2, and *uṭampu* ('body') in vv. 22 and 23. The members of

400 The word mei ('true') is a muraṇ ('paradox') or iṭakkaratakkal ('saying one thing but meaning the other'). The 'body' is a māyā ('delusion') or a 'poi' ('lie'). But ironically it is

the body mentioned are *pārvai* [v. 2], *viḻi* [v. 9], *kaṇkal* [v. 12] ('eyes'), *vāi* [vv. 2, 13] ('mouth'), *cevi* [vv. 2, 13] ('ear'), *kāl* [vv. 2, 15] ('leg'), *kai* ('hand'), *koṅkai* [vv. 4, 10] ('breast'), *itaḻ* [vv. 5, 10] ('lip'), *maṭi* [vv. 5, 20] ('lap'), *arai* ('hip' or 'waist'), *mayir*, *koṇṭai* [v. 8], *narai tirai* [v. 12] ('hair'), *taṇam* [v. 11] ('wealth,' 'chest'), *pal* ('tooth'), *kunti* [v. 13] ('back,' 'spine'), *toṇṭai* [v. 14] ('throat'), *neñcu* [vv. 14, 16, 18] ('chest'), *cuṇai* [v. 14] ('saliva'), *nā* [v. 18] ('tongue'), *kaṭai* [v. 18] ('edge of mouth'), *niṇaṅkal* [v. 24] ('flesh'), *elumpu* [v. 24] ('bone'). There are two references to the lifeless body, *piṇam* [v. 21], *cavam* [v. 22]. The body, whether alive or dead, is something which is covered and adorned (cf. vv. 4, 6, 8, 14, and 22).

The expression *nāṟum uṭampu* [v. 23] ('stinking body') is found thematically often times found in Paṭṭiṉattār corpus.[401]

Paṭṭiṉattār concludes that at the end of everything not even a handful of ashes remains.[402]

2. Women

The women are referred to both individually and collectively - as individuals and as collective members. The women are part of all the life stages:

(a) The conception occurs at the womb of a woman;
(b) At the birth of the child the women receive the newborn;
(c) The child enjoys the care and cuddles of the women;
(d) The youth are attracted to them;
(e) At the old age they are there to assist; and
(f) At the moment of death, they mourn over.

But, the overall image presented of women is very grey. She is referred to in terms of her lack of common sense (*maṭam*, cf. vv. 1, 3, 4) or in terms of her attracting eyes and physique (*mayil, tōkai, koṅkai, itaḻ*, cf. vv. 4, 5, 8, 9, and 14) or as someone who is related to a man (*maṉaivi,* cf. v. 20).

Before condemning Paṭṭiṉattār as a misogynist and conclude the argument, let us set the poem in its historical setting.[403] In South India when

called 'mei' ('true').

401 *Nāṟumuṭalai narippoti cōṟṟinai nāṉtinamuñ*
Cōṟuṅ kaṟiyumnirappiya pāṇṭattait tōkaiyartam
Kūṟummalamum irattamuñ cōṟuṅ kuḻiyilviḻātu
Ēṟum paṭiyaruḷvāi iṟaivā, kacciyēkampanē. (Tiruvēkampālai, v. 34).
SA. *Nāṟṟap pāṇṭam nāṉmuḻat toṉpatu*
Pīṟṟat tuṇṭam pēiccurait tōṭṭam... (*Iranṭāvatu Koyiṟṟiruvakaval,* lines 11-12).

402 SA. *Muṭicārnta maṉṉaru maṟṟamuḷḷōru muṭiviloru*
Piṭicāmpa rāiventu maṇṇāvatuṅ kaṇṭupiṉṉumintap
Piṭicārnta vāḻvai niṉaippatal lāṟpoṉṉiṉampalava
Raṭicārntu nāmuyya vēṇṭumeṉṟē yaṟivārillaiyē. (*Tiruttillai*, v. 7).

403 Cf. Karuppaiyā, 56-57.

Śaivism wanted to enter it had to fight a hard battle against Jainism and Buddhism. The Bhakti movement was the need of the hour. This to some extent won over Jainism and Buddhism but unfortunately ended in introducing the devadasi system. Jainism and Buddhism wanted to eliminate music and art as waste of time. But, the Bhakti movement encouraged music and art. Along with this woman also was brought in: To those who held that the woman will not accompany in the end, the Bhakti movement suggested that the company of women is a must for the present age. Even Śiva has his Śakti with him. As matrimony entered, prostitution also entered. This prostitution was made into a social and religious institution during this Bhakti movement. During the Cōla period woman came to be worshipped as Śakti. A new movement of Ma.Ma. Ma. (*maṅkai-matu-maccam*,[404] girl-drinks-sex). Jainism and Buddhism kept the woman away from men while the new Bhakti movement tied men to women. The untying happened during the time of Second Paṭṭiṉattār and Siddhas. Since Śaivism made men to be tied to women it was difficult to inculcate in them wisdom. The first task was to separate men from women. To make this possible Paṭṭiṉattār turns woman upside down. The poem *kaccittiruvakaval* is an ideal example for this. This poem is not sung to the women but to men who are flirting women. After making him understand the other side of a woman, Paṭṭiṉattār demands,

> "*itaip pōi iṉitu eṉṟu*
> *collit tiriya vēṇṭā*
> *pōkamātaraip pōṟṟutalai viṭuttu*
> *ēkanātaṉin iṇaiyaṭi iṟaiñcu*."

The whipping given in this poem is not given to the woman but to the man who has fallen on woman's physical beauty. He questions the projections made by these men. Thus, the poet's songs are from a man to a man. Hence, there is no need to bring in a woman.

Moreover, Paṭṭiṉattār does not degrade women. For example, as we have seen earlier, to the young man who praises the teeth of a woman as 'pearls' he tells that these too will pass away and she will be toothless. This is not a derogatory remark. This is the truth that the young man has forgotten and Paṭṭiṉattār makes him realize the truth.

The poem which Paṭṭiṉattār sings at the funeral pyre of his own mother is the best example to say that Paṭṭiṉattār never degraded women.

Moreover, he wants to liberate men from indulgence in sex. To drive home this lesson, he makes them understand the impermanence of the body. Tamiḻaṇṇal, who introduces Paṭṭiṉattār poems, writes the scope as "to polish the understanding, to make the men respect women and not to use them as mere

---

404 Maccam primarily means 'fish.' Since fish is the symbol of Kāmatēvan, the god of pleasure and sex, the word came to be associated with the act of sex.

pleasure-objects, to have a mind which is at peace, not to have unrestrained urge to sex one must realize the impermanence of the body. Paṭṭiṉattār's aim is to teach this. Not to give a negative outlook about woman."[405]

3. Dance

Throughout the poem one is able to perceive the dance of life. Paṭṭiṉattār is very creative in presenting this symbol indirectly. The only reference to dance is given in v. 6, *uṭaimaṇiyāṭai yaraivaṭamāṭa.* Here the verb *āṭa* ('to dance'), though does not refer to the dance of Śiva, it indirectly takes us in that direction. The seven characteristics attributed to the Lord Śiva are present in the poem: *āṭa* [v. 6] ('dance'), *koṇṭai* [v. 8] ('plait'), *piṟai* [vv. 7, 19] ('crescent'), *caṭai* [v. 19] ('plait'), *maṟai* [v. 17] ('hide,' 'scripture,' 'god'), *cuṭalai* [v. 23] ('cremation ground'), *nīṟu* [v. 24] ('ashes'). Through these images the irony[406] that is driven home is that man has forgotten the eternal dance of the Lord Śiva and has concentrated so far on his own dance.

The Lord Śiva, Śaivism believes, dances for the welfare or the functioning of the world. The dance is the symbol of unsullied wisdom and uncontaminated happiness.[407] For example, when Paṭṭiṉattār calls the Lord as '*tillaiyāṉantat tāṇṭavṉe*,' (*Tiruttillai,* v. 14) it means not only 'the Lord Śiva is the Lord of Tillai,' but also refers to the dance of Śiva, which is known as '*tāṇṭavam.*'

4. Related Opposites

The poem points out to the pole of opposites. Life is not an escape from these opposites but living out the contrasts as they are:

i. *orumātu* (v. 1) vs. *oruvaṉ* (v. 1)
ii. *vintu* (v. 1) vs. *curōnitam* (v. 1)
iii. *uruvam* (v. 3) vs. *piṇam* (v. 21)
iv. *āṭai araivaṭamāṭa* (v. 6) vs. *tukilumiḻantu* (v. 14)
v. *oḷi* (v. 5) vs. *iruḷ* (v. 12)
vi. *vaḷarpiṟai* (v. 7) vs. *matiyumaḻintu* (v. 13)
vii. *vantupukuntu* (v. 2) vs. *ventuviḻuntu* (v. 24)
viii. *vāḻvu* (v. 17) vs. *cāvu* / *cavam* (v. 22).

Paṭṭiṉattār catches hold of the core of the entire reality, i.e., the play of opposites. But, towards the end he falls into the temptation to hold on to god and to treat body as redundant. But it is through the body that one surrenders to the transcendental reality.

---

405 Cf. Karuppaiyā, 56-63.

406 "Ironic statements usually have a double meaning. The more hidden it is, the greater the intellectual satisfaction of both discerner and ironist." I. J. J. Spangenberg, "Irony in the Book of Qohelet," in *JSOT* 72 (1996) 61 (57-69).

407 Ghose, *Tyāgarāja Cult*, 126.

5. Dependence

In the poem we observe the presentation of dependence at two levels: mutual and real. The mutual dependence between a man and a woman (v. 1), the dependence of the child on parents and neighbours (vv. 3-4), the dependence that the young person shows on the young girls (vv. 7-11), the dependence of the old man on his family and friends before and after death (vv. 12ff.) – all these ring in the level of mutual dependence. There is yet another level, i.e., real dependence, which the poet realizes at the end of the poem. At v. 24 the poet makes a distinction between unreal dependence, which is on the body, and real dependence, which is in God.

H. Conclusion

In this chapter, (i) We have travelled with Paṭṭiṉattār in his historical and literary context, and have attempted to understand his poem by employing various narrative analysis tools; (ii) The characterisation brings to light the human life transition in a vivid manner; and (iii) The author, who retrospects his own life along the lines finally surrenders to the Lord Śiva.

IV. POEMS AND POETS IN DIALOGUE

The present chapter has two scopes. In section one, we place the poets and the poems side by side and look for the contextual, communicative, conceptual similarities and various differences between them and observe whether they are in duet or duel. The next section enumerates the perspectives and queries that emerge in the dialogue with the poets and us, who are distant in space and time. The method used here is that of comparative literature.

A. Poets and Poems with One Another

1. Similarities

1.1. Contextual

1.1.1. A Wake-up Call

From the external evidences we deduce that Qohelet wrote the poem in the context, when the people, who returned from the exile had to cope with life. The Torah, the Temple, and the Monarchy had no sense to them in Babylonian exile. Instead of searching for their identity and meaning in these 'failed' institutions they turned towards their own selves – human persons as ends, "created in the image and likeness of God" (Gen 1:27). They dreamt of a world where they would relive the First Creation experience, when everything was *good* and *in order*. Qohelet through this poem awakes them from their slumber so that they may begin to look within their own selves and find meaning. Qohelet justifies this by composing his poem with ample intertextual links with Gen 1-4.[408] Qohelet, who observed the destruction of the hard-held

408 "In fact, I have not come across a single scholar who denies Qoheleth's use of the Genesis material." Cited in K. Dell, "Exploring Intertextual Links between Ecclesiastes and Genesis 1-11," in K. Dell – W. Kynes, eds., *Reading Ecclesiastes Intertextually* (London 2016) 3. Dell makes three types of intertextual links: quotation (explicit, intentional reference), allusion (implicit, intentional reference), and echo (implicit, unintentional reference). "Eccl 12:7 is the often-cited parallel text to Gen 3:19 (with Gen 2:7): 'And the dust returns to the earth as it was, and the breath returns to God who gave it.' This verse, along with Eccl 3:20 forms the strongest evidence of an intertextual allusion." Dell, "Exploring Intertextual Links," 11.

institutions, came to the realization that everything is impermanent and the only permanent reality is to realize the pristine beauty that was put in each of us by the Creator at the moment of Creation. For, "Ecclesiastes and Genesis exhibit substantial agreement as to the central focus of the creation motif – that life is to be celebrated as a 'good' creation of God."[409]

Paṭṭiṉattār, on the other hand, awoke the people from their overindulging in the body and its concerns. When Śaivism entered Tamil Nadu the faiths that already prevailed were Jainism and Buddhism, which preached intellectual growth by eliminating devout practices as superstitions and arts as mere waste of time.[410] Śaivism revamped and brought back the devout practices and arts. It exalted the role of women. But, as the time went on the people were too much tied to the arts and the women. To make them understand that life is more than women, the poets such as Paṭṭiṉattār had to take a radical step.[411] They took on hand the impermanence of body and beauty of women. In order to set their mind on God and God alone people have to distract themselves from these distractions. Taking on the theme of the impermanence of the body, Paṭṭiṉattār makes a clarion call to the people to turn back to God.

1.1.2. Names Not Theirs

The internal evidence of Eccl 11:4 – 12:8 shows that the author of the poem is Qohelet. But there is no such reference to the author in *Uṭal*. From the external evidence we deduce that the poet is Paṭṭiṉattār. Both the poets hide their *literal* or historical identity behind their *literary* identities: Qohelet is known by his profession or function of preaching in the assembly. Paṭṭiṉattār is known by his origin, the village he came from, i.e., Kāvēripūmpaṭṭinam.

1.1.3. Delighted, Not Depressed

One of the key themes addressed by the poets is meaninglessness (cf. 'vanity' in Eccl 11:4 – 12:8 and *'ōr piṭi nīṟum ilāta uṭampai'* in *Uṭal*). On account of this theme, often these two poets are presumed to be pessimistic and depressed persons. The word, 'meaningless,' according to the Oxford English Dictionary, means (a) 'without meaning or signification; devoid of expression; without purpose. and (b) not possible to interpretation or logical processing.'[412] When Qohelet says that 'all things are meaningless,' he is using the word in its second signification, i.e., everything is not amenable to interpretation or logical processing for we do not know God's plan (cf. 11:4-6). There is

409 R. Johnston, "Confessions of a Workaholic. A Reappraisal of Qoheleth," in *CBQ* 38 (1976), 12-18. Here, 22.

410 Cf. Karuppaiyā, 53.

411 Cf. Karuppaiyā, 54.

412 Oxford Online Dictionary. Accessed from http://www.oxforddictionaries.com/definition/english/meaningless, on 26 April 2016.

purpose in everything, for "in the end God brings everything into judgment" (12:14). Therefore, Qohelet is not a depressed person who in his unnecessary extreme emotional pain makes a sweeping statement that nothing in the world ever has a meaning. If he were to say so, his statement will fall into the fallacy of begging the question, i.e., his very statement will become meaningless logically. Qohelet's deliberate choice to write and teach does not contradict his assertion that all is meaningless. The point Qohelet is trying to make is that we do not know the meaning. We act in vain because we "do not know the work of God, who makes everything" (cf. 11:5). Though he observes the contradictions in life (the innocent suffering, the bad happening to the good, the injustice, the poverty, the ill-governance, etc.), he agrees that everyone dies in the end, and questions the point of working for the future generations who will only destroy your efforts. He never quits searching for meaning and never once preaches that others should quit their journey.

In the same vein, Paṭṭiṉattār writes this poem not out of his frustration that everything is meaningless and will end up in ashes. All he wants to convey to the reader is that things are not permanent. Before one tries and understands the meaning of one he is already thrusted into another thing. Moreover, all that he presents in the poem are not from his own life experiences. For example, when he says that the young man spends his family inheritance on sex workers, it need not mean that Paṭṭiṉattār was flirting women. The presentation in the poem is the fruit of his curious observations of the people of his own time. Paṭṭiṉattār himself was a person who lived his life in wealth and joy. He embraced renunciation not because he was depressed about his life but because of his delight in the Lord Śiva. Nothing could delight him but the Lord.

Therefore, Eccl 11:4-12:8 and *Uṭal* are not the poems written by two depressed men, who hated the world, the women, and the body. They are not about the pointlessness of our endeavours or a cynical viewpoint of life. They are guidebooks to life. They are the reflections of two enlightened men who leave suggestions for the future. After observing the inconsistencies and the changes in human body and the world, Qohelet and Paṭṭiṉattār never ever deny the existence of God. Their faith in God is bolstered in the end. Hence, Qohelet and Paṭṭiṉattār are not pessimists, but godly sages.

1.1.4. Individual in the Crowd

The Law and the Prophets of ancient Israel emphasized relationship with God and the community. The commandment to love God (cf. Deut 6:4) emerged in the context of the well-being of the community. The community of Israel, which was collectively saved from the bondage in Egypt and was driven out of it to settle in the land of Canaan, was invited to maintain and adhere to the covenantal obligations laid out by the Lord. But, as we move to the Wisdom Literature there is a movement from the emphasis on the collective crowd to the individual person. The wise persons of Israel, instead of concentrating on the miraculous events of the Lord in history, began to concentrate on individual human life. Their aim was to bring the universalistic and transcendent implications of divine revelation to the forefront of individual human life. Human person was seen "not only by his place in the continuum of history, but also and especially by his relationship to the constancy of the cosmic order and to the God who created it."[413] The sages, from their observation, experience, and knowledge, evolve rules of behaviour - which can be to some extent applied universally – to help an individual rediscover the meaning in the world.[414] Qohelet, in line with the sages of ancient Israel, from his 'observations' and 'seeing' events 'under the sun,' advices the 'young man' to 'rejoice' and to 'remember,' for these two will make him rediscover the meaning in his life here on earth. Paṭṭiṉattār's time also marked a transition of focus from community to the individual.[415]

1.1.5. 'No' to Organized Religion

Qohelet nowhere in the book uses the title 'YHWH' to refer to God. In our poem, in all the four instances referring to God (11:5, 9; 12:1, and 7), the word he uses is 'Elohim,' the common word for 'God.' In *Uṭal*, Paṭṭiṉattār does not make use of the title 'Śiva.' In v. 17, the title *maṟaiyavaṉ,* though refers to God, points not to the Lord Śiva, but to what has been predestined by God for all human beings. In v. 24, as the poet implores before the Lord Śiva, the explicit name of the Lord is not given. Thus, both the poems reach beyond the scope of organized religions of Judaism and Śaivism. Moreover, the poems describe the concrete and universal human experiences. An individual, be a theist, atheist, non-theist, undergoes all the four life-stages described in the poems.

1.2. Communicative

1.2.1. Genre of the Text

Both the texts are in the form of poetry. The recent critical edition the HB, BHQ, renders Eccl 11:4-12:8 as a poem.[416] The major characteristics of Hebrew poetry such as parallelism, rhythm, artistic repertoire, and word-pictures are found in the text.[417] Paṭṭiṉattār's *Uṭal* is undoubtedly a poem, proven through the internal evidence – the presence of the *cantam* pattern at the beginning of the poem, the literary devices employed and images made use of, proven

413 Hogan, *Biblical Vision*, 222.

414 Cf. Hogan, *Biblical Vision*, 222.

415 Cf. Cf. Karuppaiyā, 53-54.

416 *BHQ*, 50-52.

417 Alter lists these as the major characteristics of Hebrew Poetry. Cf. R. Alter, *The Art of Biblical Poetry* (New York 1985).

through the external evidence, that the text is sung as a poem even today. Both authors have chosen the genre of poetry because of the beauty of expression that the poetry offers. The poems address both the intellect and the emotions of a reader, for poetry expresses both emotion and intellect, inseparably combined in the production of powerful communication. The beauty, imagery, and balance tap the deep psyche of the reader in a more powerful way than a treatise or an essay.

1.2.2. Imaginary Audience

Qohelet makes use of 'young man' as an imaginary audience, through whom he speaks to all the readers. For Paṭṭiṉattār, the Lord Śiva, though is not exactly an imaginary audience, he makes use of the Lord to address the listeners of the poem. Ultimately it is not the Lord Śiva who must know and understand the impermanence and insignificance of the body but the reader himself.

1.2.3. Style

Qohelet employs 32 word-pairs within the poem and Paṭṭiṉattār as many as 24. These word-pairs, from the literary point of view, help the poem stand as a unified whole. The word-pairs employed are both synonymous and antonymous. As far as the motif of human life-stage is concerned, these poems help the reader understand the blend that exists between the stages.

1.2.4. Images

Qohelet and Paṭṭiṉattār often make use of the same word-pictures or images when referring to certain key themes. Let us tabulate them as follows:

Theme	Qohelet	Paṭṭiṉattār
Conception	Sowing of the seed (11:5-6)	Semen being sowed in the womb of a woman (vv. 1-2)
Birth	Seeing the light (11:8)	The first faculty which is developed 'sight' (v. 2). The 'light' in v. 5, though immediately refers to the smile or the teeth, it still conveys the presence of life
Childhood	'Childhood,' 'black-hair' or 'dawn' (11:9-10)	'*Maḻalai*' (v. 5), '*pālar*' (v. 6)
Youth	'Young man,' 'youth' (11:9)	'the crescent' (v. 7)
Old Age	Luminaries darken, fear creeps in, energy fails (12:2-5)	Strength is lost, appearance and beauty yield, the sight fails, body weakens (vv. 12-18)

Death	'Flesh' returns to the earth while 'the life-breath' returns to God (12:7)	The messengers of the God of Death take away the life-breath, and the body becomes the ashes (vv. 20, 24)
Enjoyment	'Rejoice,' 'follow the ways of heart,' 'walk in your sight' (11:9-10)	The young man goes after the sights of his eyes and the desires of his heart (vv. 8-11)
Work	Four types of works are described in 12:3	The human person is basically a worker. He commands things to be done. ('*kaṭaṉmuṟaipēcum eṉavurainâvu*,' v. 18)
Mourning	'The doors of the street are shut, and the mourners are in the street' (12:4-5)	'The neighbours halt their work as a sign of their solidarity with the dead person and his grieved family' (vv. 21-22)

1.3. Conceptual

1.3.1. Human Person in Four Stages

Understanding and evaluating the presentation of human life-stages in the poems of Qohelet and Paṭṭiṉattār is the main focus of our research. The life-stages of a human person described by Qohelet and Paṭṭiṉattār are six: Stages '1' and '6' refer to 'no-life' or 'pre-life' and 'post-life' respectively. When these two stages are excluded, the life-stages are four:

	Stages	**Qohelet**	**Paṭṭiṉattār**
1.	Conception	'the breath of life' (11:5)* 'the sowing of the seed' (11:6)*	'semen that is as small as a semi-dewdrop mixing with ovary' (vv. 1-2)
2.	Birth	'to see the light' (11:7)	'womb opening and the baby falling on the earth' (v. 3)
3.	Childhood	'childhood' and 'black hair' (11:10)	'playing till five years old' (v. 6)
4.	Youth	'youth,' 'young man' (12:1a)	'the lively sixteen years old' (v. 7)
5.	Old Age	'the days of evil' (12:1b-5)	'body stooped and a stick in his hands' (v. 12)
6.	Death	'life-breath returns' (12:6-7)	'the messengers carry away the life-breath' (v. 20)

*In 11:5 is added "the mystery of the origin of a human being in the womb (cf. Ps 139-13-16; Job 10:11-12; 2 Mac 7:22; Qoh. Rab. 5:10) and the still simpler fact that one knows only after birth what kind of child has developed in the womb."[418]

*Targum interprets the 'sowing of the seed' in 11:6 "as a cipher for sexual activity and the procreation of children, and 'morning' and 'evening' as images for youth and old age, and it establishes thereby a connection with vv. 7ff."[419]

1.3.2. God, the Author of Life

The origin and the author of human life is God. For Qohelet it is God who 'makes all things' (11:5). He is the 'creator' (12:1) and the giver of life-breath (12:7). 12:1a is the only time "when the book of Qohelet speaks of God as the 'creator' of humankind."[420] Towards the end, the poet reiterates through a pun, for, "the reader of v. 1 expects 'death' but hears at first 'crater,' then realizes that 'Creator' was what was said. At the end of the poem, this 'Creator' is double recalled: through 'crater' (v. 6) and 'God' (v. 7)."[421] In *Uṭal* the life is extinct when the life-breath exits human body. This exit occurs according to 'what the *Lord* has *written*' (v. 17).

1.3.3. Impermanence of Reality

These two poems portray a dynamic movement. What is 'present' ('life') at the beginning is 'absent' at the end ('death'). The realities – cosmic, social, environmental, and anthropological - are portrayed as if they undergo a drastic change. This change is uncontrollable and often incomprehensible. Only reality that does not change or mutate is the 'Creator God.' 'To think about one's Creator' would then mean initially and above all to be conscious of one's own 'creatureliness' and thus also of one's transitoriness (cf. 12:7).[422] In this respect "12:1a can be understood not only as an exhortation to be conscious of one's transitoriness but also as a call to seize the opportunities granted by God for pleasure and enjoyment."[423] Yet God is also 'Creator' in that he has made everything 'beautiful' (3:11; cf. 7:14), and his 'work' is enduring, immutable (3:14-15; 7:13), and ultimately incomprehensible to human beings (3:11; 8:17; 11:5).[424] The realities are contingent and unpredictable. For Paṭṭiṉattār this

418 Krüger, *Qoheleth*, 195.

419 Krüger, *Qoheleth*, 195.

420 Krüger, *Qoheleth*, 197.

421 Krüger, *Qoheleth*, 197.

422 Cf. M. Gilbert, "La description de la vieillesse en Qohelet XII 1-7 est-elle allégorique?" in J. A. Emerton, ed., *Congress Volume*, Vienna 1980 (*VTSup* 32; Leiden 1981), 101.

423 Krüger, *Qoheleth*, 198.

424 Krüger, *Qoheleth*, 198.

realization emerges at the end of the poem, when the entire human life ends in a handful of ashes.

1.3.4. Miseries of Old Age and Death

Both the poems present childhood and youth as light and pleasure and old age and death as darkness and suffering. Fox, while evaluating the presentation of the old age and death by Qohelet, sums up:

> the poem's purpose is not to convey information; it is to create an attitude toward aging and, more importantly, death. A reader, especially a young one like the youth ostensibly addressed in this unit, may not be aware of the fear, loneliness, and nostalgia for an earlier reality irretrievably lost, which are the lot of many (and to some extent, perhaps all) of the aged, Qohelet undoubtedly among them.[425]

In the same vein, Paṭṭiṉattār also describes the old age as the time of misery and suffering. This presentation is rhetorical or pedagogical as through this presentation, Paṭṭiṉattār drives home in the mind of reader to appreciate the presence of the Creator in this constantly changing life. The allegorical interpretation of Qohelet has made us aware how the old age affects the physique of a human person.

Paṭṭiṉattār goes a step forward. He not only records the physical ailments but also presents the emotional and psychological ailments that an old man undergoes. Qohelet describes these miseries through analogies and metaphors:

v. 12	Loss of youth, loss of richness Loss of teeth and eyesight Appearance of grey hair Body is paralysed Heart treasures hatred and anger
v. 13	Body is stooped He is 'mocked at' He loses his mind Ears are hard of hearing Mouth loses its control and he continues to babble
v. 14	Unable to sleep Tormented by cough, dryness of throat The glands stop functioning Body loses its grip He is scoffed at by the women and the children

425 Fox, "Aging and Death," 69-70. Cited in Krüger, *Qoheleth*, 200.

v. 15	He loses all his respect The excretory system becomes uncontrollable
v. 16	Loss of logic in thinking and speaking Fear creeps in Loss of physical strength Looks for care and concern
v. 17	Despises everything in life
v. 18	Becomes speechless. Communicates through gestures. No in-take of food or liquids is possible.

1.3.5. Life After Life

Though life-spirit returns to God in Qohelet and the life-spirit is taken away by the messengers of the Lord Yamā, both the poets do not make mention of rebirth or life after life. For Qohelet, life ends when the 'dust returns to the earth' and 'the life-breath returns to God.' The death marks the end of human life-breath, and cremation the end of human body. Though Paṭṭiṉattār believes in the theory of rebirth, he is silent about the belief in the present poem.[426]

1.3.6. Ethics of Joy

In Qohelet and Paṭṭiṉattār, happiness is of high value. Though Qohelet meditates on mortality, his underlying thirst is to rejoice. Though our lives are a nanosecond in the history of the entire universe the call to rejoice in this minute moment is never negotiable. Life is not predictable. Things are never certain. Joy is not in the thoughts of the next or tomorrow, but in the grateful acceptance and celebration of the now and today. To rejoice is a religious act according to Qohelet, for if one does not rejoice 'God will bring him into judgment' (11:9).[427] The idea of the exhortation to the young man to enjoy

426 In the Paṭṭiṉattār corpus there have been many instances which support his belief in rebirth. Eg.

'Aṉṉai ettaṉai ettaṉai aṉṉaiyō

Appaṉ ettaṉai ettaṉai appaṉō

Piṉṉai ettaṉai ettaṉai peṇṭirō

Piḷḷai ettaṉai ettaṉai piḷḷaiyō

Muṉṉai ettaṉai ettaṉai ceṉmamō

Mūṭanāi aṭiyēṉum aṟintilēṉ

Iṉṉum ettaṉai ettaṉai ceṉmamō

Eṉceivēṉ kacciyēkampanē."

(Tiruvēkampālai Tiruviruttam).

427 Kierkegaard once wrote: "It takes moral courage to grieve; it takes religious courage to rejoice."

himself in his youth in 11:9 revolves around the theme of 'joy' in 3:12-13, 22; 5:17-19; 8:15; and above all 9:7-10.[428] The ethics of joy calls for an "application of the 'understanding' (heart) and the critical 'observation' of situations and opinions."[429] In 11:9, one finds the summary of the ethic of the book in the sense that it urges for realism, striving for what is attainable: "Enjoy yourself – but with understanding and within the framework of what is realistically possible."[430] Thus 12:1a, together with 11:9b, "summarizes the theological foundations of the ethic of the book of Qoheleth briefly and concisely: the proper attitude toward life grows out of the fact that one receives and accepts 'good' as a 'gift' and 'bad' as the 'judgment' of God (cf. 7:14). 12:1a in no way revokes or restricts the exhortation to pleasure in 11:9a, 10a."[431] The acts of 'remembering' of the Creator and 'rejoicing' are not mutually exclusive but complementary.

In *Uṭal*, the poet presents the childhood and youth as the time of enjoyment and pleasure. At the birth of the child the entire neighbourhood rejoices. The child is vested with ornaments and jewels, which is a sign of pleasure and richness. To the youth are endowed all the possibilities for rejoicing. Before the old age arrives one enjoys all the pleasures reserved to him in life. Moreover, Paṭṭiṉattār uses eschatological visions to promote a particular idea of ethics in this life, and denies the value of worldly possessions.[432]

1.3.7. Accountability of Humans

The creator God demanding an account from the human person is very explicit in Qohelet (cf. 11:9), while it is implicit in *Uṭal*. This accountability is not accompanied by any reward or punishment.

1.3.8. Meaningless Meanings

If we translate '*hebel'* in 11:8, 10, and 12:8 as 'absurd' or 'meaningless,' we understand that Qohelet considers everything 'under the sun' as meaningless. Meanwhile he never claims that 'God' gives meaning to the entire reality. He leaves this to the understanding of the readers. For Paṭṭiṉattār, the entire life is meaningless. For him all things in the world exist to end up in a handful of ashes and dust.

428 Krüger, *Qoheleth*, 196.

429 G. S. Ogden, "Qoheleth XI 7 – XII 8: Qoheleth's Summons to Enjoyment and Reflection," *VT* 34 (1984), 31.

430 Krüger, *Qoheleth*, 196.

431 Krüger, *Qoheleth*, 198.

432 Cf. Kent, *Converting Gender*, 148.

1.3.9. Invitation to Remember God

Qohelet invites the young man to remember God before the advent of evil days of old age and death. Paṭṭiṉattār mourns over his life for the forgetfulness of God with which he has conducted his entire life. The approach of Qohelet to this is 'outside-in,'[433] while that of Paṭṭiṉattār is 'inside-out.'[434]

1.3.10. Socio-Cultural Elements in the Poems

Qohelet by mentioning of the four types of people in 12:3 ('keepers of the house,' 'grinding women,' 'rich and powerful men,' and 'the looking-out-of-the-windows of women') succinctly presents the entire society. The world of Qohelet is characterized by work. Human person is primarily a worker. Paṭṭiṉattār's presentation of neighbourhood is very colourful and elaborate: the womenfolk receive and adore the child (vv. 4-5), the children are at play (v. 6), the young men are educated (v. 7), the girls in the street are attracted (vv. 8-10), the neighbourhood waits on the needy old man (v. 14), and they accompany the dead man to the cremation ground (vv. 20-24). From birth to death, a human person is the key part of the society and its culture.

2. Dissimilarities

2.1. Ethical vs. Philosophical

Qohelet's presentation of life-stages is with the aim of inculcating in the mind of the young person an ethical necessity 'to rejoice' and 'to remember.' The young person addressed in the poem has to make an ethical choice at the end of reading. Paṭṭiṉattār, on the other hand, presents a philosophical reflection on the human life-stages. The addressee of the poem, the Lord Śiva, at the end, does not respond or react. In other words, Eccl 11:4-12:8 is a rhetorical device that advices the youth, while *Uṭal* ia a lamentation over impermanence of life.

2.2. Monologue vs. Soliloquy

Eccl 11:4-12:8 is a monologue whereas Paṭṭiṉattār's *Uṭal* is a soliloquy. A monologue, (from Gk, '*monos*,' ['alone'] and '*logos*' ['word,' or 'speech']) is the speech or verbal presentation presented by a single character. The listener or the addressee does not respond or react to the message he receives. In Eccl 11:4-12:8, it is Qohelet who presents his ideas to the 'young person,' who

433 'Outside-in' means 'starting from the outside and going inward.'

434 'Inside-out' in plain English means, 'with an inner surface turned outwards' or 'having the inner surface turned outwards.' Stephen Covey taking up this term in his famous The Seven Habits of Highly Effective People has made it a life-management principle. According to him, "the 'Inside-Out' approach to personal and interpersonal effectiveness means to start first with self." See, S. R. Covey, *The Seven Habits of Highly Effective People* (London 2004), 14.

never responds or reacts to the message. The monologue of Qohelet serves as a rhetoric tool of exhortation. There is no indication whether the addressee received the message. On the other hand, a soliloquy (from Latin '*solo*' ['alone'], 'loquor' ['to speak']), is a literary device which is used to reveal the innermost thoughts of a character. Here one who talks reflects over his past and talks to himself. The soliloquy of Paṭṭiṉattār makes the reader lament over the impermanence and insignificance of the body.

2.3. Addressing Down vs. Crying Up

Qohelet, as a wise person, who has learnt life-lessons, teaches the young man, who is his virtual student. Qohelet furnishes his exhortation as a direct address to a 'young man' who is *below* him, while Paṭṭiṉattār laments before the Lord Śiva, who is *above* him. The arrow of Qohelet from 'up to down' is reversed in Paṭṭiṉattār as 'down to up:'

2.4. Spirit vs. Matter

The poem *Uṭal* seems to show that human person is a pure matter. Though it makes a reference to the 'life-breath' as taken away by the messengers of the Lord Yamā, he does not speak of its entry into a human being. The description of human conception is silent about the entry of life-breath into a human person. For Qohelet, the case is different. He describes the entry of 'life-breath' at the moment of conception and narrates its exit at the moment of death. Qohelet's description of human person as a blend of matter and spirit is very explicit whereas that of Paṭṭiṉattār is very implicit or is absent.

2.5. Individual vs. Communitarian

The dialogue in Eccl 11:4-12:8 is one-to-one while in *Uṭal* the poet dialogues with the community. Each member in the community is called to evaluate oneself as to see whether one fulfils the duty presented to him.

3. Duet or Duel

Any study on comparative literature, in the final analysis, must answer the question, 'so what?' There are contextual, communicative, and conceptual similarities and considerable dissimilarities between Qohelet and Paṭṭiṉattār and their presentation of human life-stages. Now, so what?

The similarities between the poets do not account for the dependency of one poet on the other for the following reasons:

(a) Both the poets are distant from one another in space and time. Qohelet belongs to the 3rd cent. BCE while Paṭṭiṉattār belongs to the 10th cent. CE. Qohelet might have been a Jew born in Palestine or Egypt. Paṭṭiṉattār is a Tamil born in Kāvēripūmpaṭṭinam.

(b) Both have been written in different languages and both reflect two different worldviews. Qohelet wrote his poem in Hebrew while Paṭṭiṉattār wrote in Tamil. Qohelet's poem reflects a linear worldview of life, where life begins at one point, moves in a particular direction and becomes extinct. Paṭṭiṉattār's poem reflects a cyclic worldview of life, where life begins at one point, moves, appears to be extinct, but is reborn again.

(c) The socio-cultural and religious milieu of both the poets are diverse. Qohelet's poem emerges out of post-Exilic despair and meaninglessness while Paṭṭiṉattār's poem reflects his own conversion, and acts as a catalyst evoking the devotion to the Lord Śiva.

Our placing together of these poems side by side and our narrative analysis of these reveal that the basic human experience of life-death is an archetype that is shared commonly by the entire humanity. Qohelet and Paṭṭiṉattār, the representatives of two different worldviews, still play the same chord when they present the human life-stages as four, the importance of the realization of God-factor in the lives, and the complementary contradictions and paradoxes with which human persons must put up to live.

Qohelet and Paṭṭiṉattār not only bring out the symphony present in life-stages, but they themselves are synchronized so well that we are able to get a unified view of life. The poets together create a symphony. The relationship between them is more a duet than a duel.

B. Poets and We: Perspectives and Queries

1. Is God a Cultural Memory?

Qohelet in 12:1 says to the young man 'to remember' the Creator. In *Uṭal* v. 24, Paṭṭiṉattār laments that he has forgotten to 'remember' God all throughout his life. Both the poets remember God at the wake of a catastrophe: for Qohelet, the catastrophe is 'the evil days' that are round the corner; for Paṭṭiṉattār, the catastrophe is the death and inutility of human existence. Does Qohelet take in God as a 'cultural memory' to make people always remember the evil days of Babylonian exile? For, from the time of Jerome to J. Barbour, there have been assumptions that through Eccl 11:7-12:7, Qohelet wanted to inculcate in the minds of its readers the memory of the Exile through a vivid presentation of the various images and word-pictures. And is not Paṭṭiṉattār creating a cultural memory of God in the Tamil society which was then dominated by the so-called atheistic religions Jainism and Buddhism, which emphasized the role of body and its intellect? When Buddhism preached everything as impermanent and passing, Paṭṭiṉattār, through his poem proposes an alternative paradigm: though everything changes, there is a God, who never changes, yet is the cause of every change. These poets play a key role in creating theologies for the world. They create a cultural memory and name it God.

In ANE religions, the gods leave the ruined cities. The prophet Ezekiel envisions the Glory of YHWH leaving the city of Jerusalem, which is (to be) ruined by Babylonian exile (cf. ch. 10). When the people were exiled they were literally uprooted from the Promised Land, the Land of their forefathers where stood the Temple.[435] Their hearts were restless. 'Why did God abandon us? Did God forget our sacrifices? Did not God say to Abraham that I will leave the city undestroyed if I find at least five righteous persons? (cf. Gen 18:16-33) Were all we unrighteous and unfaithful in the eyes of God? Where is God when these sufferings occur?' – these were the questions that the exiled Israelites asked. No prophet ever could console them. Even after the return to Jerusalem the questions must have lingered in their minds. To these people, Qohelet taking on the elements of the Exilic events, creates a cultural memory, which is God. Qohelet who dreams of restoration of Exile into an Eden experience, takes on the same 'Elohim' and creates a cultural memory out of Him. As we have observed earlier, Qohelet always uses 'Elohim' to refer to God and he never uses the tetragrammaton, for the Lord is absent in the Exile and it is ideal to use the distant and the remote existing God, 'Elohim.'[436]

Jerome, who replaces 'the young man' of 11:9 with 'the Hebrews,' drawing on Qohelet Rabbah writes,

> Therefore enjoy your youth O Israel…before your time of bondage comes…Before Nebuchadonosor comes, or Titus, Vespian's Son, is summoned by the prophets and their prophecies are fulfilled…When the doors of the temple are closed Jerusalem will be made humble and the Chaldean will come as if by the song of a bird, called thus in the words of Jeremiah, and the singing girls with the lute in the temple choir will become silent…the weeping and crying will wander in the street and will be hemmed in by the enemy's siege. Be happy, therefore, Israel, in your youth.[437]

Thus, for Qohelet, God is a cultural memory, the remembrance of whom will make an individual live with hope amidst despair.

Paṭṭiṉattār presents a catastrophe that happens in the human body. Body is an instrument. Through this instrument a man is able to enjoy the pleasure of a woman. It is through this he works and earns his profit. At every prayer to the Lord, a man asks for the good health from the Lord. For, if the body yields to sickness, no woman would embrace him, no profit-earning would

435 The city-lament motif in Eccl 12:2-5 is an evidence that Qohelet was conscious of this theme when he composed his poem. Cf. Barbour, *Story of Israel*, 143-46.

436 Cf. J. A. Loader, *Polar Structures in the Book of Qohelet* (Berlin 1979), 128.

437 Cited in Barbour, *Story of Israel*, 138.

be possible, and he would soon embrace death. For Paṭṭiṉattār, the body is for this temporary world. But, life is long. Through this body one is able to attain *moksha.* The body which was given to the soul or lent to the soul, instead of assisting the man in his salvific process, makes him sin all the more. The greatest of these sins is that man begins to identify himself with his body. When the body ails and dies, the man realizes it was life-breath that moved the body and it was in fact life-breath that was carrying the body. The death can happen at any time. What is necessary is to remember God, the giver of life-breath, when one is alive.

2. The God-Talk in the Poems

2.1. Two Gods: 'Creator God,' 'Created God'

The basic premise in both Eccl 11:4-12:8 and *Uṭal* is God, not man. For Ecclesiastes, "God is the ultimate standard by which all motives, and forms of behavior in human society must be interpreted."[438] God is the *summum bonum*, the source and end of all values, and the world and its phenomena is His creation.[439]

Qohelet at the first instance regards God as the Creator.[440] Creation and created order provide the background to ancient wisdom literature. "Ecclesiastes adopts the same language regarding the ways of the earth (1:4-7), the Creator (12:1), and the nature of human toil in the cosmos."[441] Leaning on the traditional religious beliefs, he affirms that God made everything in the world upright and in pristine glory. Although Qohelet has been understood to be an Epicurean or Stoic, he based his patterns of life firmly upon reverence for God and observance of the divine precepts. His basic proposition of wisdom, therefore, is that life in its manifold aspects is entirely devoid of meaning

438 There are 12 key theological themes in the Ecclesiastes: (1) There is divine supervision of all human actions 95:1); (2) The world came to existence as a new being (3:11, 14; 7:13); (3) God created the world beautiful and with utmost perfection (3:11, 14); (4) Human mind can never grasp the essence of God (7:23, 24; 5:1; 8:17); (5) Humans are composites of different elements and at the moment of death the elements disintegrate (3:12; 5:17; 11:10); (6) The failures and afflictions that affect a person are because of his own deed (7:29); (7) God does what he wishes to do and none can question his authority (8:4); (8) Man is created to attain wisdom, to fear God, and to obey His commandments (7:19; 12:13); (9) What concerns angels is not the subject matter of enquiry to man's mind (5:7); (10) The acts of divine service and devout practices are good (9:10); (11) The life-breath is eternal and returns to God when man dies (12:7); and (12) There are rewards and punishments to man's actions (3:17; 8:6, 13; 11:9; 12:4). Cf. Z. Faier, *Introduction to the Book of Qoheleth* (New York 1988), 10-11.

439 Harrison, *Introduction to the Old Testament*, 1084.

440 "Qohelet echoes traditional understanding of God as Creator albeit in different language." J. L. Crenshaw, *Ecclesiastes. A Commentary* (Philadelphia 1987), 23.

441 O'Dowd, "Epistemology in Ecclesiastes," 210.

without God.[442] Qohelet sees the world as it is.[443] He knows God only from a distance and he leads us to the conclusion to fear God, after taking us to desperation and hopelessness.[444] It is God who gives meaning to the world. Kidner says, "We face the appalling inference that nothing has meaning, nothing matters under the sun. It is then that we can hear, as the good news which it is, that everything matters – 'for God will bring every deed into judgment.'"[445]

The invitation to remember 'God' in 12:1, "marks the final demystification of Qohelet's illusory 'I'. We are not autonomous selves but creaturely, relational selves, and we are relational selves primarily in relation to God."[446]

In the rest of the book, Qohelet presents God as a hard ruler, who shows the world a grim countenance, who does not seem to love mankind, who is unpredictable, who lays down the rules and judges those who transgress them, but he does so inconsistently, and from the human perspective at least, rather erratically.[447] All truths are partial, all thinkers inadequate. Qohelet's hard and lonely theology is only one vision of the Infinite.[448]

For Paṭṭiṉattār God is the Creator and the Ruler. Man is a servant of God. Man enjoys authentic freedom only if he participates in the liberty of God. And he participates in God's freedom only by remaining subject to God. He is called to love God without constraint. God is eternal. God is a giver of life-breath. God gives meaning to human living.

Both the poets speak only about the Creator God. The 'created God' or 'no god' of organized religions are not important to them. This fact appeals to the universality of human thirst for transcendence.

2.2. God whom We Can't Pray To

Qohelet does not pray to God. Zimmermann says that Qohelet "never offers a prayer nor cries out to God for mercy though he suffered much."[449] "If prayer is 'communion' with God, Qohelet demonstrated no intimacy with God on that point. Prayer is nowhere in the book."[450] Qohelet has a deterministic view of God rather than fatalist or pessimistic. This is the reason for the absence of prayer or any direct communication with God. Humans can never change

---

442 Harrison, *Introduction to the Old Testament*, 1083-84.

443 N. Lohfink, *Qohelet. A Continental Commentary* (Minneapolis 2003), 2.

444 Kidner, *The Message of Ecclesiastes*, 14.

445 Kidner, *The Message of Ecclesiastes,* 20.

446 C. G. Bartholomew, "The Theology of Eccelsiastes," in *Words are like Goads*, 371.

447 Fox, *Time to Tear Down*, 136-37.

448 Fox, *Time to Tear Down*, 138.

449 Zimmermann, *Inner World of Qohelet*, xii.

450 Anderson, *Qohelet and Its Pessimistic Theology*, 122.

the mind of God (cf. 5:1-6; 7:16-17). This also maybe because Qohelet wants to make a silent protest against the Exile brought about by God. Even when the evil days are round the corner, there is no need for prayer. For the prayer does not bring about any change. The evil days will befall everyone of us. On the other hand, Paṭṭiṉattār's poem is a prayer to God. Though his prayer will not stop the aging process and the suffering involved in the life-stages, fixing one's mind on God will make one live a better life.

3. Human Person: Who? Why?

Greek philosophy and its derivative scholastic theology view human person rather dualistically – matter and form, body and soul, etc. That is why in popular Christian parlance we speak of offering mass for the departed souls, mission as saving souls, etc. Furthermore, human person is considered almost exclusively as self-sufficient individual (= the I-self) rather than the we-self rooted in the communitarian relationship. According to the monistic view (*Advaita Vedānta*) of Śankara, Brahman is the only reality, and the world, as it appears, is illusory. Human person is *jīvātman*. In reality, there is no difference between the *jīvātman* and Brahman. Sankhya system considers human person as made of two principles: *purusha and prakrti.* In contrast with these perspectives, the poems of Eccl 11:4-12:8 and *Uṭal* present a biblical anthropology which is unitive and holistic. For, they perceive human persons not dualistically, but unitively, not as I-self but as we-self. For instance, when the Eccl 11:10 speaks about 'flesh' it emphasizes the weak, fragile, mortal human aspect and it also underscores the aspect of relatedness. Even when there appears a contrast such as between *'flesh'* and *'life-breath'* it does not imply duality but it is only a question of emphasis. Now let us consider the anthropology of these poems.

At the outset, let us consider the anthropological terminologies used in the poems:[451]

a. Flesh. It is the substance of human physical existence and is subject to attack, injury, damage, and decay. Human persons are flesh in the form of the physical body which is weak, feeble, vulnerable, and perishable, when trouble and sickness befall it. The related word-field of 'flesh' in the poem is 'dust' (Eccl 12:7).

b. Heart.[452] At the centre of human life is the heart, which is the seat of all thought, planning, reflection, explanation, ambition, and

451 Hogan, *Biblical Vision,* 243-45.

452 The lexicographical meanings are: 1. the heart; 2. seat of vital force; 3. one's inner self; 4. inclination; 5. determination; 6. the will; 7. attention, reason; 8. the mind; 9. the conscience; 10. inside, middle. Cf. L. Koehler – W. Baumgartner – J. Stamm, *The Hebrew and Aramaic Lexicon of the Old Testament* (Leiden 2000), 13-15. SA. J. K. Bruckner, *Healthy Human Life. A Biblical Witness* (Oregaon 2012), 81.

decision. It is also the place where the whole person experiences life and suffers joy, sorrow, anxiety and fear, bitterness and hope. This process of reflection, planning and decision takes place in the hidden depths. The wholeness and integrity of the person are dependent on the clear direction and wholeness of heart. The heart refers to the "centre of the human physical and spiritual life (and) to the entire inner life of a person."[453]

c. Life-breath. In Hebrew, 'spirit' wind, breath of life, life-giving power (cf. Gen 2:7). The divine breath enters and makes one into a living being in unity and wholeness (Eccl 11:5) and when the breath departs man returns to dust (Eccl 12:7). In the face of death, man commends his spirit into God's hands and so yields his life to God (SA. *Uṭal* v. 24). Paṭṭiṉattār also speaks of this life-spirit as 'breath' in v. 18 and 'uyir' in v. 20. The Second Creation Account uses the word 'soul' (cf. Gen 2:7) to refer to the life-breath.[454]

3.1. Imago and Similitudo Dei

The first picture of human person that these poems paint is that a human person is in the image and likeness of God. Qohelet, who plays on intertextual echoes with Gen 1-11, makes a direct reference to Gen 1:26-28 when he says, 'your creator,' and 'life-breath returns to God.' The image and likeness is more spiritual than physical. For Qohelet God is a supreme sovereign, who is incomprehensible to human minds. He can never undergo mutations. But, the human physical body is susceptible to mutation. God's image is not in the physical body of a human person but in the life-breath which is present in him. For Paṭṭiṉattār the life-breath is the God-thing in human person. The body is only a container. It is the life-breath that moves the body. But, in ignorance human persons identify themselves with their physical bodies. In Roman Catholic anthropology[455] the focus is less on the origins of humankind and more on the future of humanity. Thus, even in reading the account of the creation of humankind the real concern is eschatological; it is to recognise the future that is offered as a promise of God and in which we already participate.

---

453 A. Luc, 'lev,' in *New International Dictionary of the Old Testament Theology and Exegesis,* 2:749-54.

454 "The concept נֶפֶשׁ characterizes human existence in a distinctive manner. Localized in the throat, the organ through which nourishment is taken, it calls attention to human need and desire; the longing, seeking and yearning of human beings. It also represents the seat of spiritual feeling and inner conditions. The human being is 'soul' which approximates what we mean by person, the 'I'." Hogan, *Biblical Vision*, 245.

455 Christian anthropology extensively addresses human person as created in the image and likeness of God, his or her freedom, body and soul, sin and grace, the mystery of death and of resurrection and the mystery of the personal and communitarian final destiny.

The image of God is therefore not so much something static that is given to us as something that is realised in us throughout our life by the working of the Holy Spirit as we live an authentic human life.

3.2. Human Personhood

A human being is a person-in-relation. Everyone lives out the belief of 'being as communion.'[456] In a community a person is re-shaped and re-located. Here comes into picture the ethical element. It means first care for the fellow human beings and then reach out the world of culture and the larger web of relationships between individual and communities. At last, it means care for the world of nature, so that we do not plunder and destroy it, but rejoice in it as God's good creation.[457] The poems present human person as related. The key lesson the text teaches us is simple: 'to be' is 'to be related'; 'to be' is 'to be-with'. In the final analysis, relationality constitutes human personhood.[458] The concept of personhood is understood today in terms of peoplehood.[459] Humans experience life at two extremes: isolation and identification. Relationality is the middle way between these two extreme levels.

Humans are social by nature. Paṭṭiṉattār makes the human birth as an explicit outcome of social interaction between a man and a woman. A person who is born out of a social interaction, or as a sign and fruit of such interaction, is called to interact with one another throughout his life. This innate archetype which searches for the other is active at all stages of his life: at birth he is dependent on his mother and neighbourhood, at childhood he needs the company of his playmates, at youth he is dependent on persons, who lead him to self-discovery. At old age, he becomes dependent again. Till his burial or cremation, he needs the company of the people in the neighbourhood. The relationship that exists at this realm is that of inter-subjectivity. This relation of love is characterized by immediacy, reciprocity, and availability. This relationship is constant. The wife who was at the good times of man's life is there to assist at his ill health and to mourn when he dies. Paṭṭiṉattār also mentions of another type of relationship that possibly

456 The phrase is borrowed from the title of J. D. Zizioulas, *Being as Communion. Studies in Personhood and the Church* (Crestwood 1993).

457 Cf. C. E. Gunton, "Human Being as Relational Being: Twelve Theses for a Christian Anthropology," in C. Schwöbel – C. E. Gunton, eds., *Persons, Divine and Human* (Edinburgh 1991), 141-65.

458 To put in the Heideggerian term, the world of Dasein is a 'with-world'. Being is "being-with others" [M. Heidegger, *Being and Time* (New York 1962), 155]. For Gabriel Marcel, to exist (esse) is to exist-with (co-esse) [G. Marcel, *Creative Fidelity* (New York 1964), xvii].

459 Cf. J. Kopas, *Sacred Identity. Exploring a Theology of the Person* (New York 1994), 155-60.

can exist, i.e., 'relation of functionality.' The young man, for example, looks at the girls in the streets, and goes after the sex workers. Here the young man sees another person merely as functionaries. There is no love involved in this relationship. This is a 'give-and-take' or 'take-and-give' type relationship. Here one is indifferent, anonymous, and manipulative. The other is seen as 'tool to be handled.'

Later development in social sciences has made us aware of the long-forgotten quality of a human person, i.e., relationality.[460] Overemphasizing on rationality gives an exclusive identity to a person and necessarily alienates one from the other while relationality binds all – male or female, black or white, Asian or European, Christian or Hindu, poor or rich. Only the understanding of human beings as relational, interrelated and interdependent can help us respond to the serious challenges facing humankind today.

3.3. Persons in Process

Human persons are always in the process of becoming. From conception to birth, from birth to childhood, from childhood to youth, from youth to old age, and from old age to death. At no point a person can be said that he is completely a human person. It is this 'becoming' dimension that makes the 'being' of the person. This thought is well-construed by Qohelet and Paṭṭiṉattār. Qohelet and Paṭṭiṉattār portray human beings as weak, fragile mortals destined to death and decay and at the same time they are interconnected, interdependent, and interrelated.

3.4. Persons as Suffering

The poems also present humans as suffering. The sufferings have a vocational purpose. Human beings exist at two levels: 'being' level and 'becoming' level. 'Becoming' involves change and change often entails suffering. Human suffering when accepted positively provides an occasion for personal growth. To make suffering a path involves faith, freedom, conviction and commitment. 'What has it to do with me?' This question rises at least in important moments of our life. Human persons fail to 'feel-with' the other. This is the result of our indifference. The poems challenge us today to *own* our suffering and to feel with the other in suffering. This solidarity with other ultimately emerges from inner freedom. Authentic suffering with others makes us grow as full human persons.

3.5. Cry for the Transcendent

Another anthropological dimension that emerges from the texts is the cry of the human beings for the transcendent. There is an inner dynamism in every

460 Cf. D. Goleman, *Social Intelligence. The New Science of Human Relationships* (New York 2007).

human person which makes him or her raise towards the 'transcendent.' This cry arises out of his experience of finiteness at various moments of his life. Qohelet's problem is not primarily cosmological, 'what is the world like?' but anthropological, 'what does it mean to be human?'[461] The scope of Qohelet is to rediscover the meaning of human life in the presence of God.

3.6. Human Person: Meaning-Making

Qohelet's final coda, though states that 'everything is meaningless,' the statement is not sweeping but relative:[462] human labour or toil, wisdom, principle of justice, pleasure, and religious practices seem to be meaningless at the outset, do offer man a meaning. There are certain things such as the joy that God gives, the fear of God, and God himself, which are never *hebel.* Embracing these realities will make a person find meaning in life despite life's uncertainties, incongruities, absurdities, and mysteries. Paṭṭiṉattār, when finally says that the whole life ends up in a handful of ashes, he does not negate the meaning in each stage of human life. The sociologist Peter Berger asserts that there is a fundamental human need for meaning, and that without a framework of meaning, neither collective nor individual life is possible.[463]

3.7. Human Person: Joyful

Our poems define human existence as joyful. The desire for happiness is natural and innate.[464] Qohelet proposes 'joy' as a prerogative for life. 'Remembering God' is the first step to joy. Eaton says, "The preacher wishes to deliver us from a rosy-colored, self-confident, godless life, with its inevitable cynicism and bitterness, and from trusting in wisdom, pleasure, wealth, and human justice or integrity. He wishes to drive us to see that God is there, that he is good and generous, and that only such an outlook makes life coherent and fulfilling."[465] Paṭṭiṉattār throughout the poem does not forget to mention the joy which is involved in each stage.

461 Seow, *Ecclesiastes*, 102.

462 For a discussion to see whether toil, wisdom, justice, pleasure and religion are meaningless, see V. Onwukeme, *Searching for Meaning with Qoheleth* (Longford 2012).

463 P. Berger, *Pyramids of Sacrifice. Political Ethics and Social Change* (New York 1976), 166-69. Cited in Waltke, *Old Testament Theology,* 958.

464 "The desire to happiness is of divine origin. God has placed it in the human heart in order to draw man to the One who alone can fulfill it." *Catechism of the Catholic Church*, no. 1718.

465 M. A. Eaton, *Ecclesiastes. An Introduction and Commentary* (The Tyndale Old Testament Commentaries 16. Downers Grove 1983), 48.

3.8. Human Person: Born to Die

It is the reality of death that makes rational the way of life which Qohelet commends to his readers, with its focus on living each moment of life joyfully before God rather than on the pursuit of wisdom, wealth, or any other human end that comes under the heading 'chasing after the wind.'[466] Crenshaw believes that death is important to Qohelet because its arbitrariness is troubling to him. According to Crenshaw, Qohelet is unable to find correlation between the way of life and the timing of death. Death nullifies any personal human achievement and mocks human desire for fame and lasting memory.[467] Paṭṭiṉattār's portrayal of human person as 'born to die' is evident in vv. 21-24.

4. Life Before and After

Qohelet and Paṭṭiṉattār focus on life-before-death, not life-after-death. The abstract thinking and hypothetical suppositions are not their interests.

Qohelet does not present the concept of afterlife or resurrection. His reference to the eternal dwelling place (12:5) points to eternal death (cf. 9:10). Qohelet's eschatological reflection is about the personal *eschaton* (12:1-7; cf. 3:21).[468] Though God's judgment is referred to in 11:9 (SA. 3:17; 9:5; 12:14) it is not clear if it is a judgment after death, during the life on the earth, or in a distant future. "The notion of God as judge and arbiter of all is done on earth is crucial to Qohelet's theology."[469] Qohelet also does not say that death is incurred on account of sins (cf. 1 Cor 15). Qohelet speaks about life-breath returning to God (12:7). According to Hinson, "Qohelet never intended his readers to think of the life-breath as having independent life and sharing a personal relationship with God in heaven. He meant that the power of life has been withdrawn. The departure of the spirit was part of the final break up and disappearance of the human individual."[470] Although, Qohelet does not utter a single word about afterlife he might still have the concept in his mind. However, it is interesting to observe that someone who speaks so much about death does not address afterlife, or resurrection, or eternal life.

Paṭṭiṉattār, though a staunch believer of rebirth, makes no reference to it in *Uṭal*. According to this poem, life-spirit is taken away by the messengers of the Lord of Death and the body ends up in a handful of ashes. According to Śaiva Siddhantha school, liberation is attained through the means of *charya*, *kriya*,

466 Provan, *Ecclesiastes*, 39.

467 Crenshaw, *Ecclesiastes*, 25.

468 But it is plausible that the personal eschaton which makes reference to future judgments implies the resurrection or at least life after death.

469 Ogden, *Qoheleth*, 230.

470 D. F. Hinson, *Theology of the Old Testament* (London 2001), 89.

yoga and *jnana*.[471] The path of charya involves serving Lord Śiva in a temple or religious place by performing such tasks as cleaning, cooking, carrying water, gathering flowers etc. The path of kriya involves performing devotional tasks such as worshipping the idol of Śiva, singing devotional songs, reciting the mantras, narrating stories about Śiva or doing personal service to Śiva like a son does to his father. The path of yoga involves practicing yoga exercises and meditation and contemplation. By following this path one gets an opportunity to live constantly in the company of Śiva and become his spiritual companion. The path of knowledge is the fourth path. It is the best and most direct path to the world of Śiva. The other three are actually considered inferior to it. Though Paṭṭiṉattār does not seem to propose any of these paths to attain liberation, his present poem seems to tell us that his realization is because of his knowledge.

What is necessary for Qohelet is to live this present life in a worthy manner. For that he puts forward a *material spirituality* to live the present in a worthy manner.[472] Bonhoeffer who appeals to 11:8-10 in his discussion of 'the Right to Bodily Life' notes,

> Man is a bodily being, and remains so in eternity as well. Bodiliness and human life belong inseparably together. And thus, the Bodiliness which is willed by God to be the form of existence of man is entitled to be called an end in itself...It is in the joys of the body that it becomes apparent that the body is an end in itself within the natural life. If the body were only a means to an end man would have no right to bodily joys ... This would have very far-reaching consequences for the Christian appraisal of the body, housing, clothing, recreation, play and sex. 473

Now another question arises: Is life determined by God? Does Qohelet advocate determinism or fatalism or predestination? Towner suggests,

> By the simple device of shifting the emphasis from the admitted determinism of an order in which God has already ordained everything to the human responsibility or freedom that Qohelet also admittedly affirms, the weight comes down not on a tragic fatalism – human beings in the hands of a distant, all-powerful, and arbitrary God who causes good and evil alike – but on the opportunity for human happiness in a world in which God is utterly sovereign and people are truly free.[474]

Ultimately what is needed? Since all are dying beings we are called to be more sympathetic with one another. This call involves becoming a responsible citizen, seeing the consequences of our actions, learning from our mistakes,

471 Cf. M. Dhavamony, *Love of God according to Saiva Siddhanta. A Study in the Mysticism and Theology of Saivism* (London 1971), 53-54.

472 Bartholomew, *Words and Goads*, 371.

473 D. Bonhoeffer, *Ethics* (London 1955), 113.

474 Towner, "Ecclesiastes," 284.

avoiding immediate gratification with its possibly dangerous consequences (sex, drugs, etc.), getting rid of our consumeristic and advertising tendencies, greed and compulsive shopping, and learning how to say 'no.' We are often disillusioned. That which seems to promise us happiness turns out to be sour and salty.

The centre of Eccl 11:4-12:8 is the 'young person.' In *Uṭal* as well the poet concentrates on the theme of youth at length. The youth of one's life is the time of change. The characteristics of the youth are: energy and enthusiasm, creativity and spontaneity, integrity and bias-free attitude, openness and dynamism, motivation and achievement, vision and mission, unity and solidarity, and non-conformism and discontinuity.

To remember one's creator in the days of one's youth (12:1) is not a call to vigorous service of YHWH when young, but a reminder that youth will not last. Death comes to all. Hope will be lost. Here, therefore, a sober existence, one that is tempered by the knowledge that death awaits everyone and everything. It is this final stamp on Qohelet's words that should also influence our understanding of the *carpe diem* passages as providing no more than temporary meaning.[475]

The poets offer two key lessons to the youth: (a) About the reality of decay and death and what this signifies about God and about ourselves. This is important, because young people often think of themselves as indestructible and all but eternal, and youth culture often seems designed to promote this self-understanding. (b) About the goodness of God and to be encouraged to live responsively to this goodness. This involves virtue, of course, but also involves joy. It is important to speak about both.

For the poets, death is a leveling agent. With Qohelet we have the only HB author who openly questions death. Qohelet and Paṭṭiṉattār do not romanticize or play the emotional tone of death. Death is for them a fact of life that makes all human activities abusrd.[476] Death pervades their entire poems. Our lives simply mirror the larger picture.[477]

5. Harmony of Life-Stages: Unity of the Opposites

Qohelet and Paṭṭiṉattār equally treat the unity of opposites present in the world. The contradictions and the dialectics which are in the society cater to the growth of the entire society. The human life advances through these opposites. The unity of opposites was first suggested by Heraclitus (ca. 535 - 475 BCE), a pre-Socratic Greek philosopher. Taoism, which emerged as a religious thinking during this period in China also was centered on this concept. This theory tells

475 Enns, *Ecclesiastes*, 135.

476 Enns, *Ecclesiastes*, 130.

477 Enns, *Ecclesiastes*, 134.

that the reality is a duality of polar opposites. Or the reality manifests itself in opposites. In Taoism, Yin and Yang are the manifestations. Yin stands for the characteristics of softness, passivity, femininity, darkness, the valley, and the negative, Nonbeing, while Yang refers to characteristics such as hardness, masculinity, brightness, the mountain, activity, Being. Yin and Yang bring dynamic balance of forces of movement and rest, activity and passivity, so that the balance point returns to center. Tao, the unity of the opposites emerges. The reality manifests itself in two ways at the same time.[478]

Qohelet presents the seven contradictions in the poem. The polar of opposites is a technique of merismus – of a situation in a relationship which is intended to depict a unified whole, which is employed in Sumerian and Egyptian poems as well.[479] When the opposites stand together they present a reality, where the whole is greater than the sum of its parts.

1.	'morning' (11:6)	'evening' (11:6)
2.	'light' (11:7)	'darkness' (11:8)
3.	'good' (11:7)	'evil' (11:10)
4.	'spirit' (11:4)	'flesh' (11:10)
5.	'to come' (11:8)	'to go' (12:5)
6.	'sun' (11:7; 12:2)	'moon' (12:2)
7.	'God' (11:5, 9; 12:7)	'man' (12:5)

478 As soon as beauty is known by the world as beautiful, it becomes ugly.
As soon as virtue is being known as something good, it becomes evil.
Therefore, being and non-being give birth to each other.
Difficult and easy accomplish each other.
Long and short form each other.
High and low distinguish each other.
Sound and tone harmonize each other.
Before and after follow each other as a sequence.
Realizing this, the saint performs effortlessly according to the natural
Way without personal desire,
and practices the wordless teaching thru one's deeds.
The saint inspires the vitality of all lives, without holding back.
He nurtures all beings with no wish to take possession of.
He devotes all his energy but has no intention to hold on to the merit.
When success is achieved, he seeks no recognition.
Because he does not claim for the credit, hence shall not lose it.
(*Tao Te Ching,* Chapter 2). Translated from the Italian e-version. a cura di Luciano Parinetto, Collezione 'Civiltà antiche, 1' Milano, 1999. Daode jing (Tao Te Ching) a philosophical and political text written by Laozi (Lao Tzu).

479 R. K. Harrison, *Introduction to the Old Testament* (Peabody 2004), 1083.

For every force in reality there is an equal and opposite counterforce.[480] The unity of opposites invites us to understand life in its totality and to grasp it with its dynamics, with its movement, vibrations, and dances. Moreover, the human person is part of the universal web of interconnectedness.

Loader comments on the contradictions in Ecclesiastes:

> "In all the other examples of protest literature known to us there is relaxation of tension in the end because one or another solution to the crisis is offered. But in Ecclesiastes the tension continues to the end; that is the most important characteristic of the entire book. One element is repeatedly placed in opposition to another and the frustration resulting from the tension between opposing elements is accentuated. Polarization creates tension, and tension, when continued, means frustration."[481]

Paṭṭiṉattār's poem also contains seven pairs of opposites:

i. *oru maṭa mātu* (v. 1) // *oruvaṉ* (v. 1)
ii. *vintu* (v. 1) // *curōṇitam* (v. 1)
iii. *makalirkaḷ* (v. 4) // *iḷamaintar* (v. 23)
iv. *maḻalai moḻintu* (v. 5) // *nāvuṟaṅki* (v. 18)
v. *vaḷarpiṟai* (v. 7) // *matiyumaḻintu* (v. 13)
vi. *puviyilviḻuntu* (v. 3) // *uyirkoṭupōka* (v. 20)
vii. *vantu pukuntu* (v. 2) // *ventuviḻuntu* (v. 24)

Paṭṭiṉattār's another noteworthy song *Koyil Tiruakaval* (lines 6-13) also reflects the contrasting elements found in our poem:

piṟantaṉa iṟakkum
iṟantaṉa piṟakkum
tōṉṟiṉa maṟaiyum
maṟantaṉa tōṉṟum
peruttaṉa ciṟukkum
ciṟuttaṉa perukkum
uṇarntaṉa maṟakkum
maṟantaṉa uṇarum
aruntiṉa malamām
puṉaintaṉa aḻukkām
uvappaṉa veṟuppām
veṟuppaṉa uvappām[482]

---

480 This is Newton's Third Law of Motion.

481 Loader, *Ecclesiates*, 10.

482 "Whatever is born will die
Whatever is dead will be born(again)!
Whatever appears will disappear

When we take something its counterpart also comes with us. Like in a coin, when we take its one side, the other side also comes with. Like in holding a stick, when you hold it on one end, the other end also comes with it. When we are born, death comes with it. The youth comes with old age. The health with sickness. The relationships with loneliness. The sound with silence. The satisfaction with hunger. The light with darkness. The strength with weakness. The gain with the loss.

Paṭṭiṉattār goes to the root of the reality and tells that every reality is a play or unity of opposites. But, unfortunately, he ends in upholding one and denying the other. He failed to say both the opposites have to be appreciated and lived out. Paṭṭiṉattār, who came the half way, could not make the journey full.[483]

C. Conclusion

After juxtaposing the poems and the poets side by side to compare and contrast them we have moved to questions and doubts. The comparative method used in this chapter has brought to light the dynamics present in the poems and their mutual embrace. What stands out in the comparison is that the poets are in one accord in their portrayal of human life-stages.

Whatever disappears will appear!
Whatever is big will be small
Whatever is small will be big!
Whatever is felt will be forgotten
Whatever is forgotten will be felt
Whatever is eaten becomes excretion!
Whatever is worn becomes dirt!
Whatever is pleasurable becomes hated
Whatever is hated becomes pleasurable!"
It is apt to recall the words of Qohelet, who also has a poem expressing the same mindset:
"a time to be born, and a time to die;
a time to plant, and a time to pluck up what is planted;
a time to kill, and a time to heal;
a time to break down, and a time to build up;
a time to weep, and a time to laugh;
a time to mourn, and a time to dance;
a time to throw away stones, and a time to gather stones together;
a time to embrace, and a time to refrain from embracing;
a time to seek, and a time to lose;
a time to keep, and a time to throw away;
a time to tear, and a time to sew;
a time to keep silence, and a time to speak;
a time to love, and a time to hate;
a time for war, and a time for peace." (Eccl 3:2-8).

483 Cf. Karuppaiyā, 90-93.

V. THE HERMENEUTICAL ARC

The present chapter is concerned about drawing a hermeneutical arc between the poems of our study and the entire Ecclesiastes and Paṭṭiṉattār corpus. The aim of doing this is to establish the theme of our study, 'divine-human symphony,' as the hermeneutical centre of the two poets. This chapter is developed in two stages: first, we evaluate the structure of Eccl 11:4-12:8, and situate the poem in the contexts of the Book, the Wisdom Literatuare, and the entire HB; second, we evaluate the structure of *Uṭal*, and situate the poem in the contexts of Paṭṭiṉattār corpus and entire Śaivite literature.[484]

A. Eccl 11:4-12:8 in Context

1. Evaluating the Structure

Let us pick up the key words that have emerged in our analysis of the poem and arrange in a structure to see how the poem stands as a unified whole threaded by the theme of 'divine-human symphony:'

What is 'Not Knowable'
11:4 "clouds"
11:5 "child in a mother's womb"
11:5 "life-breath to the child"
11:5-6 "you cannot know"
11:6 "sow your seed"
11:6 "the morning and the evening"
11:6 "happy outcome"

11:7 "light is sweet"

What is 'Knowable'
11:7 "eyes to see the sun"
11:8 "many years of life"
11:8 "many days of darkness"

484 Since the Śaivite literature is very wide, we will consider only two representational texts: one by Tirumūlar and another by Aruṇakirinātar.

11:9	"rejoice"
11:9	"heart," "eyes"
12:1	"remember your creator"
12:1	"years," "days"
12:2	"light"
12:2	"sun"
12:2	"clouds return after the rain"
12:3	"the day"
12:5	"human being"
12:7	"dust to the earth"
12:7	"life-breath to God"

Though the word '*hebel'* occurs three times in the poem (11:8, 10; and 12:8) we do not take it as a key word. The poem begins with the formation of a human being in the womb and ends with the disintegration of the human being into dust and life-breath. The phrase 'light is sweet' has two functions in the structure: (a) At the epistemological level, the phrase marks the transition between 'what is not knowable' and 'what is knowable.' The growth of the seed sown or the growth of the foetus is not knowable. But the sun, the light, the clouds, the streets, the men, the women, the mourners, the breaking of the jar are perceivable. Man is tossed between 'the not knowable,' and 'the knowable.' The things he knows he cannot control. In front of the process that happens in his body and in the world outside he stands mute and incapacitated. He shall not take to frustration. Rather he must pick up his spirit and must cherish the light that is sweet. (b) At the religious level, the phrase 'the sweet is the light' goes hand-in-hand with the 'God-talk' in the poem. Lest the reader jumped into the Epicurean way of eating and drinking when there is still light, the author skilfully brought in the element of 'God' at the beginning (11:5), at the middle (11:9; 12:1), and at the end of the poem (12:7). It is God who is the author of 'light,' which is 'sweet.' At each stage of life one must 'remember' the 'Creator' of the light and must 'rejoice.'

2. In the Context of the Book

Ecclesiastes is a bipolar book.[485] The polarities do not stand in contrast to one another, but beautifully pair with one another. Our scope in this section is to situate the three expressions present in our poem – (a) 'vanity of vanities,'

485 Cf. J. A. Loader, *Polar Structures in the Book of Qohelet* (Berlin 1979). Loader identifies seven polar structures in the book. By 'polar structures' the author means "patterns of tension created by the counterposition of two elements to one another." Loader, Polar Strcutures, 1. "A polar expression is close to the antithesis or counter-position." S. Bazyliński, *A Guide to Biblical Research* (Rome 2009), 179.

(b) 'light,' and (c) 'sweet' in the entire Book of Ecclesiastes and see how the theme of 'light as sweet' pervades the entire Book.

a. 'Vanity of vanities'

This expression occurs in 1:2 and 12:8. Longman recognizes two voices present in the Book - one speaker speaks in the first person and goes by the name Qohelet (from 1:12 – 12:7) , while the second speaker addresses Qohelet in the third person (in 1:2-11 and 12:8-14).[486] From Longman's argument we may deduce that 11:2 and 12:8 belong to the second speaker.

These two verses have twofold functions in the entire Book: (a) They introduce the author or the voice of the narrator; and (b) They put forward the very purpose of the book – however, stated negatively. In the thirty-eight occurrences of *hebel* in twenty-nine different verses, the superlative 'vanity of vanities' seems to be the key to both the 'front door' (1:2) and the 'back door' (12:8) of the book.[487] Looking at the negatively stated purpose one jumps to the conclusion that Qohelet is a pessimist, "who perceived that life an exercise in futility."[488] If one perceives Qohelet as a pessimist it is difficult to answer how the Book came to be read during the Feast of Tabernacles, a festal celebration of eating, drinking, and joy.[489] So, the theme of futility has yet another pole, i.e., enjoying God's basic everyday gifts (2:24-26; 3:12-13, 22; 5:18-19; 8:15; 9:7-9).[490]

Hubbard makes the summary of the book based on these two poles:

> It begins with the announcement of its basic conclusion: everything in life is futility (1:2) … That theme is illustrated with a whole chain of evidence drawn from Koheleth's personal observations – the four Demonstrations (1:4-2:26; 3:1-4:16; 5:13-6:12; 8:10-9:12). It is reinforced with clusters of proverbs – the three collections of Words of Advice (5:1-12; 7:1-8:9; 9:12-12:8) – that show the emptiness of conventional wisdom and that counsels the hearers in how to make the best of life, hard as it is. And it is punctuated with the six alternative conclusions that urge the people to set modest expectations for themselves and enjoy God's simple, everyday gifts of food, drink, work, and love. It concludes as it began with the vanity verdict.[491]

---

486 Cf. T. Longman III, "Challenging the Idols of the Twenty-First Century," 207-08.

487 Cf. W. W. Wiersbe, *Be Satisfied* (Wheaton 1990), 14-15.

488 G. W. Parsons, "Guidelines for Understanding and Proclaiming the Book of Ecclesiastes, Part I," in *Bibliotheca Sacra* 160 (Apr – Jun 2003), 168.

489 Cf. B. G. Webb, *Five Festal Garments. Christian Reflections on the Song of Songs, Ruth, Lamentations, Ecclesiastes, and Esther* (Downers Grove 2000), 106-07.

490 Parsons, "Guidelines for Understanding," 168.

491 D. Hubbard, *Ecclesiastes, Song of Solomon* (Dallas 1991), 30.

There is yet a second frame – or outer frame – to the Book, which has yet another theme:[492]

1:1 1:2 ----- inner frame: 'vanity' ----- 12:8 12:9-14

outer frame: 'fear of God'

b. 'Light'

This positive aspect of Ecclesiastes can be backed up with the analysis of the word 'light' in the Book. Qohelet uses the word 'the light' three times in the Book (2:13; 11:7; 12:2):

2:13	Then I saw that wisdom excels folly as light excels darkness.
11:7	Light is sweet, and it is pleasant for the eyes to see the sun.
12:2	before the sun and the light and the moon and the stars are darkened and the clouds return with the rain.

In 2:13 we have a simile: 'just as light excels darkness wisdom excels folly.' Here 'light excels darkness' is the universal statement, to which 'wisdom excels folly' stands in parallel.

11:7 through a synonymous parallelism extols 'light as sweet.'

In 12:2 the light is being darkened. Though the verse speaks of this in the vocabulary of a cosmic eschatology, it primarily refers to the darkness that will fall upon a human individual.

If we reverse the occurrences, we can establish a logical syllogism:

Premise 1: 'Light is darkened' (12:8)

Premise 2: 'Light excels darkness' (2:13)

Premise 3: (Therefore) 'light is sweet' (11:7).

The light is darkened in 12:2. Though the light is darkened 'the light *always* excels darkness' (cf. 2:13). Since the light excels darkness the light is always sweet. Hence, the light, the life, is always sweet. The light prevails over darkness. And life over death.[493]

c. 'Sweet'

The word 'sweet' (*mtq*) appears twice in the Book – in 5:11 and 11:7

5:11	Sweet is the sleep of labourers
11:7	Sweet is the light

The adjective 'sweet' is feminine in 5:11 and it refers to the feminine noun 'sleep,' while in 11:7 it is masculine referring to the masculine noun 'light.' Though the other occurrence of the word 'sleep' in 8:16 refers to physical

492 Cf. A. G. Shead, "Reading Ecclesiastes Epilogically," in *Tyndale Bulletin* 48.1 (1997), 68.

493 By this I do not mean 'life after death.' I intend to mean the life does have a meaning even at the ever-impending threat of death.

sleep or bodily rest (as in 5:11) the word also has the meaning of 'death.'[494] Therefore, if we take 'sleep' as 'death' in 5:11, we can reframe into:

Sweet = Sleep (5:11)
Sleep = Death
Therefore, Death = Sweet (5:11)
Sweet = Light (11:7)
Death = Light (cf. 5:11)

Through the use of the adjective 'sweet' intending to mean the two poles of life and death, Qohelet skilfully arrives at his final meaning that everything – from life to death - indeed is 'meaningful.'

3. In the Context of Wisdom Literature

To read Ecclesiastes as part of the Wisdom Literature we must concentrate on the repetition and the choice of the words. The Biblical authors did not pick words at random, but evidently made careful use of the language in ways often quite subtle and powerful.[495] This is truer of wisdom writers, for whom one of the hallmarks of wisdom was the sophisticated crafting of language.[496]

The word 'light' occurs 58x in the Wisdom Literature (19x in Psalms; 32x in Job; 4x in Prov; 3x in Eccl). In Psalms, 'light' either refers to 'the face of God' (4:6) or 'God' (27:1) or physical light (119:105). God is seen as the fountain or the source of light (cf. 36:9; 43:3). Finally, the light also functions as a metaphor for life (Ps 56:13; Job 3:16; 3:20; 33:28;).[497] Though the book of Job also uses 'light' to refer to 'God's light,' 'physical light,' dominantly it points to 'life' – in contrast to 'death as darkness' (cf. Job 3:16; 3:20; 33:28). In Proverbs the use of light is very metaphorical, as in "the path of the righteous is like the light" (cf. 4:18; 6:23; 13:9; 16:15).

The word 'sweet' occurs 7 times in the Wisdom Literature (Ps 19:11; Prov 16:24; 24:13; 27:7; Song 2:3; Eccl 5:11; and 11:7). In Ps 19:11, Prov 16:24, 27:7 the sweetness is compared to 'honey.' The 'sweet' is attributed to the sense of 'tasting.' In Song 2:3, 'the fruit of the beloved' is sweet and in Eccl 5:11 and 11:7 the 'sweet' does not apply to 'physical' sense of 'tasting,' but metaphorically appeals to the feelings.

Qohelet reflects the understanding of the 'light' in Psalms and Job and 'sweet' in Song of Songs when he handles these two words in 11:4 – 12:8.

---

494 "To sleep a perpetual sleep," (Jer 51:39, 57). "The stouthearted were stripped of their spoil; they sank into sleep; none of the troops was able to lift a hand," (Ps 76:5). "So mortals lie down and and do not rise again; until the heavens are no more, they will not awake or be roused out of their sleep," (Job 14:12).

495 Cf. Alter, *Biblical Poetry*, 167.

496 Cf. Alter, *Biblical Poetry*, 168.

497 Here 'light of life' is in contrast to 'darkness of death.'

'Light' and the absence of it strikes on the theme of life and death and since "death undermines the structures of meaning by which the wisdom tradition makes sense of life."[498]

From the theological point of view, the Wisdom Literature, for example in Prov chs 10-29, has three theological presuppositions: (i) That this is an orderly world, ruled by YHWH, its wise creator. (ii) That knowledge of this order is possible to the person who opens himself to wisdom. (iii) That the wise man who thus aligns himself with God's order will experience good things, while the fool will suffer for his folly.

In others words we can summarize these presuppositions as (a) 'order,' (b) 'knowability,' and (c) 'justice.'[499] Qohelet radically questions these three presuppositions of the Wisdom Literature. For Qohelet the order in the nature is wearying and pointless (cf. 1:4-9). In 11:4-12:8, the poet makes one aware of the possible *de-order* that can happen in the cosmos. Qohelet believes in a cyclical model of reality whereby life-breath that is given by God returns to God and the cycle continues.[500] The cyclical model of reality "leads Qohelet inevitably to his thematic declaration of the pointlessness of it in all (cf. 1:2 // 12:8)."[501] "Qohelet also attacks the traditional wisdom which affirms that God's ways are basically knowable."[502] "Like the Psalmist (Ps 139:13-16), Qohelet stands in awe at the mystery of gestation and birth – but where this led the Psalmist to worship and adoration (Ps 139:17-18), it leads Qohelet only to a deeper feeling of resignation over the unpredictability of everything (cf. 11:5-6)."[503] As far as justice is concerned though Qohelet finds no convincing evidence for this in the world, he is fully convinced that God will bring people into judgment (cf. 11:9) and will establish his justice in the end.

As far as the motifs of 'life in different stages,' 'shortness of life,' 'knowability of life and its shortness' Qohelet reflects the words of the Psalms:

Ps 39:4-5

39:4	"LORD, let me know my end, and what is the measure of my days; let me know how fleeting my life is.
39:5	You have made my days a few handbreadths, and my lifetime is as nothing in your sight. Surely everyone stands as a mere breath. *Selah*

498 J. Blenkinsopp, *Wisdom and Law in the Old Testament. The Ordering of Life in Israel and Early Judaism* (Oxford 1983), 65.

499 Cf. A. W. Jenks, "Theological Presuppositions of Israel's Wisdom Literature," in *Horizons in Biblical Theology*, 1 (Jun 1985), 43-44.

500 As opposed to this the prophets believed in a linear model of reality.

501 Jenks, "Theological Presuppositions," 58.

502 Jenks, "Theological Presuppositions," 60.

503 Jenks, "Theological Presuppositions," 61.

In Ps 39:4, the psalmist prays to the Lord that the Lord might make known to him 'his end,' and 'the measure of his days.' The verb, 'to know' is used twice here – one in hiphil and other in qal. In Eccl 11:5 too we have two occurrences of 'to know,' through the use of which Qohelet communicates the 'non-knowability' of God's plan, design, and what future holds. It is God who knows everything.

Ps 39:5 portrays how the days are mere handbreadths before God. Every human person is a mere breath before God. The words used here 'day', 'breath', and 'human person' appear in our poem as well (cf. Eccl 11:8; 11:9; 11:10; 12:1; 12:3; 12:5; 12:8).

Ps 90:9-10

90:9	For all our days pass away under your wrath; our years come to an end like a sigh.
90:10	The days of our life are seventy years, or perhaps eighty, if we are strong; even then their span is only toil and trouble; they are soon gone, and we fly away.

While Qohelet is uncertain about the number of days or years of one's lifetime, the Psalmist from his empirical experience notes that the human lifespan is seventy years for all and eighty for the strong.[504] Secondly, the Psalmist mourns over the fact that life is filled with 'toil and trouble.' The 'toil' is one of the key motifs in Qohelet. The word occurs 22x in the Book (of 55x in the HB; 13x in Pss).[505] Though Qohelet does not use the word 'trouble,' he calls human toil wearisome (cf. 10:15).

Ps 103:15-16

103:15	As for mortals, their days are like grass; they flourish like a flower of the field;
103:16	for the wind passes over it, and it is gone, and its place knows it no more.

The word used to refer to 'human person' is 'mortal,' which is alien to Qohelet. The Psalmist uses the metaphors from the vegetative world – 'grass,'

504 The lifespan of the Patriarchs and Moses are relatively longer. Adam lived 930 years (Gen 5:5), Noah 950 years (Gen 9:28), Abraham 175 years (Gen 25:7), Isaac 180 years (Gen 35:28); Jacob 147 years (Gen 47:28); Joseph 110 years (Gen 50:22); Moses 120 years (Deut 34:7); Joshua 110 years (Judg 2:8). The lifespan of Samuel, David and Solomon are not mentioned. We notice a decline in the lifespan of human persons as the time passes.

505 Eccl 1:3; 2:10-11, 18-22, 24; 3:13; 4:4, 6, 8-9; 5:14, 17-18; 6:7; 8:15; 9:9; 10:15.

and 'flower.' The word, 'wind', also is used literally. In our poem 'spirit' is used in the sense of 'wind' (11:4) and of 'life-breath' (11:5; 12:7).

Ps 139:4, 7, 11-13

139:4	Even before a word is on my tongue, O LORD, you know it completely.
139:7	Where can I go from your spirit? Or where can I flee from your presence?
139:11	If I say, "Surely the darkness shall cover me, and the light around me become night,"
139:12	even the darkness is not dark to you; the night is as bright as the day, for darkness is as light to you.
139:13	For it was you who formed my inward parts; you knit me together in my mother's womb.

The omniscience and the omnipresence of the Lord are admired at in 139:4 and 7 respectively. Moreover, the word, 'spirit' has yet another nuance, for 'your breath' means 'your presence.' In vv. 11 and 12 the Psalmist while situating himself in the physical darkness and the figurative darkness of death, extols that the 'darkness is not dark to the Lord, and the darkness is yet light to Him.' In Eccl 11:4-12:8, though there is an eclipse of light, the light wins over darkness. In 11:5 Qohelet states that the process of formation of foetus in the womb of a mother is unknown to us, whereas in Ps 139:13, the Psalmist presupposing to know the process, marvels at the life-process in the womb.

Ps 71:6, 17, 18

Psalm 71 describes human life in four stages: conception (71:6b), birth (71:6a), youth (71:17), and old age (71:18). Though Qohelet also speaks about four life stages he does not use the proper words.[506]

4. In the Context of the Hebrew Bible

The Torah and the Prophetic Literature in general talk about God's involvement in human history. But, the Wisdom Literature takes a diversion as it tends to avoid any such reference. Let us take the First Creation Story (only Gen 1:3-5) as the representative of the Torah and Isa 5, 38:12-15, and 52:13-53:12 as the representative texts of the Prophets and see how the hermeneutical arc of Ecclesiastes embraces them.

506 In Sir 30:21-25 the theme of joy that needs to be present youth is brought out well.

Gen 1:3-5

1:3	Then God said, "Let there be light"; and there was light.
1:4	And God saw that the light was good; and God separated the light from the darkness.
1:5	God called the light Day, and the darkness he called Night. And there was evening and there was morning, the first day.

Intertexts with Eccl 11:4-12:8

'light'	Gen 1:3 (2x); 1:4 (2x); 1:5 (1x) // Eccl 11:7 (1x); 12:2 (1x)
'God'	Gen 1:3 (1x); 1:4 (2x); 1:5 (1x) // Eccl 11:5 (1x); 11:9 (1x); 12:7 (1x)
'good'	Gen 1:4 (1x) // Eccl 11:6 (1x); 11:7 (1x); 11:9 (1x)
'dark'	Gen 1:4 (1x); 1:5 (1x) // Eccl 12:2 (1x)
'day'	Gen 1:5 (2x) // Eccl 11:8 (1x); 11:9 (1x); 12:1 (1x); 12:3 (1x)
'evening'	Gen 1:5 (1x) // Eccl 11:6 (1x)
'morning'	Gen 1:5 (1x) // Eccl 11:6 (1x)

The density of the intertexts between Gen 1:3-5 and 11:4-12:8 reveals to us that as God saw 'light as good,' Qohelet sees 'light as sweet.' The 'light' was created by God and the darkness is separated from it and can never overwhelm light. From the theological point of view, Qohelet, at the face of death, chaos, and destruction, dreams of returning to the First Creation, where everything was 'good.'

Isa 38:12-13

38:12	My dwelling is plucked up and removed from me like a shepherd's tent; like a weaver I have rolled up my life; he cuts me off from the loom; from day to night you bring me to an end.
38:13	I cry for help until morning; like a lion he breaks all my bones; from day to night you bring me to an end.

In 38:10-20 we see a writing of King Hezekiah of Judah when he was sick and recovered from his illness (cf. 38:9). The selected verses (vv. 12-13) express how human life is ended in a day. The end of human beings takes place in one day. This thought is in parallel with Qohelet, for in Eccl 11:4-12:8, he moves from 'years' (cf. 11:8) to 'day' (cf. 12:3) when he begins to describe death or end of human persons.

Isa 52:13 – 53:12

In the Fourth Song of the Suffering Servant (Isa 52:13-53:12) we see an anonymous chorus speaking about the birth, growth, suffering and passion, condemnation and execution, burial and glorification of the servant. The servant is born and grown 'like a young plant' (53:2). The silence of the suffering servant amidst the infirmities and oppression resounds the silence of the old and dying man who is portrayed in Eccl 12:1-6.

B. Uṭalkûṟṟuvaṇṇam in Context

1. Evaluating the Structure

Based on the word-field of 'light' we can re-structure the poem as follows:

'no light'
v. 5 *oḷinakaiyūra*
v. 24 *yaḻalkoṭupōṭa*
'no light'

There is a dynamic movement in the poem as far as the element of light is concerned. Initially there is 'no light.' The life process – the embrace of semen and ovum – takes place in the darkness of the womb. Internally the first sense that develops is sight (cf. v. 2), which has to do with 'light.' Then the baby 'sees the light' when it is born. Its sparkling smile-laddened lips are inviting to the neighbours. The baby now comes to be part of the world. The light that is inviting begins to dwindle and reaches the point of 'no light' – death. Ironically, the light (cf. 24) that is lit at the funeral pyre awakens a new enlightenment in the onlookers – here, on the poet. As the first 'light' was an invitation to acknowledge the presence of the baby in the world, the second light is an invitation to be aware of the absence of the human person in the world.

Secondly, there is also a word-play on 'moon.' The Tamils primarily calculated time in terms of the movement of the moon.[507] The poet takes on the moon by which human life is calculated, draws a metaphor and applies to human life stage. The two words that the poet use are '*vaḷarpiṟai*' and '*mati*:'

v. 6 *vaḷarpiṟaiyeṉṟu*
v. 13 *matiyumaḻintu*
v. 19 *vaḷarpiṟaipōla*

Though the same word '*vaḷarpiṟai*' is used in vv. 6 and 19, in v. 6 it refers to the 'growth (of the child)' while in v. 19 it refers to the 'shape.' V. 13 is the apex after which there is a degradation in human body. Though '*mati*' signifies 'mind' or 'mental ability,' the destruction of '*mati*' (= moon) marks the destruction of life.

The word '*mati*' is the section marker as far as the theme of 'pleasure' or 'pleasant' is concerned. When the '*mati*' dies there is no more pleasure. What follows is 'bent body,' 'sleeplessness,' 'disease,' 'cough,' 'uncontrolled urination and defecation,' 'loss of strength,' 'constant fear,' and 'anxiety.'

507 This is why the month is known as 'tiṅkaḷ' (= 'moon') and the first day of the week is 'tiṅkaḷ.'

Hence, the '*mati*' has two faces: on the one side, it causes 'pleasure,' and on the other, 'pain.' The two faces of the '*mati*' are not contradictory but complementary. The other side of the '*mati*' makes one understand the fleeting nature of life and to live life fully when there is still 'light.'

Therefore, through the metaphor of 'light' Paṭṭinattār, beautifully enumerates the human life-stages and invites us to live life fully surrendering to the Lord (cf. v. 24).

2. In the Context of the Paṭṭiṉattār Corpus

There is no consensus among the scholars as far as the number of the poems in the Paṭṭinattār corpus is concerned. We follow the opinion of T. V. Kalyānasundaranār, who has grouped the corpus under 36 *patikaṅkaḷ*. Though each patikam is a unified whole within there are yet some threads that run through ąll, such as, 'surrendering to the Lord Śiva,' 'impermanence of the world and the body,' 'the need for liberation,' and 'the belief in rebirth.'

In this section we have picked up seven stanzas from the entire corpus and see how they help us understand the *Uṭal* better and vice versa.

(i) *kaṭṭi yaṇaittiṭum peṇṭīru makkaḻuṅ kālattaccan*
veṭṭi muṟikku marampōṟ carīrattai vīḻttiviṭṭāṟ
koṭṭi muḻakki yaḻuvār mayānaṅ kuṟukiyappāl
eṭṭi yaṭivaip parōviṟai vākacci yēkampaṉē.[508]

In this poem the poet uses the metaphor of 'tree' to refer to the body. The body is the tree. God is the carpenter. The mourning that happens over the cutting down of the tree, i.e., death, as described in the poem, is similar to *Uṭal* v. 20 ('*maintaruvantuku ṉintaḻanontu maṭiyilviḻuntu maṉaivipulampa*').

(ii) *ūruñ catamalla uṟṟār catamalla uṟṟuppeṟṟa*
pēruñ catamalla peṇṭīr catamalla piḷḷaikaḷuñ
cīruñ catamalla celvañ catamalla tēcattilē
yāruñ catamalla niṉṟāḷ cataṅkacci yēkampanē.[509]

In this poem, where the poet succinctly talks about the impermanence of world realities, he surrenders to the feet of the Lord Śiva. The poet categorizes

508 'The women and children who embrace
If the carpenter of time cuts down this tree of body
Will cry and mourn until the cemetery
Not one more step they will take Lord!' (*Tiurvēkampalai*, 2).

509 'The village is not permanent; the relations are not permanent;
Hard earned name is not permanent; the women are not permanent; the children and
Property are not permanent; the riches are not permanent; in the world
No one is permanent; Only your feet are permanent, O Lord!' (*Tiurvēkampalai*, 13).

the impermanent realities into seven *ūr*, *u<u>r</u><u>r</u>ār*, *pēr*, *peṇtīr*, *piḷḷaikaḷ*, *cīr*, *celvam*, and sums up in one word *yārum.*

We have the parallels to these seven categories in *Uṭalku<u>r</u><u>r</u>uvaṇṇam*.
ūr // 'the neighbours' (v. 21)
u<u>r</u><u>r</u>ār // 'the acquaintances' (vv. 4-6)
pēr // 'the crescent moon' (v. 7)
peṇtīr // 'the women' (vv. 4, 8, 9, 14, 20)
piḷḷaikaḷ // 'the children' (v. 20)
cīr // 'the health' (vv. 12-17)
celvam // 'the property – inherited and owned' (vv. 10-11).

These seven realities are not only impermanent, but also incapable of survival in front of death. They cannot withhold a person from dying. There is no escape from aging and death except to surrender at the feet of the Lord Śiva (cf. v. 24).

(iii) *muṭicārnta ma<u>n</u><u>n</u>aru ma<u>r</u><u>r</u>umuḷ ḷōru muṭiviloru*
piṭicāmpa rāiventu maṇṇāva tuṅkaṇṭu pi<u>n</u><u>n</u>umintap
paṭicārnta vā<u>l</u>vai niṉaippatal lā<u>r</u>po<u>n</u><u>n</u>i <u>n</u>ampalavar
aṭicārntu nāmuiya vēṇṭume<u>n</u> <u>r</u>ēya<u>r</u>i vārilaiyē.[510]

In this poem, where the poet mourns over his ignorance, has the expression *piṭicāmpar,* which is found in *Uṭal* v. 24 ('*ōrpiṭinī<u>r</u>um*').

(iv) *ūṭṭuvip pā<u>n</u>u mu<u>r</u>aṅkuvip pā<u>n</u>umiṅ ko<u>n</u><u>r</u>oṭo<u>n</u><u>r</u>ai*
mūṭṭuvip pā<u>n</u>u muyaṅkuvip pā<u>n</u>u muya<u>n</u><u>r</u>avi<u>n</u>ai
kāṭṭuvip pā<u>n</u>u miruvi<u>n</u>aip pācak kayi<u>r</u><u>r</u>inva<u>l</u>i
āṭṭuvip pā<u>n</u>u moruva<u>n</u>uṇ ṭētillai yampalattē.[511]

The primordial fire is responsible for human life. This fire is lit by God. When this fire dies the person also dies. In the context of our poem, the funeral pyre that is lit (v. 24), ironically refers to the fire that is no more present in the human body.

(v) *mu<u>n</u><u>n</u>ai yiṭṭatī muppu rattilē*
pi<u>n</u><u>n</u>ai yiṭṭatī te<u>n</u><u>n</u>i laṅkaiyilē

---

510 'Though seeing the kings and all in the end
Boiling down to a handful of ashes and dust
I am not able to forget the life bound to the earth
And to embrace your feet in order to live.' (*Tiruttillai*, 7).

511 'One who feeds, one who makes us sleep,
One who binds together, one who causes the effects,
One who shows the fruits, one who ties with the thread of destiny
One who makes us dance is that who lives in Tillai.' (*Tiruttillai*, 11).

aṉṉai yiṭṭatī yaṭiva yiṟṟilē
yāṉu miṭṭatī mūḷka mūḷkavē.[512]

Here the poet talks about four kinds of fire – the fire that the Lord Śiva lit, that Hanuman lit, that his mother lit, and the poet himself has lit. The first fire created the world. The second fire liberated Sīta. The third fire gave life to the poet. The fourth fire liberates the soul of poet's mother from her body. The 'fire' – 'the light' – serves as a tool for creation and liberation.

(vi) *nāṉēnī nīyōnā ṉāmiranṭu moṉṟāṉāl*
tēṉiṉ ruciyatupōṟ ṟeviṭṭāinī pūraṇamē.[513]

What is sweeter than honey is the union of the poet with the Lord Śiva. The poet calls the Lord as 'fullness.' In our parallel literature – Ecclesiastes – there is a similar expression: 'the life-breath that was given by God returns to Him.' This life-breath is the 'light' within human persons.

(vii) *cōtiyāṉ cūḻpaṉinīr cūṟaikoḷu māṟēpōl*
nītikuru viṉṟiruttāḷ nīpeṟṟāi neñcamē.[514]

Though at the surface level 'the light' stands for 'the sun,' at the deeper level it refers to the 'Lord' who is the light and wisdom.

To sum up, *Uṭalkuṟṟuvaṇṇam,* the poem of our study, beautifully knits together all the pearls that are found in the entire corpus. The ultimate end of the poet expressed in the poem is to be freed from the impermanent body and to be intimately united to the Lord Śiva, who is the 'light,' and this union is as 'sweet' as honey.

3. In the Context of Selected Śaivite Poems

Now let us situate Paṭṭinattār's *Uṭal* in the context of the Śaivite literature. We take two poems from Tirumūlar (from Siddha Tradition) and three poems from Aruṇakirinātar (from Bhakti Tradition). *Uṭal* will fall under both the Siddha Tradition, because though Paṭṭinattār is not one of the 9 or 18 cittās held tradionally[515] he is the contemporary of the cittās, and the Bhakti Tradition, because the *pāṭuporuḷ* ('content of the song') is the Lord Śiva.

---

512 'The primordial fire lit Tiripuram.
The later fire lit Srilanka.
The fire by mother lit my abdomen.
The fire I lit let it burn.' (*Song Sung at the Funeral Fyre of the Mother*, 7).

513 'If You become I, and I become You, and We become One
It is like the taste of honey, O Fullness!' (*Pūraṇamālai*, 100).

514 'As the sun discards the eclipsing clouds
So does the feet of the Lord discards folly!' (*Neñcoṭu makiḻtal*, 32).

515 Abirāmi Antati lists 9 cittās: "Catyanātar, Catōkanātar, Ātinātar, Anātinātar, Vekuḷinātar, Mātaṅkanātar, Maccēntranātar, Kaṭēntranātar, Korakkanātar." The Tamil Siddha tradition

The Tirumūlar corpus is tradionally known as Tirumantiram. Tirumantiram is one of the Tamil Śaiva canonical literature known as *Tirumuṟai.*[516] The Tamil Bhakti movement[517] promoted a sense of sacred centred on the Temple while Tirumantiram proposed an alternative religious vision centred on human body.[518] Tirumantiram is also the pioneering work of the Tamil Siddha tradition.[519] According to Zvelebil, Tirumantiram is the "encyclopaedia of authentic spiritual experience on almost all levels."[520]

The Tirumantiram speaks about the centrality of human body in the conceptual scheme of ancient Tamils. In the ancient Tamil society which

---

names 18 of them: "Patañcali, Akastiyā, Kamalamuṉi, Tirumūlar, Kutampai, Korakkar, Tanvantiri, Koṅkanār, Cāttamuṉi, Vāṉmīkar, Rāmatēvar, Nantīsvarar, Iṭaikkāṭar, Maccamuṉi, Karuvūrar, Pōkar, Pāmpāṭṭi, and Cuntaranantanār."

516 Though the term muṟai has several meanings in Tamil, it denotes, in this context, a body of religious texts arranged in a certain order or an individual text placed in that order. "Tiru" means divine, sacred or auspicious. Śaiva works are grouped into 12 classes known as Tirumuṟai. Though the whole Tamil Śaiva canon is in metrical form, a distinctive terminology is used for individual components of the canon. The first seven Tirumuṟai are known as Tēvāram, the eighth comprises Tiruvācakam and Tirukkōvaiyār. The ninth Tirumuṟai includes two texts Tiruvicaippā and Tiruppallāṇṭu and the Tirumantiram is known as the tenth Tirumuṟai. Whereas various compositions are included in the eleventh Tirumuṟai, a single text called Periyapurāṇam constitutes the twelfth Tirumuṟai. The Śaiva canonical works cover approximately a period of 700 years. See K. Zvelebil, *The Smile of Murugan. On Tamil Literature of South India* (Leiden 1973), 185-87.

517 The Tirumantiram belonged to the bhakti era that began in the Tamil linguistic –cultural area in the 6th century ce. The region lying south of the Vēṅkaṭa hills was recognised as the Tamil country during the bhakti period, as in the Caṅkam age. Two or three centuries immediately following the Caṅkam period is designated as Kalabhra interregnum in the history of Tamil literature, during which "the zenith of Jaina and Buddhist influence in South India was achieved." Stein notes, "these cults [Jainism and Buddhism] co- existed peacefully with each other and with indigenous forms of religion." The late classical works Paripāṭal, and Kalittokai, several didactic works and the twin epics Cilappatikāram and Maṇimēkalai were composed during this period. This period of relative peace in the religious arena was followed by the bhakti period which was marked by religious acrimony and violence spurred by the conversion of kings to Śaivism by saints. The Tamil bhakti movement that was spearheaded by the three "Tēvāram" saints was centered on temple and pilgrimage, and Śiva, the presiding deity of the temple constituted the theme of devotional hymns. Poet-saints called upon all members of Tamil society to participate in the worship of Śiva envisioning the formation of devotional communities irrespective of gender and caste distinctions. Thus, the object of the movement was to unite the Tamil society under the banner of temple-based Śaivism, thereby to enervate Jainism and Buddhism that had wielded influence in the Tamil country from long before the Common Era. See I. Peterson, *Poems to Śiva. The Hymns of the Tamil Saints* (Delhi 22001), 9-10.

518 This realization comes from Tirmumantiram 85.

519 Cf. T. N. Ganapathy and K. R. Arumugam, *The Yoga of Siddha Tirumūlar. Essays on the Tirumantiram* (Quebec 2006), xvi-xvii.

520 K. Zvelebil, *Lexicon of Tamil Literature* (New York 1995).

valorized the ideals of love and war held the body in a very high position. The body is referred to as *uṭampu*, *uṭal*, *mey*, and *yākkai* in the texts. The body is perceived as the primary medium for expressing emotions. In the following poems *Tirumūlar* underlines the necessity of a human body:

Uṭampār a̲liyil uyirār a̲livar
Tiṭampaṭa meiññana̲ñ cēravu māṭṭār
Uṭampai vaḷarkkum upāyam a̲rintē
Uṭampai vaḷarttē̲n uyirai vaḷarttēnē.[521]

Uṭampina̲i munna̲m i̲lukke̲n r̲iruntē̲n
Uṭampina̲uk kuḷḷē yur̲uporuḷ kaṇṭēn
Uṭampilē uttama̲n kōyilkoṇ ṭāṉyeṉr̲u
Uṭampina̲i yāṉirun tōmpukiṉ r̲ēṉē.[522]

The Lord dwells in human body. His presence is the life-spirit. This indwelling presence of the Lord is possible only as long as there exists body. Therefore, taking care of the visible body is equal to taking care of invisibile life-spirit, i.e., God. Tirumūlar goes to the extent of describing ways and means of attaining immortal body, '*kāyacitti*.' What is to be noted is that unlike the systems which emphasized the ephemerality of the physical body, Tirumūlar appreciated and adored the body to the extent of preserving the body to make the soul continue to exist in it. Tirumūlar also is the proponent of Aśṭāṅka Yōkā ('the eightfold path), which sheds light on caring for the body and mind. His Yōka presupposes the necessity of human body. The highest goal of yoga is the attainment of a non-dualistic union with the Lord Śiva whereby one reaches the bliss and the power (siddhi) at the same time. According to Tirumūlar salvation is possible only through body. He advocates that 'love is God' and unity of mankind to God is possible.

Now let us turn to see the poems from Tiruppukal̲ of Aruṇakirinātar,[523] who is one of the well-known persons in the Śaivite Bhakti tradition.

---

521 'When the body dies life also dies.
When one dies attaining wisdom becomes impossibile.
Hence, learning the art of taking care of the body.
I took care of my body to take care of my life.' *Tirumantiram*, 724.

522 'Earlier I considered my body a mistake
Later I saw the life-spirit within the body
Since the Good One has His Temple in the body
I am resolved to take care of the body.' *Tirumantiram*, 725.

523 Aruṇakirinātar belongs to the 15th century. He hails from Tiruvaṇṇāmalai. He himself being indulged in pleasure-seeking, after attaining enlightenment sings songs devoted to the Lord Murukan̲. When many other saints of his age attained enlightenment through their merits - penance, self-denial and struggle, Aruṇakirinātar achieved it through grace of God. He is said to have composed as many 16,000 songs, of which only 1365 have

karuvaṭaintu patturra tiṅkaḷ
vayirriruntu murrippa yinru
kaṭaiyilvantu tittukku lantai...vaṭivākik
kaluviyaṅke ṭuttuccu ranta
mulaiyaruntu vikkakki ṭantu
katariyaṅkai koṭṭitta valntu...naṭamāṭi
araivaṭaṅkaḷ kaṭṭicca taṅkai
iṭukutampai porcuṭṭi taṇṭai
avaiyaṇintu murrikki ḷarntu...vayatēri
ariyapeṇkaḷ naṭpaippu ṇarntu
piṇiyulanru curritti rinta
tamaiyumunkaru paiccittam enru...peruvēnō.[524]

In this poem the poet mentions the five stages of life: conception, birth, childhood, youth, and old age. He, during his youth, when going after the 'rare women,' longs for the grace of God. This poem is parallel to *Uṭal* as long as the description of human stages is concerned. The poet is very brief in his description of the old age – he uses only a single word '*vayatēri*.' Unlike Paṭṭinattār, who describes the process of aging and death in detail, Aruṇakirinātar is very brief and and succinct.

vanitaiyuṭal kāya ninru utiramati lēyu runṭu

been retrieved. His anthology known as Tiruppukal is an exposition of the qualities of the Lord Murukan - His Beauty, Benevolence, Knowledge, Bravery, and Courage. Tiruppukal, which is composed after the cantam style (like *Uṭalkurruvaṇṇam*), is a standing evidence for the poet in Tamil literary skills. Through Aruṇakirinātar Śaiva Siddhanta took a new direction as he brought the Lord Murukan to the centre stage.

524 'Being conceived in my mother's womb
I spent ten months over there
and developed into a full form;
Finally, I arrived in this world
As a little baby.
They took me out, washed me
And made me suck my mother's breast for milk.
I was laid on the floor and I cried;
I clapped my little hand; I crawled;
I walked;
I wore gold chains around my waist
I wore anklets and earstuds
I put on golden ornaments
And so adorned, I matured and grew up glowingly.
I reached adulthood
I sought the company of dear girls
I suffered from numerous diseases
Had enough of running around
When will I ever get your gracious blessings?' *Tiruppukal*, 9.

vayirilneṭu nāḷa laintu...puvimītē
maṉitaruru vāki vaṇtu anutiṉamu mēva ḷarntu
vayatupati ṉāṟu ceṉṟu...vaṭivākik
kaṉakamulai mātar taṅkaḷ valaiyilmika vēyu ḻaṉṟu
kaṉivatuṭa ṉēya ṇaintu...poruḷtēṭik
kaṉaporuḷe lāmi ḷantu mayalilmika vēya lainta
kacaṭaṉeṉai yāḷa vuṉra...ṉaruḷtārāi.[525]

The content and the expressions in the above poem are parallel to *Uṭal* vv. 2, 7, 9-10, and 24. The ultimate plea of the poet is that he might be filled by the grace of God.

Kaṭṭaḻaku viṭṭut taḷarntan kiruntumuṉam
Iṭṭapoṟi tappip piṇaṅkoṇ ṭatincilarkaḷ
kaṭṭaṇame ṭuttuc cumantum perumpaṟaikaḷ...muṟaiyōṭē
veṭṭaviṭa veṭṭak kiṭañcaṅ kiṭañcameṉa
makkaḷoru mikkat toṭarntum puraṇṭumvaḻi
viṭṭuvaru mittait tavirntuṉ pataṅkaḷuṟa...uṇarvēṉō
paṭṭaruvi neṭṭaik karavuñcam piḷantukaṭal
muṟṟumalai vaṟṟik kuḻampuṅ kuḻampamuṉai
paṭṭaayil toṭṭut tiṭaṅkoṇ ṭetirntavuṉar...muṭicāyat
taṭṭaḻiya veṭṭik kavantam peruṅkaḻuku
nirttamiṭa rattak kuḷaṅkaṇ ṭumiḻntumaṇi
caṟcamaya vittaip palaṉkaṇ ṭucentiluṟai...perumāḷē.[526]

---

525 'Being confined in the womb of the mother drying up her body,
rolling over in the blood gathering strength,
and suffering for many a day in her womb,
finally, I took a human form and arrived on this earth.
I grew up everyday and attained the age of sixteen,
becoming a handsome youth,
I roamed around a lot being ensnared by
whores with beautiful bosom;
I hugged them with passion and
Went about in search of wealth
I squandered away all my large riches
I am a stupid fool having indulged in
Delusory lust and wandering aimlessly.
Kindly bless me with your grace and take charge of me!' *Tiruppukaḻ*, 195.

526 'The handsome and robust body became worn out.
The five sensory organs that once ruled the body
Were thrown into confusion and disarray.
The body turned into a corpse
That was carried by a few for a fee.
Large drums were beaten in a ritualistic manner
to the meter of music
People marched in a group following the corpse,

This poem is parallel to vv. 19-24 of *Uṭalkuṟṟuvaṇṇam.* What is unique in the poem is that the Lord Śiva is called *perumālē.*[527]

Now we have two extremes: Tirumūlar who advocated the importance and the indispensability of the body and Aruṇakirinātar, who sees the body as an instrument for sin and wants to shed it away as soon as possible. This difference of opinion is basically because of their difference in the understanding of God: For Tirumūlar, God is an immanent reality, who takes shelter within the created realities – in our context, the body of the human person. Aruṇakirinātar sees God as transcendent, as an external reality. There exists a chiasm between God and the life-spirit within a human person. The body is an obstacle to bridge the chiasm. Therefore, shedding off the body is a necessary prerequisite to be united to God.

Now, where do we situate Paṭṭinattār? Chronologically Paṭṭinattār (10th cent.) stands between Tirumūlar (8th cent.) and Aruṇakirinātar (15th cent.). Between 8th to 10th centuries there might have been a lot of insistence on the body that people forgot God and were tied up with taking care of their bodies, entertaining them and enjoying pleasures through them. Paṭṭinattār had to do a hard task of untying these cords and liberate them. To balance the extreme of over-indulgence, Paṭṭinattār goes to another extreme of negation of the body. Aruṇakirinātar, who comes later, who must have heard and read of Paṭṭinattār, follows his footsteps in advocating 'the negation of the body.' Theologically speaking, in Paṭṭinattār, we see a beautiful blend or symphony of an immanent and transcendent God – God is immanent because His life-spirit is within us (cf. *Uṭal* v. 20) yet transcendent as He can be prayed to (v. 24).

C. Conclusion

The hermeutical arc drawn between our texs and their respective corpus makes us understand the imperative of divine-human harmony in living out the transition in each life stage. Such a harmony is both a gift and a task.

And a few simply rolled along the path,
While some cleared the way for the funeral procession.
When will I escape this myth called life
And learn to seek the way to attain your hallowed feet, my Lord?' *Tiruppukaḻ*, 38.

527 Perumāl is the epithet for the God of Vaishnavism – the Lord Vishnu. This title is used to refer to the Lord Murukā. This is an instance of syncretism between Śaivism and Vaishnavism.

VI. DIVINE-HUMAN SYMPHONY

This final chapter summarizes the key points of our study and help us understand the perspectives of Qohelet and Paṭṭiṉattār on life transition.

Qohelet and Paṭṭiṉattār – as we have established in Chapter Two – seem to divide human life-stages into four. The description of life-stages is more vivid in *Uṭal* than in Eccl 11:4-12:8. Paṭṭiṉattār's presentation reflects three conceptual components – biological, psychological, and social.

Paṭṭiṉattār divides human life stages into four:

Stage 1: 'Welcome' (0-5 years)
Stage 2: 'Independence' (5-16 years)
Stage 3: 'Interdependence' (17-60 years)
Stage 4: 'Dependence' (60+).

The stage 1, described in vv. 3-6, refers to the birth of a human person. The newborn baby is welcomed into the family and the neighbourhood. In other words, the baby is introduced to the 'significant other' and the 'generalized other.'[528] The family members and the neighbours pamper their child with their fondling kisses. They adorn him with dresses and pearls.[529] The child *imitates* the family and the neighbours acquiring from them the linguistic skills and and is *socialized* in their cultural and religious identity.

In stage 2, described in v. 7, which refers to the childhood or early adulthood, the child passes through a period of learning and discovery. The *vaḷarpiṟai* enjoys considerable amount of freedom and independence. He learns religion and art from a wise teacher. This stage is characterized by tremendous growth – in body and mind.

In stage 3, described in vv. 8-11, the middle adulthood, a man earns and yearns. Though Paṭṭiṉattār describes only one side of this stage, i.e., a man wasting away his resources on sex workers, the reader can still decipher the

528 Mead uses the terms 'significant other,' and 'generalized other' to refer to the people who are 'more influential' and 'less influential' respectively. Cf. G. H. Mead, *Mind, Self, and Society* (Chicago 1962), 154-59.

529 Paṭṭiṉattār in fact talks of a child who is born with a silver spoon in mouth.

other part, i.e., a man working and acquiring wealth. The man also is married and begets children. Entering into a marriage was seen as a social obligation. In the words of Freud, this stage is characterized by *lieben und arbeiten* ('love' and 'work').[530] The family relationships, the work, and the life in the society make him an interdependent being. A man becomes committed to his love and work.

In stage 4, elaborated in vv. 12-18, referred to as the old age or late adulthood, the man is beset with physical and psychological ailments. This is the time of reversal. The time of *tēipiṟai,* the moon dies out. The body weakens. The mind is fearful. The movement is restricted. The sensual organs do not respond. He is now a dependent person – for his food and locomotion.

Though Qohelet's presentation is not as orderly as that of Paṭṭiṉattār, still we may deduce well-knit life-stages:[531]

Stage 1: 'Potentiality & Hope' (Birth) [vv. 11:8]
Stage 2: 'Autonomy & Playfulness' (Childhood) [vv. 11:9]
Stage 3: 'Passion & Enterprise' (Youth) [11:9-12:1a]
Stage 4: 'Impotence & Despair' (Old Age) [12:1b-5]

Stage 1: The 'child' who sees the light is filled with hope and is potential to become the way it likes. One will never be able to predict its course of life.

Stage 2: The depiction of this stage is very obscure.

Stage 3: The young man's passion is portrayed through the word-pictures of 'walking,' 'eyes,' and 'heart'. He is both 'flesh' and 'heart.' The flesh makes him accomplish his endeavours. The heart enables him to fix his desires.

Stage 4: Qohelet presents this stage very metaphorically. There is a reversal of life as we saw above in Paṭṭiṉattār. The man becomes physically independent and emotionally desperate.

530 Though this phrase is not found in the voluminous work of Freud's writings, "Bettelheim, a German speaker who had far more intimate contact with Freud than any other contemporary authority, held that Freud saw the good life as one that is filled with meaning by the enduring, mutually helpful relations that we have with the people we love, and through knowing that we are working in ways that help others live better lives." Cf. V. Daniels, "Lecture Notes on Sigmund Freud and Psychoanalysis," in https://www.sonoma.edu/users/d/daniels/freud_notes.html (accessed on 20 November 2016, 10:00 am).

531 Qohelet Rabbah proposes seven stages of life based on the motif of 'vanity' in Ecclesiastes: "The seven 'vanities' mentioned by Qohelet correspond to the seven worlds which a man beholds (i.e., the seven stages of life). At a year old he is like a king seated in canopied litter, fondled and kissed by all. At two and three he is like a pig, sticking his hands in the gutters. At ten he skips like a kid. At twenty he is like a neighing horse, adoring his person and longing for a wife. Having married, he is like an ass (working hard for a livelihood). When he has begotten children, he grows brazen like a dog to supply their food and wants. When he has become old he is (bent) like an ape." (Qoheleth Rabbah 1:2).

Blending these two presentations let us derive a unified plot of human life:[532]

Stage One: 'Mimicry.' We are born in this world utterly helpless. We are dependent entirely for our survival, health, and learning. We learn by watching and mimicking others. If we imitate well, we are appreciated and if not admonished. There is a constant thirst for approval and validation. At this stage we learn to function within a given society.

Stage Two: 'Self-discovery.' At this stage we learn, we develop a self-identity, and identify what makes us unique and different from others. With a lot of trial-and-error and experimentation, we imbibe new values, we meet new persons, and we visit new places.

Stage Three: 'Commitment.' After having identified our strengths, weaknesses, opportunities, threats, limitations, and boundaries, we attain an enlightenment that life is limited and one cannot have everything. At this stage we maximize our potential in life. We build our legacy. We ask questions: what will I leave behind when I am gone? What will people remember me for? Who will cry when I die? What will I give to others?

Stage Four: 'Legacy.' Our energy and circumstances no more allow us to pursue our goal any further. Our mortality and finiteness begin to threaten us face-to-face. We move towards oblivion and emptiness.

Now, let us highlight from the poems the salient features that would serve as the life-lessons for our life journey which is in Divine-Human Symphony:

1. Sow Your Seed

This seems to be another way of saying, 'live your life' (Eccl 11:6). The word-picture of 'sowing-a-seed' occurs constantly in the Bible. Of them three instances stand out: (a) "The one who sows sparingly will also reap sparingly, and the one who sows bountifully will also reap bountifully" (2 Cor 9:6); (b) "Those who sow in tears shall reap with shouts of joy" (Ps 126:5); and (c) "If you sow to your own flesh, you will reap corruption from the flesh; but if you sow to the Spirit, you will reap eternal life from the Spirit" (Gal 6:8). What we reap or what we earn out of life depends only on what we have sown. Qohelet exhorts us to sow bountifully and cheerfully.

2. Rejoice

Qohelet invites his reader to rejoice – to rejoice even when one's life is short (Eccl 11:8-9). His invitation to rejoice is not an antidote to suffering or sadness in the world. But he presents 'joy' as an existential feeling. Often times our joy is at the mercy of someone or something else. We even let our joy be stolen.

532 The titles used in this unified presentation are borrowed from E. Becker, *The Denial of Death* (California 1987) and M. Manson, http://markmanson.net/four-stages-of-life, (accessed on 15 February, 2016, 10:00 am).

Joy is an inner light which glows by itself when all the covering layers are removed.

3. Remember

Qohelet calls the reader to 'remember' two things: (a) the shortness of life; and (b) the Creator (11:8; 12:1). When we are alive we have the life-breath in us and when we die the life-breath returns to the Creator. Therefore, as St. Paul says, "If we live, we live to the Lord, and if we die, we die to the Lord; so then, whether we live or whether we die, we are the Lord's" (Rom 14:8). The first prerequisite is to gain a wise heart. The Psalmist beautifully prays, "So teach us to count our days that we may gain a wise heart" (Ps 90:12). Though there seems a distiction between remembering the shortness of life and the Creator, the distinction becomes extinct because as soon as one realizes the shortness of life his mind raises itself to the Creator.

4. Fulfill Your Dreams and Desires

Another exhortation of Qohelet to the young man is "to follow the inclination of your heart and the desire of your eyes" (11:9). "The heart walks after the eyes" (Job 31:7). Here Qohelet does not go against the Pentateuchal prohibition (cf. Num 15:39). But, in line with what he has said earlier in his Book (cf. Eccl 2:24; 3:12, 13, 22; 5:18; 8:1) he counsels that the duty of enjoying is one's lot and part. Hertzberg sees two parallel injunctions in Qohelet: "You cannot anticipate the future, so work in the present; life is beautiful and death is dark, so enjoy yourself in the present."[533]

Qohelet does not advocate Epicurean way of reacting to life. But, his invitation is a proactive response to life.

5. Begin with the End

Qohelet advices the young man to begin everything with the end. The end is God on the one hand, and the final judgment on the other. When the end is kept in the mind the beginnings are always focused.

6. Do not Worry

The next lesson by Qohelet is to remove sorrow, sadness, and worry. 'Worry is like a rocking-chair. It gives you something to do. But it takes you nowhere,' thus goes a saying. Jesus also strikes the same chord when he says, "Do not worry about your life, what you will eat, or what you will drink, or about your body, what you will wear. Is not life more than food, and the body more than clothing?" (Mt 6:25).

533 H. W. Hertzberg, *Der Prediger* (Gütersloh 1963), 203, 204.

7. Remove Pain from Your Body

Our human mind often works not on the principle of good and bad but on the principle of pleasure and pain. Though it is good to get up early in the morning and do physical exercises, the mind suggests the body to sleep more because it is pleasurable to sleep and painful to exercise. This lesson of Qohelet can be taken as a reminder to us to take care of our bodies. After the body-spirit dichotomy of the Greeks our Christian theology also has taken a pro-spirit and anti-body mode. Pain or suffering is treated as something which has a salvific value. Qohelet does not subscribe to a pain-free living, but guides the young man to be free from pain internally and externally.

8. Work, Relax, Relate

The allegorical section on old age (12:2-6) gives these three principles of work, relax, and relate. For Marx, human person is a 'worker.' For Heidegger, he is a 'being-with.' There is yet another dimension, i.e., a 'relaxer.' We need to find meaning in our work, rest, and relationships. For if our meaning is not in the created realities, or in the realities that create everyday, where lies the meaning? Qoheleth Rabbah gives a metaphor of a man who is fled from the executioner. The executioner runs after him. The people who see him running in vain say to him: 'run less that you have not to make a longer return' (cf. 12:2). All our running is to be a running towards the Creator. He, the executioner(!), always has the upper hand. There are traces of predestination or determinism in Qohelet (cf. 11:9) and Paṭṭiṉattār (cf. '*vētan eḻutiyavāṟu,*' in *Uṭal* v. 17). Amidst all this happiness is to be our goal. It is meaning in life that gives happiness. As Harari notes,

> Happiness is not the surplus of pleasant over unpleasant moments. Rather, happiness consists in seeing one's life in its entirety as meaningful and worthwhile. There is an important cognitive and ethical component to happiness. As Nietzsche puts it, if you have a why to live, you can bear almost any how. A meaningful life can be extremely satisfying even in the midst of hardship, whereas a meaningless life is a terrible ordeal no matter how comfortable it is.[534]

9. Let Go

The final end of all humans is to let go – to let go of the body, and to let go of the spirit. The words of Jesus to Peter worth cited here: "Very truly, I tell you, when you were younger, you used to fasten your own belt and to go wherever you wished. But when you grow old, you will stretch out your hands, and someone else will fasten a belt around you and take you where you do not wish to go" (Jn 21:18).

---

534 Y. N. Harari, *Sapiens. A Brief History of Humankind* (London 2014), 437.

'Old age' is a blessing. It symbolizes fullness of life. "Death and birth are to be viewed as parallel processes: just as man is born with a cry, tears, and a sigh, so he dies. He is born with his fist clenched as if to say, 'the whole world is mine,' and he dies with open hands as if to day, 'I have inherited nothing from this world,' (Qoheleth Rabbah. 5:14)."[535]

10. Power and Purpose

All throughout the stages the power we enjoy is human autonomy. But, this human autonomy has a goal, i.e., to realize the presence of the power of the Creator-God. "Ecclesiastes reminds us, first, that human autonomy will never serve as an adequate basis for life and thought. But, second, it alerts us to the difficulty of decentering the self, the 'I,' from its pretended autonomy. Ecclesiastes gives us the idea of the depth of transformation involved in moving away from human autonomy to a life centered in God."[536] The main obstacle to living well in the world is that mortal beings consistently refuse to accept their mortality and finitude.[537] Like Gilgamesh we too search for immortality.[538] We want to deny death. We are autonomous. We are capable of knowing what must be done, yet incapable of knowing what wisdom is. We are creatures. That is why we are called to "remember the Creator in the time of our youth, and in the youth of each thing: situations, societies, associations, cultures, political relations, and churches."[539] We can never become like God (cf. Gen 3). The poets Qohelet and Paṭṭiṉattār persuade us of the futility of this ongoing human quest and thus to save us from a life that is itself characterized by futility, and a handful of ashes. "Though the future remains unknown,

---

535 H. Rabinoswicz, "Death," in *Encyclopaedia Judaica*, vol. 5 (Detroit 2007), 511.

536 Bartholomew, *Words and Goads*, 386.

537 D. C. Fredericks, *Coping with Transience. Ecclesiastes on Brevity of Life* (Sheffield 1993).

538 Gilgamesh is given the following answer:
"Gilgamesh, whither rovest thou?
The life thou pursuest thou shalt not find.
When the Gods created mankind,
Death for mankind they set aside,
Life in their own hands retaining.
Thou, Gilgamesh, let full thy belly.
Make thou merry by day and by night.
Of each day make thou a feast of rejoicing,
Day and night dance thou and play!
Let thy garments be sparkling fresh,
They head be washed; bathe thou in water.
Pay heed to the little one that holds on to thy hand,
For this is the task of mankind." Cited in Jonston, 'Workaholic,' 142.

539 O'Dowd, "Epistemology in Ecclesiastes," 216.

there is hope in the present that arises from the discipline of remembering the creator: daily taking joy in his gifts of food and work."[540]

11. God, the Final Word

The literally final word in the poems is GOD. God is the end, who / which is the beginning of all our beginnings and ends. To God we surrender.

12. Light that Enlightens

In Paṭṭiṉattār's *Uṭal,* the poet is enlightened at the final light in the funeral pyre. At this he looks back the entire human life-cycle. He yields himself at the feet of the Lord to be ruled by Him. Though the poem does not spell out the life-lesson other than surrendering to God, elsewhere Paṭṭinattār presents the ideal way of an enlightened person:

pēipōṟ ṟirintu piṇampōṟ kiṭantiṭṭa piccaiyellām
nāipō larunti naripō luḻaṉṟunaṉ maṅkaiyarait
tāipōṟ karutit tamarpō laṉaivarkkun tāḻmaicollic
cēipō lirupparkaṇ ṭīruṇmai ñāṉan teḷintavarē.[541]

In sum, the texts of our study give three insights for facing the life transition: (i) Put God first in everything you do. Everything that one is, has, and does is by the grace of God. What you do for God and with God is permanent, and what you do for you and with you is but temporary. (ii) The power of discipline and routines. Greatness does not come from giving in to every single desire that you might have in any given moment. Discipline is a decision not compromised. Each life stage needs discipline. Routines create consistency in discipline. And (iii) You are attached to what / whom you serve. Service and attachment go hand in hand. To be at the service of others and of God is the ultimate expression of love.

540 O'Dowd, "Epistemology in Ecclesiastes," 216.

541 'He will wander like a demon, sleep like a corpse,
Will eat what is given like a dog, will search like a wolf,
Will respect every woman as his mother, will be meek towards all,
Will place himself like a child…one who is wise.' *Tiruttillai*, 76.

EPILOGUE

Task Accomplished

The comparative reading of Ecclesiastes 11:4-12:8 and Paṭṭiṉattār's Uṭalkūṟṟuvaṇṇam on human life transition has been done as follows:

We recorded the first impressions of the texts, established the texts as narrative poems, recognized the metaphors of 'light' and 'sweet' and felt the rhythm of human life-stages. After surveying the scholarly literature on the texts, we found out the lacunae and the need to fill them through a synchronic study.

Then, after establishing the historical, theological, and literary contexts of the poets and the poems, a close reading of the texts was done through the narrative analysis tools of structure, setting, style, characterisation, and themes and motifs.

The close readings of the poems were juxtaposed to see their contextual, conceptual, and communicative similarities and dissimilarities. A few queries were raised in the process.

After drawing a hermeneutical arc between their respective corpus, we, finally established, that the life transition becomes easier when one, fixing the eyes of God, enjoys in each stage 'the light which is sweet.'

The study shows that both these texts (i) use 'light' as a metaphor to 'life;' (ii) divide human life-stages into four and underline the transition in each moment of life; and (iii) emphasize the divine-human symphony as a pre-requisite to experience light as sweet.

Task Ahead

In our research we have encountered three wisdoms: (i) Wisdom of Ecclesiastes and Paṭṭiṉattār, which is manifest in their respective texts; (ii) Wisdom of the readers, past and present, who in their finite understanding and limited capacity have attempted to go near the text, which is a *mysterium tremendum et fascinans*; and (iii) Wisdom of God. The poets have tried to comprehend this wisdom in a capsule, but it is incomprehensible. Our answers have brought more queries, not vice versa. Our wisdoms need to surrender to the Third Wisdom, which surpasses poets, poems, and us. In that surrender we will realize that 'life changes' and 'life is short,' and in each transition one needs to 'rejoice' and 'remember.' And the point of arrival is 'divine-human symphony,' which becomes the point of departure as well.

LITERATURE

Texts and Tools

ĀRUMUGANĀVALAR, *Tamizh Ilakkanam - Tamil Grammar* (Chennai 1993).

ALSTER, B., *Studies in Sumerian Proverbs* (Copenhagen 1975).

ALTER, R., *The Art of Biblical Narrative* (New York 1981).

_____, *The Art of Biblical Poetry* (New York 1985).

BAZYLIŃSKI, S, *A Guide to Biblical Research* (Rome ²2009).

BERLIN, A., "Introduction to Hebrew Poetry," in *New Interpreter's Bible*, Vol. IV (Nashville 1996), 301-315.

BOTTERWECK, J.- RINGGREN, H. eds., *Theological Dictionary of the Old Testament* (Grand Rapids 1997-2006), I-XV.

BROWN, F. - DRIVER, S. - BRIGGS, C., *A Hebrew and English Lexicon of the Old Testament* (Oxford 1996).

BROWN, R. E., - SCHNEIDERS S. M., "Hermeneutics." In eds. BROWN, R. E., FITZMYER, J. A., & MURPHY R. E., eds., *The New Jerome Biblical Commentary* (Bangalore 1990).

ELLIGER, K. – RUDOLF. W., eds., *Biblia Hebraica Stuttgartensia.* Fifth Critical Edition (Stuttgart 2006), 1352-53.

EVEN-SHOSHAN, A., *A New Concordance of the Bible.* Thesaurus of the Language of the Bible: Hebrew and Aramaic Roots, Words, Proper Names, Phrases and Synonyms (Jerusalem 1990).

FISCH, H., *Poetry with a Purpose* (Bloomington 1988).

FITZMYER, J. A., *The Interpretation of the Bible in the Church.* Pontifical Biblical Commission's Document. Text and Commentary (Roma 1995).

FOKKELMAN, J. P., *Reading Biblical Narrative. An Introductory Guide* (Louisville 1999).

JENNI, E. - WESTERMANN, C. eds., *Theological Lexicon of the Old Testament* (Peabody 1997), I-III.

JOÜON, P. - MURAOKA, T., *A Grammar of Biblical Hebrew* (Roma 2006).

KOEHLER, L. - BAUMGARTNER, W. - STAMM, J., *The Hebrew and Aramaic Lexicon of the Old Testament* (Leiden 2000).

LEVINE, E., *The Aramaic Version of Qoheleth* (New York 1981).

LISOWSKY, G., *Konkordanz zum hebräischen Alten Testament* (Stuttgart 1981).

LONGMAN, T., *Literary Approaches to Biblical Interpretation* (Grand Rapids 1987).

MARGUERAT D. - BOURQUIN Y., *How to Read Bible Stories. An Introduction to Narrative Criticism* (London 1999).

MUTHUKUMARAN, P., *Tamil Marapu* - Tamil Tradition (Chennai 2002).

O'CONNOR, M., *Hebrew Verse Structure* (Winona Lake 1980).

PETERSEN, D. - RICHARDS, K., *Interpreting Hebrew Poetry* (Minneapolis 1992).

PONNAIAH, N., *Tamililakkaṉamum Uraiyamaippum - Tamil Grammar and Prose Structure* (Colombo 1958).

POWELL, M. A., *What is Narrative Criticism? Guide to Biblical Criticism* (Minneapolis 1990).

RAJAM, V. S., *A Reference Grammar of Classical Tamil Poetry* (Philadelphia 1992).

SCHENKER, A. – et al, *Biblia Hebraica Quinta* (BHQ) (Stuttgart 2004), 50-52.

SCHÖKEL, A., *A Manual of Hebrew Poetics* (Rome 1988).

SKA, J. L., *Our Fathers Have Told Us. Introduction to the Analysis of the Hebrew Narratives* (Rome 1990).

THIRUMURUGAN, R., *Ilakkaṉam Inikkiratu - Sweet Grammar* (Pudhucherry 2006).

TOV, E., *Textual Criticism of the Hebrew Bible* (Minneapolis ^{2}2001).

WALTKE, B. K. - O'CONNAR, M., *An Introduction to Biblical Hebrew Syntax* (Winona Lake 1990).

WATSON, W. G. E., *Classical Hebrew Poetry. A Guide to Its Techniques*, JSOTS 26 (Sheffield 1984).

Cittar Pāṭalkaḷ Tokuppu III. Paṭṭiṉattār Pāṭalkaḷ (Project Madurai E-Edition 2003).

On Ecclesiastes 11:4-12:8

ANDERSON, W. H. U., *Qoheleth and its Pessimistic Theology* (New York 1997).

_____, "The Poetic Inclusio of Qoheleth in Relation to 1:2 and 12:8," in *SJOT* 12 (1998), 203-13.

_____, "Ironic Correlations and Skepticism in the Joy Statements of Qohelth," in *SJOT* 14/1 (2000), 67-100.

BAAB, O. J., *The Theology of the Old Testament* (New York 1949).

BAILEY, L. R., *Biblical Perspectives on Death* (Philadelphia 1979).

BAKER, D. L., *Two Testaments, One Bible. A Study of the Theological Relationship between the Old and New Testaments* (Downers Grove, Ill. [2]1991).

BARTHOLOMEW, C. G., *Reading Ecclesiastes. Old Testament Exegesis and Hermeneutical Theory* (Roma 1998).

BARR, J., *The Garden of Eden and the Hope of Immortality* (Minneapolis 1992).

BARTON, G. A., *A Critical and Exegetical Commentary on the Book of Ecclesiastes,* ICC (New York 1993).

BONORA, A., *Qohelet: La Gioia e la Fatica di Vivere* (Brescia 1987).

BRIDGES, C., *Ecclesiastes* (Carlisle [2]1961).

BROWN, W. P., *Ecclesiastes.* Interpretation: *A Bible Commentary for Teaching and Preaching* (Louisville 2000).

_____, "The Didactic Power of Metaphor in the Aphoristic Sayings of Proverbs," in JSOT 29 (2004), 133-54.

BRUNS, J. E., "The Imagery of Ecclesiastes in 12:6a", in *Journal of Biblical Literature* 84 (1965), 428-30.

BULLINGER, E. W., *Figures of Speech used in the Bible* (Grand Rapids 1999).

BURKES, S., *Death in Qoheleth and Egyptian Biographies of the Late Period* (Atlanta 1999).

CANEDAY, A. B., "Qoheleth: Enigmatic Pessimist or Godly Sage?" in *Grace Theological Journal* 7 (1986), 21-56.

CANTORE, E., "La sapienza biblica, ideale religioso del credente," in *RivBib* 8 (1960), 1-9.

CASTELLINO, G. R., "Qoheleth and His Wisdom," in *Catholic Biblical Quarterly* 30 (1968), 15-28.

CHILDS, B. S., *Biblical Theology of the Old and New Testaments. Theological Reflection on the Christian Bible* (Minneapolis 1992), 95-118.

CLEMENS, D. M., "Death in Qoheleth," in *Journal of Near Eastern Studies* 61 (2002), 71-73.

CLINES, D. ed., *The Poetical Books* (Sheffield 1997).

CRENSHAW, J. L., *Ecclesiastes. A Commentary* (Philadelphia 1987).

_____, "Book of Ecclesiastes," in *Anchor Bible Dictionary*, Vol. 2 (Doubleday 1992), 271-80.

_____, "The Expression of *Mî Yôdēa'* in The Hebrew Bible," in *Vetus Testamentum* XXXVI, 3 (1986), 244-88.

_____, *Old Testament Wisdom. An Introduction* (Louisville 1988).

_____, "The Shadow of Death in Qoheleth," in J. G. GAMMIE – W. A. BRUEGGEMANN, eds., *Essays in Honor of Samuel Terrien* (New York 1978).

DAHOOD, M. J., "Canannite-Phoenician Influence of Qoheleth," in *Bib* 33 (1952), 191-221.

_____, "Qoheleth and Recent Discoveries," *Bib* 39 (1958), 302-18.

_____, "Qoheleth and Northwest Semitic," *Bib* 43 (1962), 349-65.

_____, "The Phoenician Background of Qoheleth," *Bib* 47 (1966), 266-77.

D'ALARIO, V., *Il Libro Del Qohelet: Struttura, Letteraria e Retorica* (Napoli 1993).

DAVIDSON, R., *Ecclesiastes and the Song of Solomon* (Philadelphia 1986).

DAVIES, B. C., "Ecclesiastes 12:1-8 - Death, an Impetus for Life," *Bibliotheca Sacra* 148 (July - Sep1991), 298-318.

DAY, J. et al. eds., *Wisdom in Ancient Israel.* Essays in Honour of J. A. Emerton (Cambridge 1995).

DELITZSCH, F., *Biblical Commentary on the Song of Songs and Ecclesiastes* (Trans. M. G. EASTON, Grand Rapids [2]1950).

EATON, M. A., *Ecclesiastes. An Introduction and Commentary. The Tyndale Old Testament Commentaries* 16 (Downers Grove, Ill. 1983).

ELLUL, J., *Reason for Being* (Grand Rapids 1990).

ENNS, P., *Ecclesiastes* (Grand Rapids 2011).

FARMER, K. A., *Who Knows What is Good?* A Commentary on the Books of Proverbs and Ecclesiastes. ITC (Grand Rapids 1991).

FOLLINGSTAND, C. M., *Deictic Viewpoint in Biblical Hebrew Text* (New Jersey 2001).

FOX, M., "The Meaning of Hebel for Qohelet," in *JBL* 105/3 (1986), 409-27.

_____, *Qoheleth and His Contradictions.* JSOTS 81 (Sheffield 1999).

_____, *A Time to Tear Down and a Time to Build up. A Rereading of Ecclesiastes*. Grand Rapids, 1999.

FREDERICKS, D., *Qoheleth's Language. Re-evaluating its Nature and Date* (New York 1988).

_____, "Life's Storms and Structural Unity in Qoheleth 11:1 – 12:8," in *JSOT* 52 (1991), 95-114.

_____., *Coping with Transience. Ecclesiastes on the Brevity of Life* (Sheffield 1993).

GARRETT, D. A., *Proverbs, Ecclesiastes, Song of Songs. New American Commentary* (Nashville 1993).

GAULT, B. P., "A Reexamination of 'Eternity' in Ecclesiastes 3:11," in *Bibliotheca Sacra* 165 (Jan – Mar 2008), 39-57.

GEORGE, A., *The Epic of Gilgamesh* (London 2000).

GIANTO, A., "The Theme of Enjoyment in Qoheleth," in *Bib* 73 (1992), 528-32.

_____, "Human Destiny in Emar and Qoheleth," in *BETL* 136 (1998), 473-79.

GILLMAN, N., *The Death of Death. Resurrection and Immortality in Jewish Thought* (Woodstock 1997).

GINSBURG, C. D., *The Songs of Songs and Coheleth* (New York [2]1970).

GINSBURG, H. L., *Studies in Koheleth* (New York 1950).

GOLDBERG, L., *Ecclesiastes. Bible Study Commentary* (Grand Rapids 1983).

GOOD, E. M., *Irony in the Old Testament* (Sheffield [2]1981). Chapter 6, "Qoheleth: The Limits of Wisdom."

GORDIS, R., *Koheleth - The Man and His World. A Study of Ecclesiastes* (New York [3]1968).

_____, *Poets, Prophets, and Sages* (Bloomington 1971). Chapter 14, "The Wisdom of Koheleth."

HAYMAN, A. P., "Qoheleth and the Book of Creation," in *JSOT* 50 (1991), 93-111.

HOLM-NIELSON, S., "On the Interpretation of Qoheleth in Early Christianity," in *Vetus Testamentum* 24 (1974), 169-77.

HOPKINS, D. C., *The Highlands of Canaan. Agricultural Life in the Early Iron Age* (Sheffield 1985).

HUBBARD, D. A., *Beyond Futility* (Grand Rapids 1976).

_____, *Ecclesiastes, Song of Solomon.* Communicator's Commentary (Dallas 1991).

ISAKSSON, B., *Studies in the Language of Qoheleth.* With Speical Emphasis on the Verbal System (Stockholm 1987).

KAISER, W. C. Jr., *Ecclesiastes.* Total Life (Chicago 1970).

KIDNER, D., *The Wisdom of Proverbs, Job and Ecclesiastes* (Downers Grove, Ill. 1985).

KNOBEL, P. C., "The Targum of Qohelet," in *The Aramaic Bible* 15 (Edinburgh 1991).

KRÜGER, H. A. J., "Old Age Frailty versus Cosmic Deterioration? A Few Remarks on the Interpretation of Qohelet 11:7-12:8," in SCHOORS, ed., *Qohelet in the Context of Wisdom*, 399-412.

KRÜGER, T. *Qoheleth.* Hermeneia Series (Minneapolis 2004).

KUGEL, J. L., *The Idea of Biblical Poetry. Parallelism and its History* (Baltimore 1998).

LEAHY, M., "The Meaning of Ecclesiastes 12:2-5," in *Irish Theological Quarterly* 19 (1952), 297-300.

LEANZA, S., "Eccl 12:1-7: L'interpretazione Escatologica Dei Padri e Degli Esegeti Medievali," *Aug.* 18 (1978), 191-207.

LEUPOLD, H. C., *Exposition of Ecclesiastes* (Grand Rapids 1966).

LICHTHEIM, M., *Ancient Egyptian Literature.* II. *The New Kingdom* (Berkeley 1976).

_____, *Ancient Egyptian Literature.* III. *The New Kingdom* (Berkeley 1980).

LOADER, J. A., *Ecclesiastes. A Practical Commentary* (Grand Rapids 1986).

LOHFINK, N., *Qoheleth. A Continental Commentary* (Minneapolis 2003).

LONGMAN, T., *The Book of Ecclesiastes. New International Commentary of the Old Testament* (Grand Rapids [3]1998).

LONGMAN III, T., "The 'Fear of God' in the Book of Ecclesiastes," in *Bulletin for Biblical Research* 25.1 (2015) 13-21.

_____, "Challenging the Idols of the Twenty-First Century: The Message of the Book of Ecclesiastes," in *Stone-Campbell Journal* 12 (Fall 2009), 207-16.

MAZZINGHI, L., *Ho Cercato e ho Esplorato.* Studi sul Qohelet (Bologna 2001).

MCKANE, W., *Proverbs.* A New Approach (London 1970).

MCNEILE, A., *An Introduction to Ecclesiastes* (Cambridge 1904).

MICHEL, D., *Qohelet* (Darmstadt 1988).

MILLER, D. B., *Symbol and Rhetorics in Ecclesiastes* (Atlanta 2002).

_____, *Symbol and Rhetoric in Ecclesiastes.* The place of Hebel in Qoheleth's Work. (Atlanta 2002).

MURPHY, R. E., *Job, Proverbs, Ruth, Canticles, Ecclesiastes, and Esther* (FOTL 13, Grand Rapids), 1981.

_____, *Ecclesiastes.* Word Biblical Commentary 23A (Texas 1992).

OGDEN, G. S., *Qoheleth* (Sheffield 1987).

_____, "Qoheleth XI 1-6." In *Vetus Testamentum* 32 (April 1982) 158-69.

_____, "Qohelet 11:7-12:8: Qohelet's Summons to Enjoyment and Reflection," in *Vetus Testamentum* 34 (1984), 27-38.

ONWUKEME, V., *Searching for the Meaning with Qoheleth* (Longford 2012).

PIOTTI, F., "Osservazioni su alcuni paralleli extrabiblici nell'allegoria della vecchiaia (Qohelet 12:1-7)," in *Bibbia e Oriente* 19 (1977), 119-28.

PROVAN, I. W., *Ecclesiastes, Song of Songs.* NIV Application Commentary (Grand Rapids 2001).

RAPHAEL, S., *Jewish Views on the Afterlife* (Northvale 1994).

RAVASI, G., *Qohelet, Il Libro Più Originale e Scandaloso Dell'antico Testamento* (Torino 1988).

RINDGE, M. S., "Mortality and Enjoyment. The Interplay of Death and Possessions in Qoheleth," *Catholic Biblical Quarterly* 73 (2011), 265-80.

SAWYER, J.F.A., "The Ruined House in Ecclesiastes 12: A Reconstruction of the Original Parable," in *Journal of Biblical Literature* 94 (1975), 519-31.

SCHÖKEL, L. A., *A Manual of Hebrew Poetics* (Rome 1988).

SCOTT, R. B. Y., *Proverbs, Ecclesiastes* (AB 18, Garden City 1965).

SEOW, C. L., *Ecclesiastes.* A New Translation with Introduction and Commentary (AB 18C, New York 1997).

SHEAD, A. G., "Reading Ecclesiastes Epilogically," in *Tyndale Bulletin* 48.1 (1997), 67-91.

SOGGIN, J. A., *Israele in epoca Biblica.* Istituzionali, feste, cerimonie, rituali (Torino 2000).

TAMÉZ, E., *When the Horizons Close.* Rereading Ecclesiastes (New York 2000).

TAYLOR, C., *The Dirge of Coheleth in Ecclesiastes XII.* Discussed and Literally Interpreted (London 1874).

TOWNER, W. S., "The Book of Ecclesiastes. Introduction, Commentary, and Reflections," in *New Interpreter's Bible*, Vol. 5, 265-360.

VAN DER WAL, A. J. O., "Qohelet 12:1a: A Relatively Unique Statement in Israel's Wisdom Tradition," in SHOORS, in *Qoheleth in the Context of Wisdom*, 413-18.

VON RAD, G., *Wisdom in Israel* (trans. J. D. MARTIN, London 1972).

WHITLEY, C. F., *Koheleth. His Language and Thought.* (BZAW 148, Berlin 1979).

WHITWELL, C., "The Variation of Nature in Ecclesiastes 11," *Journal for the Study of the Old Testament* 34.1 (2009), 81-97.

WHYBRAY, R. N., *Ecclesiastes* (Sheffield 1997).

_____, *The Good Life in the Old Testament* (London 2002).

_____, "Qoheleth, Preacher of Joy," in CLINES, D. ed., *The Poetical Books* (Sheffield 1997), 188-98.

YOUNGBLOOD, R. F., "Qoheleth's Dark House (Eccl 12:5)," in *Journal of the Evangelical Theological Society* 29/4 (Dec 1986), 397-410.

ZUCK, R. B., "God and Man in Ecclesiastes," *Bibliotheca Sacra* 148 (Jan – Mar 1991), 46-56.

_____, ed., *Reflecting with Solomon.* Selected Studies on the Book of Ecclesiastes (Grand Rapids 1994).

On Paṭṭinattār's *Uṭalkūṟṟuvaṇṇam*

ADAIKALASAMY, M. R., *Tamil Ilakkiya Varalāṟu* (Madras [7]1981).

AṄKAMUTTU, Ā., *Paṭṭiṉattār Tiruppāṭalkaḷ* (Chennai 2008).

ARAVAANAN, K. P., *Kavitaiyiṉ uyir, uḷḷam, uṭal* (Madras 1976).

AROKIASWAMI, M., *The Classical Age of the Tamils* (Madras 1972).

AMALORPAVADASS, D. S. ed. *Indian Christian Spirituality* (Bangalore 1982).

BEROFSKY, B., *Liberation from Self. A Theory of Personal Autonomy* (Cambridge 1995).

Burrow, T. - Emeneau, M.B., *A Dravidian Etymological Dictionary* (Oxford ²1984).

Caldwell, R., *A Comparative Grammar of the Dravidian or South-Indian Family of Languages,* J. L. Wyatt & T. Ramakrishna Pillai, eds. (New Delhi ³1974).

Coward, H. G., *Studies in Indian Thought* (New Delhi ²1996).

Dhavamony, M., *Love of God According to Saiva Siddhanta. A Study in the Mysticism and Theology of Saivism* (London 1971).

Ganeri, J., *Philosophy in Classical India. The Proper Work of Reason* (New Delhi ²2001).

Gnanasambandan, A. S., *Ilakkiyak Kalai* (Madras ²1964).

Irigary, L., *Between East and West. From Singularity to Community* (New Delhi 2005).

Joshi, O. P., *Introduction to Hinduism* (Jaipur 2004).

Kalidas, R. *History and Culture of the Tamils. From Prehistoric Times to the President's Rule* (Dindigul 1976).

Kalyānasundaram, K., *Siddhar Paadalgal Thoguppu - A Collection of Siddha Poems* (Madurai 2003).

Kalyānasundaranār, T. V., *Paṭṭiṉattār Pāṭalkaḷ* (Chennai ⁴2010).

Kapoor, S., *A Short Introduction to Saivism* (New Delhi 2002).

Karuppaiyā, P., *Paṭṭiṉattār.* Oru Pārvai (Chennai 2012).

Kersten, F., *Phenomenological Method. Theory and Practice* (London 1989).

Kingsbury, F. – Philips, G. E., *Hymns of the Tamil Śaivite Saints* (Madras 1921).

Klostermaier, K. K., *Hinduism. A Short Introduction* (Oxford 2006).

Kōpālaṉ, Vē., *Paṭṭiṉattāṭikaḷiṉ Pātalkaḷ* (Chennai 2001).

Kōtaṇṭarāmaṉ, Cu., *Vētamum Caivamum* (Chennai 2014) [E-book]

_____, *Oru Vācakam.* Tirumuṟai Kaṭṭuraikaḷ (Chennai 2014) [E-book]

Maria Selvam, A., *The Song of Songs and Ancient Tamil Love Poems. Poetry and Symbolism* (Roma 1988).

Nārāyaṇavelpiḷḷai, M., *Paṭṭiṉattār Vāḻvum Vākkum* (Chennai 2013).

Paramacivam, C., *Naṟṟamiḻ Ilakkaṇam* (Chennai ⁸2008).

Parsons, H. L., *Man East and West. Essays in East – West Philosophy* (Amsterdam 1975).

Peterson, I. V., *Poems to Śiva. The Hymns of the Tamil Saints* (Delhi 1991).

Pillai, K. K., *A Social History of the Tamils,* vol. 1 (Madras ²1975).

Purnalingam, M. S., *Tamil India* (Madras ³1963).

Ramamurthy, A., *The Philosophical Foundations of Hinduism* (New Delhi 2000).

RICE, S., *Hindu Customs and Their Origins* (New Delhi 1986).

SIRCAR, M. N., *Life, Thought, and Mysticism in India* (New Delhi 1978).

SUBRAMANIAN, K. R., *The Origin of Saivism and its History in the Tamil Land* (New Delhi 1985).

SURYAMURTHY, S., *Cintaṉaikku Teḷivu Tarum Cittar Pāṭalkaḷ* (Chennai 2014).

TAMIZH PRIYAN, *Siddhar Bhathiragiriyarin Gnanapulambal* (Chennai 2013).

THIRUMURUGAN, *Siddhar Paadalgal* (Chennai 2012).

TIWARI, R., *Foundations of Indian Culture* (Jaipur 2001).

TURNER, R.L., *A Comparative Dictionary of the Indo-Aryan Languages* (London ^{2}1973).

VELLAIVARANAN, K., *Tolkāppiyam.* Tamiḷ Ilakkiya Varalāṟu (Chitamparam 1957).

VINEETH, V. F., *Self and Salvation in Hinduism and Christianity* (New Delhi 1997).

WINSLOW, M., *A Comprehensive Tamil and English Dictionary* (New Delhi 1984).

ZVELEBIL, K., *An Introduction to Tamil Classical Prosody* (Madras 1972).

_____, *The Smile of Murugan* (Leiden 1973).

_____, *The Tamil Literature* (Leiden 1975).

_____, *Lexicon of Tamil Literature* (New York 1995).

_____, *Companion Studies to the History of Tamil Literature* (New York 1992).

_____, *The Siddha Quest for Immortality* (Oxford 2003).

_____, *The Poets of the Powers.* Magic, Freedom, and Renewal (London 1973).